ITALIAN NATIONALISM:
From Its Origins to World War II

By
Ronald S. Cunsolo
Professor of History
Nassau Community College

AN ANVIL ORIGINAL

Under the general editorship of
Louis L. Snyder

ROBERT E. KRIEGER PUBLISHING COMPANY
Malabar, Florida

1990

Original Edition 1990

Printed and Published by
ROBERT E. KRIEGER PUBLISHING CO., INC.
KRIEGER DRIVE
MALABAR, FLORIDA 32950

Library of Congress Cataloging-in-Publication Data

Cunsolo, Ronald S.
   Italian nationalism / Ronald S. Cunsolo—Original ed.

   p. cm.
   "An Anvil original."
   Bibliography : p.
   Includes index.
   ISBN 0-89874-938-7 (alk. paper)
   1. Nationalism—Italy—History. 2. Italy—Politics and
government—20th century. 3. Italy—Politics and
government—1789-1900. I. Title.
DG568.5.C86 1989
320.5'4'0945—dc19   88-34380
                                                            CIP

7   6   5   4   3   2

TO
AUDREY
Love and Truth
Beauty and Friendship

CONTENTS

PART II Proletarian and Imperialist Nationalism

PART III Readings

PREFACE

A people living contiguously can have ethnic identity, psychological affinity, cultural similarities, and like religious sensibilities, and still not be nationalist. The above state describes patriotism. Nationalism is experienced when sufficient numbers of the same people strive to unite into a comprehensive political structure, to be governed by uniform laws, and be served by the same or compatible social and economic institutions. Patriotism has been the rule for the Italians and nationalism the exception. For most Italians, "Italy" has been a protean substance, connoting different forms, derived from Italy's long and varied past. As a consequence, the birth of Italian self-consciousness has been late. When it appeared, it was neither linear in growth nor overpowering in force. Before nationalism could germinate and flourish, public sentiment had to be delivered from the Roman Imperium, Roman Catholic universalism, and Renaissance transnational humanism, based on allegiance to the city-state republics. With no comparable past to detain or encumber them, peoples elsewhere in Europe were well on their way toward creating states along ethnic-political lines before the Italians began to think in similar terms. Competing views of Italy became so deeply imbedded in the Italian mind that it has been impossible to dislodge them completely. Perhaps as a result, nationalism was at first more greatly determined by the need to oust foreign powers from the peninsula than by a willful desire to live together as Italians in one all-inclusive state. Moreover, whether we are dealing with the Neo-Guelph movement, which became prominent in the decade of the 1840s, or with the liberal and democratic movements which reached their climax with the unification of Italy in 1861, or we are concerned with the authoritarian nationalist movement of the twentieth century, nationalism in Italy was always a minoritarian enterprise. Indeed, the failure or refusal of more Italians to become involved in the former became a major factor for the latter. The lingering diverse conceptions regarding Italy helped to insure the defeat of the later conservative or quasi-totalitarian edition.

Professor Thomas J. Spira, Editor of the *Canadian Review of Studies in Nationalism*, is to be commended for the wide publicity given to nationalism and for the use of the Review as an organ for the transmission and exchange of information among scholars in the field. Thanks are expressed to Ms. Edith Forbes, Aurelia Stephen, and Francis Scarinci of the Reference and Research Unit of the Nassau Community College Library for the diligence and promptness with which they pursued my requests for books, some difficult to obtain. I appreciate the assistance of Professor Giorgio Spini of the University of Florence in tracking down source materials in Italy. My gratitude is extended to Dr. Louis L. Snyder, General Editor of the Anvil Series, for the opportunity given me to contribute this volume.

Ronald S. Cunsolo
Garden City, New York

PART I

LIBERATION AND UNIFICATION NATIONALISM

CHAPTER 1

ETHNOGRAPHIC AND LINGUISTIC BACKGROUND

TERRITORY. Continental Italy is a peninsula which juts out of Central Europe like a long boot, jabbing toward North Africa. It is girdled by the Alps on the north, the Ligurian and Tyrrhenian Seas on the west, the Adriatic and Ionian Seas on the east, and the Messina Straits and the Mediterranean on the south. When the Italian tribes federated with the Roman Republic in 275 B.C., and the islands of Sicily and Sardinia on the south and west were annexed in 241 and 238 B.C. as a result of the First Punic War with Carthage (264–242 B.C.) what was known as "Italy" became formally denoted. It comprises 120,000 square miles, about the size of New Mexico, with a population today of 58,000,000.

An expanse of land is given the simple name, land. When it is being occupied and acquiring organizational form, it begins to assume the characteristics of a territory. As people live on the same land, look at identical landscapes, toil adjacent soil, fish in surrounding waters, sail in nearby rivers, and are exposed to the same elements of climate and weather, they are drawn together and become bound to the territory, while simultaneously differentiated from other peoples. Greek writers, such as Plato and Archimedes, saw Italy constituting a whole, even though it was divided among the Italic tribes and their own people had established immigrant settlements in Naples and Sicily. Roman historians from Livy and Virgil to Tacitus approached the area as a unit, the heartland of the Roman Empire. It was the Florentine poet Dante Alighieri (1265–1321) who began to give Italy descriptive details. He located and depicted its regions, stressing natural frontiers, and delimiting Italy's reach, particularly on the northeast. In his *Divina Commedia* (1321), Dante spoke of "beautiful Italy" as "the garden" of the Medieval Empire. He set the northeastern border at the Gulf of Quarnaro, short of the Istrian Peninsula and the Dalmatian coast, a demarcation which had twentieth-century nationalists wince in pain. Francesco

3

Petrarca (1304–74), Dante's fellow-Florentine, went beyond. Italy to Petrarch was not a nostalgic relic or an exciting memory but a land blessed by salubrious climate, rich soil, plentiful forests, water resources, and distinct confines to boot. One inspirational line from his letter, *Ad Italium*, "Beautiful country/ which the Appennines divides and the seas and the Alps encircle," has been repeatedly cited.

The descendants of Livy, Virgil, Tacitus, Dante, and Petrarch continued to delineate, to amplify, and to present Italy as a geographic ensemble, separated by Providence from the rest of Europe and the world. As the nation-state advanced, a number of writers in the 1500s and 1600s explained that Spain, France, England, and Russia were aspiring to achieve territorial congruence with the set of environmental circumstances bequeathed to each. During the 1700s and 1800s, patriotic spokesmen appealed to the logic of location, climate, and specific land features to lay claim to the enormous possibilities nature had in store for Italian freedom. No section was to be omitted from the campaign for liberation. Italians were called upon to follow the example of the Romans who understood the potentialities of the area, and had the ingenuity and the capacity to mobilize them for the benefit of the inhabitants of the peninsula and, ultimately, for all mankind. Historic destiny went hand-in-hand with geographic fulfillment. In their train came the nationalists who interpreted the factors of geography and history as conferring on the peninsula not only a regime of independent political entities but, more importantly, an inalienable right to a single unitary state. (*See Reading No. 1*.)

PEOPLE. One school of thought has it that the name *Italia* is derived from the Latin *Vitalus*, meaning life. If that is correct, the people who inhabited the peninsula and eventually were called Italians did not enter history as conquering hordes or sea plunderers, devoted to the gods of war and the hunt, but as settlers and farmers, engaged in peaceful pursuits, inclined toward fertility cults. No precise origins can be claimed for peoples. All people are emigrants, and the Italians are no exception. A main influx was of the Indo-Europeans whose habitat was between Scandinavia and the Russian steppes. The Indo-Europeans, who spoke a language from which Greek, Latin, and German were derived, participated, about 2500 B.C., in a huge migration, with one branch penetrating into Italy, several dispersing into other areas of Central and Western Europe, and another reaching India. The Greeks and the Etruscans were later arrivals, the former crossing the Adriatic and the Ionian between 750–550 B.C., while the latter infiltrated the region between the Arno and Tiber rivers, 600–510 B.C. Many anthropologists submit that another racial component may have filtered through from North Africa. These immigrants mingled with the indigenous population to form the Italian people, divided into the Italic tribes, the ancestors of the Romans, Tuscans, Ligurians, Piedmontese, Venetians, Lombardians, Umbrians, Neopolitans, Sicilians, etc. Federation with Rome and the Social Wars (91–88 B.C.), which the Italiac tribes undertook against what they were persuaded were undue Roman encroachments, resulted in a harmonious blend of Roman citizenship with local autonomy.

Once the Western Empire crumbled (476 A.D.), the many states which cropped up dramatized and fixed in the popular mind the ethnic diversity of the peninsula. The painstakingly slow and tantalizing evolution of the notion of an Italian nationality can be illustrated in many ways. A 1265 A.D. official listing of the student body at the University of Bologna classified the students into two categories: those who came from the peninsula and those who hailed from beyond the Alps. The former were given the assignation "the three nations," which were identified with Lombardy, Tuscany, and Rome, the latter including all of southern Italy. Social types and comic characters were regional stereotypes. The Florentine Giovanni Boccaccio (1313–75) wrote in Dante's Italian but his scoundrels and rogues were Milanese, Roman, and Neapolitan, but never Florentine. Four centuries later, the playwright Carlo Goldoni (1707–93) utilized villains and sharpees from every section of Italy except from his native Venice. Two of the leading personalities in the rise of Italian self-awareness, Pietro Verri (1728–97) and Antonio Genovesi (1713–69), advertised their major works as the efforts of a "Milanese" and "Neapolitan." Perhaps they were compelled to defer to reality, since the use of "Italian," suggesting one definable people, would have raised suspicions over the political implications. The same patriots and others equally decried the sectarian spirit among Italians, which they perceived was caused by the popular belief that the Italians were a heterogeneous "race." (*See Reading No. 2.*)

Of all the participants in the drive for Italian unification, no one campaigned more passionately for the inclusion of all Italians, north and south, than the Genoa-born Giuseppe Mazzini (1805–72). His championing of a unitary republic was designed to draw rulers and people together to the overarching demands of the common fatherland. Ambiguities and naïveté aside, Mazzini ardently maintained that the spontaneous cooperation of all the people and classes of society in the crucible of unification would of itself forge the national character. Giuseppe Garibaldi (1807–82) shared the same outlook. His invasion of Sicily and Naples in 1860 was planned to insure the incorporation of southern Italians in the new country being built. Unlike Mazzini and Garibaldi, Camillo Cavour (1810–61) approached Italy in the traditional manner, as composed of "nations" and "races." It is reported that in 1861 Massimo D'Azeglio, the former Liberal Piedmontese prime minister, deflated the congratulatory mood set off by unification with his sober observation to Premier Cavour that Italy having been made, there still remained the task of making Italians. Cavour's reply was that the making of Italians was infinitely more challenging and difficult than all the wars of Italian unification combined. A centralized state, adroitly using education and its many service instrumentalities, would in time transform many people into one. Residual differences among all these nationalists notwithstanding, through their thinking and doing, sufficient numbers of Italians came around to the idea that all the inhabitants of the peninsula were Italian and deserved to become members of one, united Italy, for which they were prepared to hope, pray, sacrifice, and die. (*See Reading No. 3.*)

LANGUAGE. A mother tongue, along with a feeling of kinship and sense of shared territory, is another prerequisite of nationalism. In his study of the languages of the Italic tribes, the historian and philosopher Giambattista Vico (1668–1744) concluded that words proceeded from the social urgings of people through which they grasp and recall important events in all their richness and subtleties. People, language, intellectual state, moral consciousness, and historical happenings interact. It has been said that Italy's more than thirty dialects became permanent or semipermanent fixtures due in large measure to the many political divisions of the country. They represented an oral or vocal aspect of political decentralization. Because he gave Italy a national idiom, Dante was hailed by the nationalists of the 1700s and 1800s as the father of the Italian nation. His *Divine Comedy*, written in the native Tuscan, became exceptionally praiseworthy, and because of this the Tuscan dialect gradually became accepted as the standard literary language of the Italian-people. As we have intimated, Italian had a rough road to travel. More copies of the *Divine Comedy* were sold between 1815–48 than in the preceding two hundred years. Prelates and theologians associated Latin with the Bible, Christianity, the church, and papacy, all God-given. The church vigorously opposed the printing of the Scriptures, thus depriving the Italians of a superior inducement to learn to read, as well as impeding the advance of a popular medium. For another thing, any move toward Italian was bound to provoke a backlash among city and rural poets who openly resented any degree of prominence obtained by Italian at their dialects' expense.

Elsewhere in Europe, as the state expanded its political control and tightened administration, the language spoken in the capital became the official tongue. It was no accident that one of the results of the One Hundred Years War (1337–1453) between England and France was that England dropped the use of the French language in public use since the Norman conquest in 1066. Since the dynastic tie appeared severed, it was foolish to continue with French. Italy, with no process of state building, was adversely affected. The establishment of foreign regimes also interfered with the acceptance of Italian. Out of instinct, dependency, and for ingratiating purposes, upper and middle class Italians took on the language of the occupying powers. The dramatist Vittorio Alfieri (1749–1803) informs us that he did not begin to study Italian until 1775, when he was twenty-six years old. Italian was proscribed in his Piedmont homeland in favor of French and the provincial dialects. It was the assignment of the literary nationalists to press for the adoption of Italian as the mother idiom. They argued, as we shall see, that a national language, national authors, and a national literature were essential for the development of an effective public spirit, a treasure Italy sadly lacked. In 1754, Genovesi incited quite a stir when he broke with practice and decided to conduct his famous course on civil economy at the University of Naples in Italian rather than Latin.

CHAPTER 2

IN SEARCH OF ITALY

A USABLE PAST. Such designations as "pre-Roman Italy," "Roman Italy," "Renaissance Italy," and "Roman Catholic Italy," among others, presuppose that there were various Italies before the Italy which eventuated in 1861. These several editions of Italy became an interminable issue for generations of patriots and nationalists. They were forced to grapple with which version was to serve as the model of the new Italy and which was to be discarded. Debates were intensified because spokesmen did not envision unification as an end in itself but as the point of departure for Italy's glorious world role. Such a divisive and disruptive subject became a hindrance to the growth of national consciousness. Still, Italy could not be united until a workable compromise was reached over which Italy was genuine and worthy of emulation.

THE LEGACY OF ANCIENT ROME. The Roman Empire had vast range, extending from Hibernia (Ireland) on the northwest to the Indus River on the southeast, the Danube on the north and the coastal area of Africa on the south. It contained about 75,000,000 people of different nationalities and levels of culture. It had durability and based position and power not so much on ethnicity as on Roman citizenship, available to all according to the dictates of political prudence, social peace, and good will. This daring experiment in an international system of law and order presided over by Rome was not easily forgotten. Following the collapse of the western axis of the empire in 476, four major states or empires emerged, each advertising itself as the sole custodian of Roman universality, while their respective heads publicized themselves as the logical heir to Caesar's seat in Rome. The four were the Eastern Roman Empire, Charlemagne's Frankish Kingdom, the Holy Roman Empire of the German Nation, and the Roman Catholic Church. Italy became the battleground of their conflicting ambitions. The attraction exercised by Roman universality is illustrated by the titles formulated by Otto I, following his coronation as Holy Roman

Emperor in Rome by Pope John XII, in 968. Among the terms of reference were *Imperium Romanorum*, *Imperium Caesarianium*, *Imperium Octavianium* [Roman Empire, Caesar's Empire, Octavian's Empire]. Boniface VIII, pope between 1294–1303, frequently substituted the imperial dress and regalia for papal vestments. "I am Pope, I am Caesar" was his characteristic explanation.

CAMPANILISMO. Italians attempted to exploit to their advantage the clash of rival interests. They turned inward to the web of relationships being worked out between the major city and its countryside. Urban centers gradually absorbed rural districts into their jurisdiction. The degree of assimilation taking place and the broadening network of responsibilities assumed by the metropolitan area is best symbolized by the *campanile-torre* (belfry-tower), first planned and erected in Florence by one of the early Renaissance masters, Beniamino Giotto. A type of localism came into being, called *campanilismo*. Translated, it meant that one's sole political allegiance was to one's city, whose *piazza* (public square) was conveniently accessible, and whose main cathedral and bell were visible and audible to all the citizenry. Pride, opportunity, and mutual jealousies prompted Venice, Genoa, Pisa, and other maritime cities to venture forth and break the power of the Moslems over the Mediterranean and adjoining sea lanes. Vast economic possibilities presented themselves as Venice and Genoa became the middlemen in the burgeoning trade between Western Europe and the Middle East and as the same cities provided the shipping, ports of embarkation, and nautical knowledge for the crusades called by the popes to wrest control of the holy places of Christendom from the Moslems. Lure of profit and the advance of commerce radiated their impact far and wide.

In north and central Italy, noble class families transferred themselves from the agrarian sections to the cities and towns and eventually went into banking, commerce, manufacturing, and government. Those of the lower classes who migrated to the cities and towns became artists, craftsmen, and shopkeepers. The accelerating awareness of the dawn of a new world and of the social responsibilities attending wealth helped to secure the patronage and resources of mind, soul, and spirit for the cultural flowering of the Renaissance. Increased confidence motivated cities to become more bold and to capitalize more fully on the animosities between the Empire and the papacy for the liberty and autonomy associated with the Era of the Communes (1000–1250).

CAMPANILISMO AND THE UNIVERSAL EMPIRE.

One occasion arrived with the advent of Frederick I, called *Barbarossa* (Red Beard) by the Italians, to the imperial throne in 1152. To thwart Frederick's plans for the consolidation of his power over the peninsula, self-governing cities of Lombardy, led by Milan, joined, in 1168, in the Lombard League. The coalition decisively defeated Barbarossa at the Battle of Legnano, 1176, thereby crushing Frederick's imperial pretensions over Italy. Legnano can be considered a victory for inter-Italian cooperation only in a limited vein. True, the battle cry of the Lombard League was "the Fatherland and Liberty." What was understood by fatherland was the individual city-commune and by liberty its right to be independent and free from any form of coercion. That was the vision of Italy the participants cherished. On the morrow of the smashing triumph, *campanilismo* became more entrenched. The mood of collaboration vanished once the foreign danger had been eased. Frederick's troops had been recruited in Italy, which also prevented the war from acquiring national or nationalist overtones. The trade guilds and entrepreneurial corporations not only set standards but also encouraged interregional competition. Another example of exclusivism occurred in 1395, when Gian Galeazzo Visconti was elected Duke of Milan. The major metropolis was overpowering to the extent that not only the city-commune took its name from it but also the city-republics that represented, as the historian Jacob Burckhardt observed, the indispensable political foundations of the Renaissance. It was the Duchy of Milan and not of Lombardy, the Republic of Florence, not of Tuscany.

CAMPANILISMO AND THE UNIVERSAL CHURCH.

The pope, the bishop of Rome, was spiritually revered as the Vicar of Christ and by many of the devotees as the authentic political descendant of the Caesars. The church claimed title to Rome and the States of the church which cut the peninsula in two. The papacy opposed the German emperor's hegemoniac ambitions and it fought any initiative in Italy which might lead to a national state, as it was taking shape in the West, and which had engendered bitter strife with the Holy See. The Vatican encouraged the cities of Lombardy to organize the Lombard League and then, after victory, maneuvered against its perpetuation out of fear that the League might become an agency for transpeninsula cooperation, which would jeopardize the church's dominant position and temporal power. Caught between the Empire and the church, Italians tried to use one as a buffer against the other. The *Guelfi* (Guelphs) were the Italian counterpart to the German Stauben Dynasty and its German supporters, arch enemies of Frederick's Italian connection. They believed that the liberty of the Communes could only be safeguarded by courting the active favor of the Church and popes. *Ghibellini* [Ghibellines], from the German Hohenstauben Dynasty and Frederick's backers in Germany, disputed the Guelph rationale. Dante was the most prestigious and vocal exponent of the Ghibelline view. He argued that the political framework was broader than the religious and that the German emperor's right to total sovereignty was not founded on papal privilege or church concession but on the divine will. The papacy was not the guarantor of the peninsula's peace but the power which kept it in turmoil.

CAMPANILISMO AND RENAISSANCE HUMANISM.
During the Renaissance, 1300–1550, Italians experienced a re-legitimization of political localism along with another universalism, that of arts and letters. Deliberately or unwittingly, Italians reached out toward a patrimony of culture. Qualifications for belonging were a cultivated mind, a cosmopolitan outlook, and a rigorous civic conscience. It was natural for Italians to esteem Renaissance Italy as the true Italy, the essence of the Italian genius. Concentration on cultural pursuits and a corollary ascription to a cultural globalism disarmed the Italians and left them unprepared to meet the threat to the future stemming from the Empire and the church and the rising national monarchies of France, Spain, and later of Austria. They were oblivious to the temptation posed to foreign states by a peninsula cut into bits and pieces. Charles VIII and the French descended into Italy in 1494,

the Spanish were drawn into the Italian cockpit in 1500 through King Ferdinand, followed by King Charles I (later Emperor Charles V), and then the Austrian Hapsburgs.

The prevailing Italian state of mind is reflected by many writers, particularly by the political theorist Niccolò Machiavelli (1469–1527). Like Dante and Petrarch, Machiavelli assailed the political manipulations of the papacy and the scandalous intrigues of the papal court. He was one with Petrarch in disclosing that the ancient Roman patriotic spirit and fighting qualities had not been extinguished but had been deflected and dispersed among the militias and mercenary forces of the many municipalities. In his better moments, Machiavelli invoked a liberator in the guise of a military commander, a shrewd statesman and master diplomat, a "pope-prince" who would galvanize Italy's numerous states and drive out "the new barbarians." (*See Reading No. 4.*) Machiavelli, however, did not become a proponent of unification. He ended his explorations by reducing his hopes for an enabling prince to a delusive chimera. A would-be savior would simply be no match for the popes, emperors, and despots who depended on regional animosities and inter-republic bickering to protect their positions. Captivated by the sustained high activity of the Renaissance, Machiavelli could not surmount its narrow political base.

REASSESSMENT: THE ATTACK AGAINST ITALY'S ROMAN PAST. The destruction of the political equilibrium which had been established among the states of Renaissance Italy provided an impetus for a reappraisal of multi-and international institutions, such as the Roman Empire and the Roman Catholic Church., A major breakthrough in the examination of Italy's past was achieved by the Neapolitan sage, Vico. In *De antiquissima italorum sapientia* (*On the Ancient Wisdom of the Italians*) (1710), he employed philology to prove that the vocabulary in daily use by the Etruscans was of a profound and abstract nature and, therefore, could not have been attributed to Rome's civilizing mission. Vico's probing into the pre-Roman era bore fruit in several directions. An objective compilation, free of adulation, Gerolamo Tiraboschi's *Storia della letteratura italiana* (9 vols.; 1772–81), opened with Etruscan poets. Another noteworthy undertaking was that of Ludovico Antonio Muratori

(1672–1750), who assembled thousands of the major source materials of Italian history. Firsthand acquaintance with the testimentary evidence of Italy's past provoked shock over what the Modenese Muratori denounced as the brazenly novel dictatorial rule introduced by the Caesars. His favorite Italy, as it was for Alfieri, was Medieval Italy, particularly the Italy of the Communal Era, because of the tight mutuality between urban and rural areas, the intimate political loyalties, and the stability represented by Christian institutions.

A number of histories were produced, which focused on Italy's pre-Roman antecedents. Since the Romans had revolted against the Etruscans in 509 B.C., and had begun by that date their domination of the peninsula, Etruria and Etruscan became the code terms for the Italic tribes. Many among the historians involved gravitated from a fanciful Etruscanophilism to a stark Romanophobia, understandable given their purposes. A Rome heralded by all the peoples in the West as the progenitor of nations was too broad a shared paternity to assist people in search of their spiritual moorings. Giuseppe Micali's *Italia avanti il dominio dei romani* (*Italy before the Roman Dominion*) (1810) affirmed that the Italians were literate and sophisticated in their own right. There was an Italy in the formative stage under the generous and judicious Etruscans. In his *Delle rivoluzioni d'Italia* (3 vols., 1769–1770), Carlo Denina condemned the Romans as vultures who did not organize the peninsula but commandeered its resources for their selfish ends. One of the fateful results was that when the Roman Empire disintegrated, Italians found it impossible to mobilize their energies and prevent Italy from being overrun by foreigners.

This anti-Roman exegisis was climaxed by the Neapolitan political figure, Vincenzo Cuoco (1770–1823), with his *Viaggio di Platone in Italia* (*Plato in Italy*) (3 vols., 1804–06). Cuoco deferred to the authoritative philosopher who lectured his countrymen on the matchless accomplishments of the ancient Italians, above all of the Etruscans, who were adjudged to have had a civilization superior to that of Greece and Rome. Indeed, it was the Italians who brought civilization to the Greeks. Had the Romans not interfered and allowed the indigenous cultures to take their natural course, the situation would have resulted in peninsula unification. The Italians were not without faults of their own. They had lowered their guard and allowed themselves to be seduced by promises of peace, security, and prosperity. Written at a time when many nationalists expected Napoleon to unite the peninsula, Cuoco's message was also meant to be a warning against the forgetting of history's lessons. Napoleon was simply interested in subjugating Italy and impressing her within the French *imperium*, as the Romans and contemplated with the Italic peoples.

REASSESSMENT: THE ATTACK AGAINST THE UNIVERSAL CHURCH. Many were the forces which independently and concertedly undercut the church's position in society. The vigor with which the Holy Roman Empire and the Emperor pushed their interests acted as a counterweight. Dante's endorsement of their prerogatives remained a concern with which the papacy had to reckon. The Italian vernacular was a worrisome abomination. Renaissance humanism made substantial inroads. Then there was the Protestant Reformation, 1517, with its emphasis on personal salvation rather than institutional religion. The rise of Protestant state churches, biblical scholarship, the more rational explanation of creedal precepts, and the consolidation of the national hereditary monarchies combined to undermine the catholicity of the Roman church. Sundry reform movements, such as the Cluniac, Cistercian, Dominican, and Franciscan, enriched the church with their newer approaches to piety and religious living but their appearances were also symptomatic of the low spiritual climate prevailing in the upper echelons of the church. More demanding and controversial were the Jansenists, anticlericals, and Freemasons.

Jansenism, named after Cornelius Jansenius (?–1638), Bishop of Ypres, called for a purified church, a sanctified priesthood, and a restructuring of the papacy to resemble the simplified organizational leadership exemplified in the New Testament Church. Whether high church dignitaries or humble clerics, state ministers or lay writers, Jansenists were outspoken in assailing the temporal power and the pope's claims to infallibility. The pope was to become what God intended a pastor to be, the shepherd of Christ's flock, and the executor of the church councils' will. Because the Jesuits had arrogated control of education, they were seen as most doctrinaire, inclined to venality and laxity, and possessed of an incorrigible urge to foment jurisdictional disputes among Catholic societies, the Jansenists singled them out for sharp rebuke. It was primarily due to Jansenist mounting pressure that the Jesuits were expelled from most countries by July 1773, the order dissolved by Clement XIV, and most of the posts vacated immediately filled by Jansenists. In the moment of triumph, Jansenist excesses and disabilities came to the fore in bold relief. Its dogmatic spirit alienated many. Statesmen in the Italian states backed away, thinking it better than to be embroiled in another round of bickering between an aroused Ghibellinism and an outraged Guelphism. Jansenism was criticized for being elitist and deficient in rank-and-file appeal. It engendered cries of Protestantism and Germanism. With the shift in sentiment, popes found it conveniently advisable to censure and ban Jansenist teaching in stages, the final blow falling at the close of the 1700s. Jansenism managed to leave a lasting mark on nationalists from Mazzini to the famed novelist Alessandro Manzoni (1785–1873), and from Cavour to Gioberti, however different their political philosophies. Within the church it brought forth a liberal Catholicism which was antitemporalist and for political separation of church and state.

Anticlericalism was a more intellectual offensive carried on within the framework of the search for Italy. It was a product of the Enlightenment. Because of the church's monopolistic control, Italian schooling was heavy on the abstract and the theoretical, and weak in the practical arts and social commitment. The historian and jurisconsult Pietro Giannone (1676–1748) ridiculed church learning for its sterile erudition and its intolerance. Galileo's attitude was strongly recommended and was to be copied, characterized by objectivity, a holy curiosity, and a saintly disposition toward uncovering the processes of the natural world. The focal point of reference of anticlerical protests was the church's political power. Italy could never be thoroughly cleared of foreigners until and unless the church's hold was permanently broken. The States of the church had to be relinquished and the church's exceptional privileges elsewhere were to be rescinded. No modern state could coexist with them. Arguments previously aired from Dante to Machiavelli regarding the insidious manner in which the papacy maneuvered to keep Italy split were reiterated and given a keener edge. Political citizenship represented the coming consciousness. A Catholic and papal Italy would not do. The emergent civilization had to develop its parallel set of loyalties and its own unchallengeable nexus of relationships. Anticlericals maintained that an impartial investigation would undoubtedly prove that the church-papal assertions to rulership and temporal power were not biblically founded but rested on lies.

The church retaliated with suppression, excommunication, forced exile, and censorship. Although many anticlericals declared themselves within the Christian Church, the litany of grievances they presented and the radical remedies they proposed were too far-reaching to be accepted except to a small minority of thinkers. Guelphs, papists, and clericals succeeded, as they had with the Jansenists, in lumping anticlericals with Protestants, Deists, outright atheists, and also with the outlawed Jansenists. Anticlericalism had to await the onset of modern culture. Popes and churchmen fulminated against it but anticlericalism was formally outside of the church and was able to penetrate restricted but sensitive areas of Italian society, where it remained a lively current of thought.

Due to its zeal and contentious mood, enemies lampooned Freemasonry as "the Society of Jesus of the Enlightenment." Its avowed goal was the brotherhood of all people. Between 1733 and 1780, lodges were organized in Florence, Rome, Turin, Genoa, Milan, and Naples. To the Freemasons, the Catholic Church was the enemy. They took up the themes discussed by the Jansenists and anticlericals, and clamored for an Italy of independent states, the church deprived of temporal power, and the papacy divested of princely trappings. Its progressive and humanitarian aims to the contrary, Freemasonry in Italy reduced itself to a crude and vitriolic form of anticlericalism, bordering on the psychopathic. Italians could not relate to it. Freemasonry was accused of being a cabal of undesirables, anti-Catholic and anti-church. The elaborate organization, the secrecy with which it conducted its business, together with the mysterious rituals, left Italians convinced that Freemasonry belonged to the occult and the diabolical. More than 300 papal denunciations were issued from 1738 to 1900. Freemasonry survived and won additional members over the church's implacable hostility to reform and to a more open society. By 1865, there were 185 lodges in Italy, all thriving, with the number of adherents unknown. A select minority of public personalities from Francesco Crispi to Garibaldi and to Benito Mussolini belonged. As a movement, Freemasonry did not participate in Italian liberation or unification. The fact, however, that it did not hesitate to confront the church and the papacy, who were against unification, contributed to the strengthening of the idea that the Italy to be born anew was not a confessional Italy, linked with the church and papacy, but a separate and secular Italy.

MAZZINI AND THE MISSION OF THE THIRD ROME.

The assaults against the Roman Empire and the universal Church were only indirectly related to Italy's liberation and unification. Not so with Mazzini and Gioberti who integrated both within their schematics and targeted their outpourings on the ideological orientation of postunification Italy. As a son of the Enlightenment, Mazzini subscribed to peace, altruism, and progress. His attention was arrested by organized movements, those grand and imaginative undertakings of a cosmic nature through which mankind was inspired to march onward. Because history and life turn primarily on spiritual dynamics and not on materialist determination, Mazzini brought the heavenly and the terrestrial together in his famous slogan, "God and the People." Small wonder, then, that "the Duties of Man are sacred." Italy, with her third appearance, following the Roman Empire and the Medieval church, was to lead the world to brotherhood under God. The purpose of the new Italy was to bring about the liberation of all peoples and make possible their incorporation within a supranational order, which would promote perpetual peace and unlimited progress. (*See Reading No. 5.*)

The many volunteers from Austria's and the Ottoman Empire's subject minorities who flocked to Garibaldi's Thousand: Poles, Serbians, Albanians, Magyars, Ruthenians, and took part in the liberation of the south in 1860, offered momentary reality and immediate promise to the Mazzinian prophecy. The parent of many subsequent and spontaneous international brigades for the cause of self-determination, the foreign contingents were drawn from Mazzini's Young Europe. On a more limited plane, within the Italian context, the need was for the coordination of all nationalist elements and have them collaborate for the liberation and unification of the peninsula. With Mazzini, it was more of a spiritual crusade and for moral upliftment than a sheer political campaign, as he went about rallying and educating his audiences to his exciting dream. Mazzini's more immediate hopes for Italy seemed on the brink of a realization in the tumultuous days of 1848–49, when his Roman Republic called for a constituent assembly of the Italian states, which would nullify the temporal power of the church, give Rome back to the Italian people, mobilize energies for a war of liberation against Austria, and create the Italian unitary democratic republic.

GIOBERTI AND THE ITALIAN PRIMACY. Born in Turin, April 5, 1801, Gioberti entered the priesthood and later left it for politics and governmental service. Having been implicated in revolutionary activities, he was arrested in 1833, tried, and imprisoned. When set free, Gioberti repaired to Paris and then to Brussels, where he completed the monumental *Del primato morale e civile degli italiani* (3 vols., 1843). As Gioberti unravelled Italian "superiority," there was not anything of merit that he did not ascribe to Italian creative impulses. Italy was the geographic center of the earth and the most inventive and cosmopolitan of countries. Through all the upheavals and alien subjugations, Italy had retained a form of unity and cohesion with Christianity and the church establishment. The church, "a spiritual monarchy," like the Roman Empire, Communes, and Renaissance city-republics, was another institution quintessentially Italian. Implicit in Gioberti's *Primacy*, as in Mazzini's *Mission*, was Vico's cyclical theory of history. The distinguished service Italy had performed for humanity in the past was a peg on the future. Her right to liberation and independence, and her involvement in another round of praiseworthy labor for mankind was premised on Rome, the Renaissance, and Catholicism. A unified and restored Italy would stem the advance of Protestantism, which Gioberti charged was an apostate religion with a veneer of piety. A fully revitalized Italy would also rid the world of the French radical variant of the Enlightenment and the Mazzinian version, whose naïve notions of egalitarian democracy and republican government would spell society's doom.

Gioberti, like the historian and statesman Cesare Balbo

(1799–1859), held that the only true and viable nationalist doctrine was Neo-Guelphism, the "Neo" originally prefixed by the anticlerical revolutionaries Gabriele Pepe and Giuseppe Ferrari. So intertwined were the fortunes of Italy, the church, and the papacy that the only hope for unification lay in a papal-church initiative. To Gioberti, the pope was an Italian prince, and he seemed to have had in mind the "pope-prince" of Machiavellian stamp. It was because of the deepest appreciation of the undeniable presence of the church and papacy on Italian soil and their irrefutable importance for Italian destiny that Gioberti espoused the unification of all Italy with the pope as the spearhead and the church as the rallying force. Gioberti proposed a confederation, embracing Piedmont in the north, the Church States in the center, and the Kingdom of the Two Sicilies in the south, each with its own ruling house, and the pope as titular president. Gioberti's confederative policy was designed to foster a general transformation under the papacy, by which all Italians were to be reunited and the country reawakened to its responsibilities as "the universal fatherland and regenerating nation of the human family." *(See Reading No. 6.)*

CAVOUR'S HISTORICISM. Count Camillo Benso di Cavour was born in Turin on August 10, 1810, of noble stock, with his mother a descendant of a Swiss-Genevan Calvinist ancestry. He attended military academy, where he excelled in the humanities rather than the sciences. On the subject of Italy's usable past, which manifestation of Italy commanded imitation, and what was to be the external outlook of a unified Italian state, Cavour marched to a different tune from Mazzini and Garibaldi. He rejected Luigi Mercanini's Hymn to Garibaldi because it was jingoistic, gory, and in bad taste. It is surprising how little, if anything at all, Cavour had to say about Italy's mission, the Roman Empire, pre-Roman Italic tribes, the Communes, Renaissance, and the Medieval Church. There was no stirring drama to be re-enacted, or apocalyptic purpose to be resumed, with Italy the main protagonist or central actor.

Cavour's perception of reality, his understanding of historical forces, was antithetical to Mazzini's and Gioberti's. History could not be accelerated in tempo to accommodate Mazzini's great leap of faith any more than it could be rolled back to entertain Gioberti's new-fangled medievalism. Unviconian, history, for Cavour, did not repeat itself. According to Cavour's way of thinking, there was no precedent to support Mazzini's hypothesis of a unification through a mass, creative act of the people. The French and Russian states, to cite two examples, began with a center, the *Ile de France* and the Duchy of Muscovy, respectively. Each gradually enlarged its domain to the limits suggested by geography, language, statecraft, and good fortune. As for Gioberti's confederation, it was nonsensical to assume that the times would sanction a confederation rather than the unitary, national state. If a democratic republic was unhistorical because untimely, and a federated Neo-Guelph order was antihistorical because outdated, the times, it appeared, might possibly allow the moderately liberal, monarchical, constitutional state. In contrast to Mazzini and Gioberti and their followers, the democratic republicans, the Neo-Guelph and monarchical federalists, respectively, Cavour opted for a state-articulated and government-directed nationalism, based neither on the people nor on popes and princes but on dynastic, political, administrative, social and economic institutions. The fact that Italy was made that way vindicated Cavour's grasp of current forces and historical realities.

CHAPTER 3

ROOTS OF ITALIAN NATIONALISM

DEFENSIVE NATURE. Nationalism was hammered out on the anvil of foreign occupations and papal-church meddling in politics. The nation-state was only accepted as a last resort to eliminate them once and for all. Articulate Italians would have been delighted had the balance of power achieved among the Italian states during the Renaissance been preserved and, when overturned, restored. Having established a new particularism with the city-state republics and having thrust toward a global humanism, Italians were forced to retreat to the intermediate stage of organized life, that of the nation-state. This backtracking was a painful experience, and it occurred while the center of economic gravity was shifting from the Italian maritime city-state republics on the Mediterranean to the states which were well along in the process of building the nation-state and which were strategically situated on the Atlantic seaboard. Nationalism for the Italians was not a primary choice but one imposed by a more realistic understanding of the world. Italians were first concerned with the liberation of the peninsula; only much later did they take to unification as the final solution. Liberationists were not inherently unificationists, nor did liberation and the desire for unification automatically complement one another.

AT LOW EBB. It would be an error to think that Italy stagnated overnight or that Italians suddenly lost their creative genius. In spite of repression and the stifling atmosphere chargeable to the foreign powers, church, and despotic states, a spirit of inquiry still characterized sectors of Italian society from the 1500s to the 1700s. Italians contributed to mathematics, experimental science, engineering, philosophy, theology, nautical knowledge, and instrumental, concert, choral, operatic, and orchestral music. On the whole, the years were marked by a general loss of vigor. The cultural leadership was fast fading. With minor exceptions, the rigidity in religion found correspondence in the sphere of politics. There was a blanket refusal to come to terms with newer forces. The trend was toward absolutism in the papal states, the occupied areas, the Duchy of Savoy, and toward aristocratic republics in Florence, Milan, Genoa, and Venice. It was the union of the throne and the altar to protect entrenched interests.

Once at the center of overseas trade, Italy was now relegated to the periphery. During the 1500s, Genoese bankers remained in an ascendant position but the bulk of their financial dealings were not fielded in Italy but went to finance Spain's European and transoceanic ventures. The irrepressible Turkish advance, following the capture of Constantinople in 1453, eroded the Venetian presence in the East. The victory registered at Lepanto (1571) by Venice and her allies was but a reprieve. In short order, Turkey resumed her march north and westward, disrupting traffic in the Eastern and Central Mediterranean, the Aegean, Ionian Seas, and the Adriatic. The Barbary pirates of North Africa ravaged shipping in the Central and Western Mediterranean as their forefathers had from pre-Roman days and their descendants after them. The crucial place assigned colonies by the mercantilist school of economics had limited appeal, if any, to Italians. Survival was the main priority. The future belonged to the unified states of Portugal, Spain, France, Netherlands, and England, which expanded overseas and established impressive colonial empires. With the decline in commercial activity, most of the surplus capital available from 1600 on was put into land. Estate ownership became the mainstay and cutting edge of society. The failure of regimes in occupied Italy to stimulate private initiative through judicious tax policies, road construction, and subsidies, combined with the downward trend to trade to move people from the cities and towns to the countryside. Milan's population, 300,000 in 1400, dwindled, under Spanish rule, to 100,000 in 1500. The city's 70 woolen mills were reduced to 5. If pockets of agricultural revitalization resulted in the northern and central regions of the peninsula, in the south those who owned the large holdings, called *latifundia* from Roman times, rented them to upper bourgeoisie capitalist farmers who drove hard bargains with peasants and day laborers, whose lot steadily worsened. By 1600, begging and paupery reached endemic proportions in the south.

Italians sheepishly adopted the customs and mannerisms of the invaders. Upper classes studied and spoke French, Spanish, and German. Dante's Italian was dropped in public communications and polite discourse. The dialects were also held in contempt. During the Spanish period, speech patterns and scribal formulations became as pompous and as stilted as the prevailing baroque style in architecture and sculpture. Whereas it had been the custom to refer directly to individuals with the simple singular second person of *tu* and plural *voi*, the replacements became *Lei* and *Loro*. *Vostra Signoria* (Your Lordship), *Eccelenza* (Excellency), and *Vostra Magnificenza* (Your Reverence) became the new words of salutation. Such discriminatory airs and high sounding titles widened the gap between the upper and lower classes.

As a take-off from the baroque, the houses of the wealthy became more palatial, with a superabundant use of elegant facades and bulging cornices, large balconies, worked marble, and pressed ornamental iron grills. Estate grounds featured elaborate gardens, which resembled parks, with massive trees and broad bushes, large flower beds, swirling lanes, and spectacular water falls cascading into huge basins or artificial lakes. Rambling vines were everywhere. Garments and vestments, whether men's or women's, were of heavy brocade, studded with buttons, and lavishly adorned with gold and silver amulets. French sartorial tastes were hardly less flamboyant than the Spanish, with the ridiculous scarf and the equally bizarre handkerchief cropping out of the sleeve cuff. The Italian *moda* was translated from the French *mode* to describe the increasing dependence of the Italian noble class on the latest French fashions. By 1630, men wore their hair to the shoulders and powdered wigs became commonplace. Female social pace setters by midcentury also adopted the wig and made it, pretentious and grotesque, a requirement of high coiffure.

Culinary arts were not exempt from the flair for display and for substituting foreign forms for native ways. Florentines had exported their cuisine to France and the French subsequently transformed it into their own. Austrians appropriated veal cutlet *alla Milanese* and turned it into *weiner schnitzel*. The positions were reversed. Italian aristocratic families boasted of a French chef or of an Italian cook who had learned his craft in France. French wines were preferred to the Italian, with the label readily identifiable, solid evidence that the partakers were connoisseurs of the finest. The *Caffé*, indoors or out, became a familiar sight among the upper middle classes and nobles as a refreshment station, where coffee, tea, and chocolate were served, to assist the habitués or those who stopped by to chatter or as they grappled with major issues. In the eighteenth century, roast beef, steak, pudding, and beer, all borrowings from the English, graced the menus and dinner tables of the *bon vivant*. Tobacco took hold by 1700. Cigarettes were confined to the lower orders and the military, while pipes were the rage of the bourgeoisie and the gentry. Due to the high cost of importation, cigars attracted a small clientele among the well-to-do.

All this was indicative of a culture that was self-indulgent and hostage to foreign fads, with little thought of sacrifice for Italy. Such a shallow outlook and frivolous temper, which indiscriminately copied the social etiquette and moral code of Italy's enslavers, did not condemn the latter as the destroyers of Italian independence but, instead, inspired exaltation of them as Providence's chosen vessels to set the world a right and "to return Italy to her golden age." That the situation could inspire revulsion is poignantly illustrated by the number of Italians, from explorers and merchants, economists and biblical scholars, to generals, who sought refuge in emigration and exile. Exposed to newer currents of thought, some of the expatriates, like Alfieri and Pietro Verri, returned to work for the liberation of the peninsula and Italy's reintroduction to the mainstream of continental life.

PROTESTORS AND PROTESTS. Nineteenth-century historians, impatient over the slow and torturous progress of nationalism, dismissed the sixteenth and seventeenth centuries as ones of stultifying conformity and rank dilettantism, of general unconcern for the peninsula's loss of freedom. The characterization is unfair. In spite of the persecutorial climate fostered by the post-Tridentine church, foreign regimes, and their princely Italian cohorts, there still remained those who could neither be forced to leave nor be silenced. They spoke out forcefully and advised their countrymen on the direction Italy had to take even if they did not exactly chart the course. The nucleus of a national liberation campaign was laid, which was to pick up momentum and acquire definable shape over the years. By the nineteenth century, it became a mature, many-sided nationalist movement, climaxed by an irrepressible call for national self-determination.

Apparently, there was sufficient vitality in Italian society for it to nourish its own critics. To begin with, the blind and fanciful emulation of foreign ways was labelled "apish" and "monkey-like." The abject submissiveness and absence of self-esteem were revolting. Patriots put Spain under public rebuke. The revolts in Naples and Palermo in the 1640s, although not ideological, were proof that not all Italians acquiesced to Spanish misgovernment. Aroused by the resounding defeat of the Spanish Armada in 1588, with a loss of 25,000 men, thoughtful men undertook a review of Spanish rule and Italian attitudes. In one broadside following another, they exposed the incorrigible defects and precarious nature of Spanish domination which, they argued, only maintained itself because of the connivance of the church, princes, and the upper classes. Reminiscent of Machiavelli, they blamed Italy's worsening plight on the mutual antagonism of Italian leaders. All forms of foreign rule were contrary to God's will and open to his wrath. Vico rejected the baroque style because, he charged, it had come from Spain and was in conflict with the plain classical tradition adhered to by Italians from Italic days. Pietro and Alessandro Verri and their associates who flanked the *Caffè* held up to scorn the moral weaklings who were bought by official sinecures and vain titles of recognition. International developments gave the complaints an exceptional relevance. Having begun in 1580 his half-century of rule as Duke of Savoy, Charles Emmanuel I labored to seize Spanish Lombardy and secure the royal crown for himself. To prepare for the possibility, he commissioned agents to undertake an educational campaign throughout Italy. The pending war was to be a crusade of all Italians against the common enemy, Spain. Spain immediately issued an ultimatum demanding demobilization of Savoy's army. Sympathetic to the liberating context in which he thought the conflict was cast, the writer Alessandro Tassoni reacted with *Filippiche contro gli spagnuoli* (*Philippics against the Spanish*) (Rome, 1614). (*See Reading No. 7.*) He and those of like mind were disheartened as their pleas for concerted action went unheeded and Charles and Savoy were left to face Spain alone and were defeated. In the aftermath of failure, Carlo Antonio Pilati and Mario Rigotti, among others, turned to Venice, hoping that the Venetians, having lost their commercial empire, could be persuaded to concentrate their energies on Italy, the fatherland, and work for an Italian rebirth. One can almost detect in their appeals a veiled hint for unification, as well as liberation.

DATING OF THE RISORGIMENTO. The *Risorgimento* was the general awakening that occurred in key sectors of Italian society, climaxed by the unification of the peninsula's people. It was a multidimensional phenomenon. In determining the beginning of the *Risorgimento*, historians favor political-diplomatic-military developments because they tend to be quantifiable and convergent. There is no unanimous agreement on the actual start of the upsurgence of the Italian people. There are scholars who choose 1601, when the Treaty of Lyons was signed between Savoy and France. It marked Savoy's renunciation of territorial designs westward on France and the redirecting of her expansionist aspirations toward the peninsula. The path was cleared for Charles Emmanuel's campaign to oppose Spain in a war for Lombardy. Implicit is an admission that Savoy's ambitions were incremental and that they culminated with Piedmont's leading role in the unification of Italy under the House of Savoy. Others have cited the epochal and critical importance of June 4, 1690, when Victor Amadeus II (1675–1730) of Savoy was invited to join the Grand Alliance against the aggressive intentions of Louis XIV and France. An Italian state had become sufficiently significant to be urged to enter a coalition of European powers against the disturber of the peace. The War of the League of Augsburg (1686–97) offered Savoy the opportunity to gain valuable military experience, although defeats forced Savoy to sign a separate peace in 1696, which restored the prewar boundaries.

A number of students of Italian nationalism have regarded Savoy's involvement in the War of the Spanish Succession (1701–13) as the inauguration of the *Risorgimento*. It confirmed Savoy's status in continental affairs. The Peace of Utrecht which ended the conflict had Austria replace Spain in Lombardy and in Naples and Sardinia. Austrian policies, if far from liberal, were less repressive than her predecessor's. Utrecht also enlarged Savoy's holdings to include Sicily. With an enlarged domain, Savoy became the Kingdom of Piedmont and Amadeus was elevated to the kingship. Here is the initiation of the relationship of Savoy-Piedmont with Italian fortunes. In 1720, Sicily was exchanged for Sardinia, and the territory over which the Savoys ruled was called the Kingdom of Piedmont-Sardinia, or simply Piedmont for our purposes. Consistent with political-diplomatic-military considerations, individuals like Gioberti chose 1848 as the *annus mirabilis* because of the uprisings in several parts of the peninsula and the war of liberation and for an Italian confederation fought single-handedly by Piedmont against Austria. The late historian Luigi Salvatorelli objected to what he detected was a pro-Piedmontese interpretation of the *Risorgimento*. As Savoy or as Piedmont, the Savoyards were driven by their own family dreams, and were only converted to liberation and unification when the nationalist bandwagon was moving and threatened to isolate or overwhelm them. Salvatorelli drew on the thinking of Giosue Carducci (1835–1907), Italy's greatest postunification poet, to underscore 1748 as the pivotal year. The Treaty of Aix-la-Chapelle, which ended the War of the Austrian Succession (1740–48), left Italy almost completely under its own rulers. Momentous cultural developments, political and liberation ideologies, reform movements, renewal philosophies and unification strategies tended to crystallize in subsequent years.

APPEAL TO HISTORY. Vico was a pioneer and representative figure in the use of Italy's past for revival. His *Ancient Wisdom of the Italians* showed civilization in Italy antedating the Romans; *La scienza nuova* (*The New Science*) (1725) illustrated the successive existential phases all people experience in their lifetime. *Corsi e ricorsi* (*occurrences and reoccurrences*) Vico named them, consisting of birth, infancy, youth, maturity, old age, and death. Then the process repeats itself. The future is unfailingly revealed in history, "the new science," premised on the divine will. Based on Vico's historical cycles and language derivations, expectation spread that Italy would shortly be resurgent. Foreign intrusions and internal factionalism were signs of death. Since language was not a random selection but an emanation of the historical-social-cultural milieu, the fact that Italian was gradually replacing Latin meant that Italy was on the verge of being reborn, if not as a state, certainly as a people. As if to mark the transition, Vico's *New Science* was penned in Italian, in contract to his earlier works written in Latin.

Determined to find in Italy's past a historical imprimatur for her deliverance, Cuoco, Denina, Micali, Tiraboschi, and Giuseppe Maria Galante spurred national thought and contributed towards helping Italians overcome their sense of obligation to Rome. The existence of a peninsula of independent states before Rome set a historical precedent and served to educate patriots and foster optimism. Tapping history as the singular authority motivated the former priest, historian, and incredibly prodigious antiquarian, Muratori. Burdened because Italians, unlike other major people, lacked documentary verification of their glorious past, he decided to fill the void, which he proceeded to do with *Rerum italicarum scriptores* (*Documents of Italian Events*) (28 vols., 1723–51), covering the period 500–1500 chronologically, and the collateral effort, *Annali d'Italia* (*Annals of Italian History*) (12 vols., 1752–54), which went over the same ground with interdisciplinary, interpretive ideas. In the sense that Muratori supplied a usable store of historical facts, he has been acknowledged as the architect of Italian history. One must, however, stop short of acclaiming Muratori a political nationalist. If he succeeded in amassing Italy's evidentiary heritage, Muratori's declared preference was for the Italy of the Communes and not that of a possible national state.

Just as Muratori was relating national awareness to historical knowledge, Gian Vincenzo Gravina (1664–1718) linked ancient law and modern jurisprudence to historical-social consciousness. Giannone's *Storia civile del regno di Napoli* (2 vols., 1729–31), published in Britain following his excommunication, proved to be a milestone in enlarging the scope of historical inquiry to include the evolution of civil, political, and religious institutions. No subject, not even the church, was immune. History was the only method given to man to get at the real and the authentic, to get away from the hagiographical approach to Etruria, Roman Empire, Communal Era, the Renaissance, the church, and the papacy.

APPEAL TO ECONOMICS AND JURISPRUDENCE. Among the array of economists and economic writers, Pietro Verri and Genovesi stand out because they were progressive and they struggled for the implementation of their ideas. Having been advisor to Empress Maria Theresa of the Hapsburg Empire, Verri abandoned Vienna and its social world, to apply his time and talent to economic problems, specifically related to the foundations of a stable economy. Allowed to return to his native Milan, Verri undertook archival research on the cause of the city's protracted economic depression. He blamed the downturn in economic activity on the negative policies of the foreign powers. The low quality of public life, discouragement of capital formation, and the loss of private initiative prevented anything resembling a work ethic from being instilled. Verri lashed out at the heavy taxation, numerous internal tolls, and, above all, at the archaic, ludicrous Spanish decisions and practices. Chief among them was a decree of 1573, which declared the vocation of the merchant to be degrading. This had the intended effect of condemning traders to social inferiority while extolling the virtue of the nobles and of property values. The Milanese aristocracy became steeped in landlord inertia and the middle classes lost interest in business pursuits. The flight from the city ensued and manufacturing shops were closed.

A product of the Enlightenment, Verri was convinced that state action could bring about economic upliftment and that the resulting benefits stood to be a gain even for the state, which would profit from greater tax yields. He advocated measures which would restore economics to its rightful place by removing the stigma the Spanish had attached to commerce and industry. The Verri brothers (Pietro and Alessandro), Cesare Beccaria, Paolo Frisi, and other economists and jurisconsults founded the *Accademia dei Pugni* (*Academy of Fisticuffs*) in 1769. The youthful aristocrats who joined the club represented an intellectual vanguard which combatted complacency on all levels of life. With Pietro at thirty-three the oldest, and Alessandro at twenty the youngest, the embattled members championed reason, common sense, and opposed the dead hand of the past. The intelligentsia was urged to leave its ivory tower of scholarly reflection and to get into public affairs, and to educate itself and the people on the momentous issues of the day.

Concerning Genovesi, his cultural surroundings may have been provincial but they did not prevent him from developing a broad and sensitive outlook. A citizen of the Kingdom of Naples and Sicily, Genovesi, trained in philosophy and theology, devoted the major part of his career to agriculture, banking, commerce, and industry. On November 5, 1754, Genovesi was appointed to the chair of political economy at the University of Naples, the first such chair endowed in Europe. Genovesi's use of Italian instead of Latin and his introduction of a new field of learning were unheard of since the institution, established in 1204, had resisted all attempts at innovation in curriculum and instructional methods. Genovesi immediately acquired a reputation as a gifted communicator, who could touch the hearts and stir the minds without engaging in the arid dialectics typical of many academicians. The Neapolitan professor drove hard for the removal of remnants of feudalism in the south and the unleashing of the productive capacities of the people. State intervention in the economy was only justifiable in the event imbalances appeared, which posed a threat to the public welfare. Genovesi also became an ardent spokesman for an updated and mass system of education, founded on free elementary schooling, which would not indoctrinate or frustrate the growth of all facets of the human personality into an integrated whole. A modern state, he pointed out, needs citizens who could think independently and responsibly and not be manipulated like blind sheep.

Many of the 30,000 students who went through Genovesi's classes absorbed the master's teaching and passed them on. Cuocco was deeply influenced and he in turn was a factor in shaping Mazzini's dedication to his national ideal. *Gherardo* D'Arco's *Dell' armonia politica-economica tra la città ed il suo territorio* (*On the Political-Economic Harmony between the City and Its Hinterland*) (1771) shows a Genovesian imprint. The author drew an analogy between the human anatomy and the body civil and politic. A sound social-political organism did not crowd all activity in metropolitan centers any more than a healthy person concentrated all his blood and oxygen supply in the brain. An even distribution was imperative. Congestion in a number of Italian cities resulted in rural unemployment and depopulation. The isolation between cities and towns, between urban and farm areas, had to be bridged by an abiding appreciation of similar stakes and shared concerns. Roads were needed for the promotion of an exchange economy. Inter-regional antipathies were to be healed.

Theoretical, philosophical, scientific, and historical, Gaetano Filangieri's *Scienza della legislazione* (6 vols., 1822) also incorporated Genovesi's admonition, and Giannone's, Vico's, and the French Montesquieu's as well. He wanted education to be expanded to include agricultural and technical studies. The wise legislator, Filangieri contended, inculcates the principle of obedience to law by encouraging self-discipline and by formulating legislation that emancipates and does not enslave. A durable and effective legal system does not promulgate laws that are artificial accretions, but laws which are organically derived from the total framework of a people's history, in harmony with the character and the experience of the citizenry. True to the essential quality of law, Filangieri conceived of an Italian awakening through exemplary and workable laws.

It would be a distortion to claim the economists and legal experts were proponents of unification. Like the historians, they were at best liberationists. They conceded to their regional affiliations. Nationalism was slow-going. They were not determined to galvanize economics or jurisprudence as instruments for a national state. Not yet. Nevertheless, economic analysis and juridical exposition had an advantage over political or historical elucidation because unitary implications could be lifted without being explicit and without being offensive to the defenders of the *status quo*. The corrective measures prescribed for regional ills, if accepted, were bound to cause ripple effects, eventually engulfing all Italy. A multiplicity of states and political divisions produced separate and disjointed economies, segmented transportation networks, and conflicting court procedures, most injurious to each region and to the peninsula. Informally or by indirection at least, generations of bankers, manufacturers, and merchants, as well as professionals, were being informed that the evolving world required broader economic and legal structures than that provided by regional, petty states. (*See Reading No. 8.*)

LITERARY AND LINGUISTIC FERMENTATION. No piece in the emergent mosaic of nationalism was more evident than the exchanges and polemics in literature and language. This was a normal function of a groping self-assertiveness, intensified by the hurt to Italian pride caused by foreign critics, who took notice of Italian borrowing from the French and Spanish and reviled Italian as a medium which did not lend itself to serious reflection and intelligent conversation. In retaliation, the

Accademia della Crusca (Academy of Chaff) was established in 1590 in Florence. As a society of letters, the *Crusca* attempted to purify Italian by purging it of foreign words and usages. It sought a return to pristine Italian, the language utilized by Dante, Petrarch, and the Renaissance lyricists. The effort was negative since the arbitrary restrictions it imposed shackled imagination and discouraged experimentation.

L'Arcadia (The Arcadian Society), founded in Rome in 1696 with papal tolerance, was another reaction to foreign denigration of Italian and also a counter-attack against the pedantry and pomposity associated with Spanish. A return to simplicity, naturalness, and spontaneity, identified with Latin classical formulations, would rehabilitate Italian and confirm Italy's preeminence in letters. Immediately, over one thousand writers throughout the peninsula entered the lists to avenge the Italian and to preserve Italy's literary greatness. Arcadian prose productions were polished, very neat, and lifeless. They violated the Viconian thesis of the contingent relationship between concepts and consciousness. Emphasis on classicism harked back to a peninsula subordinated to the Roman Empire or tied to a meddlesome church. Opponents argued that Italians were to develop their own vocabulary and style, like the English, French, and Spanish, to equate with the Italy faintly coming into view. Out of step with the times the Arcadian movement by 1775 slipped into irrelevance.

A literary enterprise which merits review is *Il Caffè*, the voice of the Milanese Academy of Fisticuffs. It was modeled after the English *Spectator*. During its two-year existence, 1764–66, the *Caffè* launched and sustained acrimonious complaints against the dull, trivial, and imitative nature of Italian literary works. To the *Caffè*, the *Crusca* and the *Arcadia* were symptoms of *passatismo*, residues of a bygone era. Sound literature had the merits of innovation and the perceptive and accurate observation of life in all its diversity. The world was dynamic and not static, as the *Crusca* and the *Arcadia* savants supposed. Vico and his disciples aside, the *Caffè* collaborators sanctioned the outright incorporation of non-Italian expressions, or their Italianization, or the invention of Italian equivalents. This would give Italian the plasticity authors needed in order to modernize their craft and explore current concerns. The brief duration of the periodical suggests that it was too shrill and premature.

If collective endeavors proved disappointing, individual efforts did not slacken but became more numerous and energetic. Francesco Algarotti's *Saggio sulla necessità di scrivere nella propria lingua (Essay on the Necessity to Write in One's Own Tongue)* (1750) explained that Italian writers had to embrace Dante's Italian for the sake of ethnic pride and because it was pliable and expansive enough to accommodate the most discriminating of literary tastes. The Piedmontese governmental functionary, Gian Francesco Galeani-Napione, in a study, appropriately entitled, *Dell' uso e dei pregi della lingua italiana (On the Use and Value of the Italian Language)* (2 vols., 1819), sketched the mutuality he believed existed between literature and public mores. If he stopped short of declaring that an effective and inspired author writes for the masses, he summoned Italian writers to the noble task of promoting the linguistic unity of the Italian people, particularly important due to the political fragmentation of the peninsula and regional separatist feelings. That Galeani may have been nearing the partnership the dramatist Alfieri saw between cultural and political nationalism is demonstrated by the plan he submitted in 1791 to the Piedmontese King Victor Amadeus III (1773–96) for an Italian confederation.

As literary personalities in the eighteenth century became bolder and translated foreign masterpieces into Italian, a question arose about the suitability of Italian for the translations, or whether the Italian versions could stand up to the originals. Such prominent writers as Melchiorre Cesarotti, Scipione Maffei, and Anton Maria Salvini were not sanguine. The frequent use they made of *arrichire* (to enrich) and *arrichimento* (enrichment) was proof that the Italian was an impoverished and unfit medium. Consequently, it was the responsibility of the translator to expand the Italian by deliberately appropriating foreign words, idioms, compound nouns, grammatical terms, even sensory euphemisms and sentence construction. Still fluid, Italian seemed to invite additions without jeopardizing structure, sacrificing its uniqueness, and destroying cohesiveness.

How this could be done was partly shown by Giuseppe Parini (1729–99) and Cesarotti. Parini, Italy's most renowned eighteenth-century poet, translated the classics with the avowed purpose of removing the inaccuracies and misconceptions which had crept into extant editions and also to elevate tastes and cultivate civic virtue. In *Il Giorno* (*The Day*), a four-part work (1765–1801), the Milanese Parini employed the epic stance, sensationalist sentiment, realistic terms, parody, satire, and comedy. Words were utilized that were direct and lucid and which also had sense appeal, suffused with emotion. Cesarotti, encouraged by Francesco Algarotti, renounced the classics and probably brought Vico's ideas to extreme conclusions. The age that was dawning demanded its own set of concepts, words, and expressions, although such feelings as love, peace, joy, fear, sorrow, hatred, and the like were inherent in human nature. It was incumbent on the translator to be keenly aware of freedom versus literalness or, as he put it, faithfulness or unfaithfulness, to what the original author had in mind. Cesarotti severely censured straight translations as the product of vapid grammarians, who were either stupid or unconcerned with differences in sentence structure between languages and the inescapable nuances in idiom meaning and interpretation. Paolo Rolli's *Il paradiso perduto* (*Paradise Lost*) *di Giovanni Milton* (1783) received rare commendation as a prize example of a translation which met the test Parini and Cesarotti were setting.

It was only a matter of time when the investigatory attitude came to grips with the lofty place occupied by Dante. In 1757, Saverio Bettinelli, a future partisan of the *Caffè*, inscribed *Lettere virgiliane*. Hypothetically despatched by the Roman sage from the beyond, the letters were a devastating exposé of the Florentine's exaggerated credentials as a superb communicator and seer and, secondly, a shocking criticism of the general worth of Italian literature. Dante's celebrated *Divine Comedy* was too cumbersome, excessively esoteric, defective in organization, flagrantly unclassical and, most damaging of all, pathetically irrelevant. What Dante had given Italy was, potentially, a national tongue. That was praise enough. For Bettinelli, the better way by which to honor the man was by gaining facility with his vernacular and making it germane, by refining and extending it, by using it to publicize and clarify the peninsula's many problems. Following his compelling anti-Dante exhortations, Bettinelli published *Dodici lettere inglesi* (*Twelve English Letters*) (1766). Unquestionably, Bettinelli was crossing the line into literary nationalism. He lamented the absence of a cultural core which would motivate Italy's cultural giants to pool their talents and resources for the development of a national and higher artistic, literary, intellectual, and scientific life. (*See Reading No. 9.*)

THE THEATER. Quite naturally, the debates over literature and language spilled into the realm of the theater. In the 1600s, what remained of the *commedia dell'arte* (art comedy) had slumped into listless improvisation, deficient in lines and plot, and with routine characters. In the 1700s, the estheticism of the Arcadian school underwent, through Goldoni, a transformation to more modern depictions. That also became stale and repetitious. The revived *commedia* featured itinerant actors and actresses who stylized in the public mind regional caricatures. Dressed in tight, colored costumes, clowns and buffoons spoofed aspects of local living. The raucous laughter elicited by Pulcinella, Colombina, Pantaleone, Brighella, and Stenterello was no longer amusing to the new breed of Italians nor to foreign lovers of Italy. Sectional patterns were overdrawn, at the expense of national similarities. To these sensitive souls, Italians were being unfairly described by their own as silly, superficial, unstable, and alienated from one another. Instead of uniting Italians, the stage was polarizing them.

Humiliated, Goldoni abandoned Italy for France. The theater had to await Alfieri, who would make it a centripetal force, and a channel for education, the transmission of political ideals without neglecting social virtues and cultural values.

DISSEMINATION OF LEARNING. A logical outcome of the fermentation was the organization of national culture and the professionalization and circulation of knowledge. Brought to mind is Voltaire's quip that Italy could do with fewer marble pillars and more good reading materials. During the 1700s and 1800s, many universities were reorganized and, where possible, placed under secular authority. Chairs dedicated for centuries to antiquated subjects were replaced with posts in the fields of public law, political economy, the physical and natural sciences. Erudites in Muratori's lineage produced noteworthy anthologies, bibliographies, dictionaries, and encyclopedias in many areas of learning. Giovanni Crescimbeni's *Storia della vulgar poesia*

(*History of Vulgar Poetry*) (1698) was a collection of Italian poetry from Italic times to 1698. In a more popular vein, there were catalogues on various themes, and all-inclusive journals, which featured articles on foretelling the future, astrological observations, and gossip columns. Periodicals of sundry types were established of an Italian and continental nature. The *Giornale de' Letterati d'Italia* (Venice, 1710–30), founded and directed by Apostolo Zeno offered a check list of Italian literary impresarios and their accomplishments, to offset disparaging comments from across the Alps. Fernando Galiani's *Dialetto napoletano* (1779) was a dictionary of Neapolitan usages and forms. A distinct import from France, the salon provided a format and opportunity where participants could thrash out any topic deemed worthy of attention. The 1700s reflected the potentialities of women, first articulated by Reformation studies. Women were found in salons in Florence, Milan, Rome, Venice, and elsewhere. Several women of noble ancestry opened their salons and hosted the gatherings of native and foreign sophisticates.

THE REFORMIST IMPULSE. In its non-French aspects, the Enlightenment achieved an immediate fruition in the eighteenth century through the enlightened despots. Great store was placed on the king and his ministers at the nerve center of the country and could mandate studies, issue edicts, promulgate decrees, and promote laws that would make the state more benevolent, government more efficient and less costly to run. In Italy, as elsewhere, remedial efforts were not substantial enough, and rulers lost their zeal for reform as subjects, especially middle class and aristocratic liberals, became impatient for more sweeping measures. Still, what was done should not be minimized.

In Lombardy, the number of tax exemptions enjoyed by the church were reduced, a physiocratic program for agriculture inaugurated, public works created jobs, the institution of poor relief alleviated suffering, administrative centralization was completed. As a result, Lombardy's population soared from 1,200,000 in 1759 to 1,500,000 by 1782. The reform contagion in Tuscany led to the removal of the exclusive guild system and the lifting of internal tolls. A freer economy was encouraged.

Torture and the death penalty were abolished, an example of the impact had by Beccaria's seminal essay, *On Crime and Punishment*, first published anonymously in 1764. On the morrow of the dissolution of the Jesuit Order, 1776, Scipione de' Ricci, Bishop of Pistoia-Prato, and of Florentine extraction, thought of reconstructing the Catholic Church in Tuscany along Jansenist lines. Meanwhile, Piedmont's rulers, Amadeus I and Amadeus II, made administration more efficient, deprived the nobility of its tax exempt status, and reorganized the army. Charitable institutions were secularized, to the dismay of the prelates, and at the satisfaction of the anticlericals and the Freemasons. Genovesi was advisor of the Tuscan-born Bernardo Tanucci, who served the Bourbon Kingdom of the Two Sicilies for over forty years as chief minister and also in lesser capacities. He tapped political economists and legal experts for state posts, many of them proteges and former students of Genovesi. Working together, a modest beginning was achieved in making the civil code less oppressive, with confiscatory imposts and censorship eased, a limit placed on the number of monasteries, and the church's tax privileges reduced.

Although it would be a disservice to claim that a genuine nationalist movement had been conceived, we can conclude that it was appearing in embryonic form. It was on the way; it was becoming visible. Something of a nationalist temper was stirring in the Italian breast. Through many interactions, regional biases and intersectional rivalries were slowly giving way to a national perspective. Problems, whether political or economic, literary or linguistic, were increasingly being approached as the concerns of all Italians. Patriots from throughout the peninsula were becoming acquainted with one another. The area of activity was steadily enlarged and Italians were getting into public life. Numbers of the valuable liberal intellectuals and the progressive gentry were being exposed to the national cause. The reform experience injected a strain of realism in thinking and planning. What was missing was full-fledged cultural and political nationalism, the popular element, and the clearly understood need for territorial unification and not just the liberation of the peninsula from foreign rule and papal interference. And the agitation had to be coupled and sealed with a willingness to sacrifice for the common objective.

CHAPTER 4

THE EVOLUTION OF ITALIAN NATIONALISM

IMPACT OF THE FRENCH REVOLUTION. The Revolution and its Napoleonic aftermath accelerated Italian thinking on liberation and unification. The issues were gradually forced into the public domain. Patriots, in increasing numbers and with greater vigor, faced the comparative merits of liberation and unification, and how each or both were to be achieved. Furthermore, if unification was the preference, was the form to be republican, monarchical, or confederative? Commitment on internal direction was also slowly coming to the fore. Republican unificationists tended to be Democrats, Monarchists, Liberals, while Confederationists' inclinations went from a mild liberalism to a cautious progressivism. Republicans and monarchists, democrats and liberals, attempted to refine, reinforce, and sell their views by identifying their aspirations for Italy, where possible, with analogous or comparable aspects of the revolution.

The outbreak of the Revolution was greeted in many parts of the peninsula with enthusiasm and keen anticipation. The *Tricolor* was raised and prominently displayed, although Austrian police and the security guards of her client states disrupted any manifestation of support for the revolutionary ideals. The Venetian aristocrat and Francophile Giovanni Pindemonte published a broadside in which he pronounced the death knell of the old order, thanks to the heroic act of the French people. Such slogans as Liberty, Fraternity, and Equality, and the Declaration of the Rights of Man and the Citizen, passed on August 27, 1789, were proof positive that what was taking place in France had meaning for all peoples. Italian refugees and delegations from Lombardy, becoming increasingly restless under the Austrian yoke and anxious to steer French opinion to Italy's behalf, fraternized with the Parisian populace, and distributed gifts to the press. The solidarity of all peoples was eloquently proclaimed. Attempts were undertaken in Italy to organize support for the Jacobins, the French radicals, in open and clandestine fashion.

A number of democratic political sheets were founded, from the *Democratico Imparziale* (*Impartial Democrat*) of Bologna to the Florentine, *Il Democratico* (*The Democrat*). Galeani's *Idea di una confederazione della potenze d'Italia* (1791) drew much attention. The author advised Italians to avail themselves of the opportunity that an inevitable war presented. It was necessary for Italians, Galeani explained, to work in unison if they intended to realize their liberation and unification. As he elucidated upon his proposal for a confederation, Galeani tackled both the question of liberation and political unification. Because he specifically addressed the many Italian states as "powers," and their rulers as "potentates," and he espoused a confederative norm, Galeani illustrated realism. By shying away from a unitary state, the Piedmontese civil servant also confirmed the extent to which traditional patterns of regional loyalties and cultural differences were imbedded in the Italian psyche.

Urges for liberation also came from France. The *Sanscoulettes*, spokesmen for the more downtrodden of French society, infiltrated into Piedmont and Tuscany, and tried to convince Italians to strike a unanimous blow for freedom. Out of sincere interest, and also, one suspects, to open up another front against reactionary Europe, the French National Convention, on October 19, 1792, promised direct assistance to all oppressed people who revolted against despotic rule. When war erupted in April 1792 and the invasion of France seemed imminent, Victor Amadeus III (1773–96) of Piedmont sent inquiries to fellow-princes for an Italian league to cooperate and prepare for any eventuality. Several thousand police agents were recruited, mainly due to the energetic labors of the Dukes of Modena and Parma. The Kingdom of Naples pledged to send two regiments of cavalry by August 1794 at the earliest. After Piedmont's conquest by the French in 1792, Alfieri and Galeani bristled with anger and scorn because of what they decried was another shocking example of peninsula unconcern and undue Italian doubts over Amadeus's intent. State inertia and distrust had prevailed again as it had with Charles Emmanuel I of Savoy and his initiative in 1614.

The French Liberal monarchical constitution put in force on

July 14, 1790 was a boon to the Italian unification monarchists. Their satisfaction was short-lived for, on September 21, 1792, the National Convention decided on a republic. If the Italian unificationist liberals and monarchists could not relate to the change from constitutional monarchy to Jacobin radical republicanism, the unificationist republicans and democrats were ambivalent for the moment. They favored a republic because it created a close partnership between the rulers and the people and among the people themselves. Mass reprisals, fanaticism, the execution of Louis XVI on January 21 and Marie Antoinette, October 16, 1793, and the armed conflict raging between France and monarchical Europe, were disillusioning. Apparently, Jean-Jacques Rousseau's precept of the general will was no deterrent against majority tyranny. The disestablishment of the Catholic Church, through the Civil Constitution of the Clergy, July 14, 1790, provoked consternation among church officials and Italian clerics and also injured the sensibilities of moderates and lay Catholics. Pius VI's condemnation of the Revolution gave many Italians second thoughts about what was transpiring in France. It is not surprising that the bulk of the nobility and the bourgeoisie, and the Liberals and Confederationists, concluded that the church's political and social conservatism was the only guarantee against the revolt of the masses.

The implication for the national cause was that just as Italian patriotism was being transformed into nationalism, and nationalists were slowly and painfully converging on the political-territorial problem, that is the goal of peninsula-wide liberation and unification, the social question was simultaneously raised. Nationalists of all persuasions reached out to attenuate the harmful effects stemming from the seeds of discord unfortunately being sown by way of France. They publicly deplored the turn in France to violence and illegalities and stressed that the path to Italy's future was through constitutionalism and interclass collaboration, leaving the institutional framework, whether republic or monarchy, to be determined by unfolding events.

NAPOLEONIC INTERLUDE. Dashed hopes quickly revived, soared, and peaked when Napoleon Bonaparte became commander of the French forces in Italy, early in 1796. With his Italian name and ancestry, nationalists believed to a man that

Napoleon would use his resources for liberation and possibly for unification. Napoleon did nothing to deflate Italian optimism. The graciousness with which Napoleon, on March 26, 1796, received pledges of good will from some of Italy's leading citizens was a good omen. An announcement of March 31, addressed to "the Soldiers of Italy," reinforced the morale of the 40,000 troops which comprised "the army of Italy." It had a vital part in Napoleon's defeat of an Austro-Piedmontese force of 80,000 men, on April 11. On May 15, the Peace of Paris was signed, and Napoleon soon thereafter entered Milan as the liberator Machiavelli had perhaps envisioned.

In this atmosphere conducive to high expectations, Italians took to their pens to inspire Napoleon and to galvanize themselves to action. There was a mingling of liberationist and unificationist sentiment in the outpourings. In May 1796, the *Giornale della società e degli amici della libertà e dell'uguaglianza* (*Journal of the Society and Friends of Liberty and Equality*) and the *Società popolare*, both Milanese democratic organs, urged on Napoleon the proclamation of all Italy's liberation as an established fact. On October 1, the new government installed in Lombardy by Napoleon offered a prize for the most original essay on the question, "Which Form of Free Government Suits Italy Best?" Melchiorre Gioja's entry won. Such common denominators as geography, territory, language, nationality, religion, and compatible customs decreed that Italy should be united into one republic. This may have been the first clear-cut exposition on the subject. (*See Reading No. 10.*) Appeals were also drafted and sent to the Directory Government in Paris. The Parthenopean Republic, which had been organized in January 1799 by Neopolitan revolutionists and French assistance, requested French collaboration for the clearing of the peninsula of all foreigners and the ordaining of one mighty republic for Italy. Undoubtedly, the culmination in the faith placed in Napoleon and France for Italian emancipation was represented by the encomium and petition the youthful literary genius Ugo Foscolo dispatched to "*Bonaparte Liberatore.*" (*See Reading No. 11.*)

Prospects for Italian liberation and unification did not square with an objective evaluation of reality. The idea that Napoleon and France would be surrogates or accomplices of Italian liberation and unification was shown to be a dead letter by the Treaty of Campo Formio, negotiated by Napoleon with Austria, and signed in October 1797. The surrender of Venetia to Austria was unforgivable. Italians held Napoleon primarily responsible as did many Frenchmen. Napoleon had deliberately fanned national feelings for personal gains. In his *Jacopo Ortis* (1802), a broken Foscolo told his countrymen that had the Italians contested for Venetia they inescapably would have been vanquished in body and despoiled again, but they would have spared their souls of the shame and guilt of indifference, betrayal, and misplaced trust.

Any assessment of Napoleon's many maneuvers must include the restraints under which he labored. Italians may not have surmised it, but neither the Directory, which set the policy, nor Napoleon, whether before or after he became emperor in 1804, desired an Italy which might some day rival or threaten France. Present in French official circles was the fear that Austria would fight to the finish to prevent any attempt at a liberated and unified Italian state which appeared to be a French satellite. It would have been impossible to proceed because Italians could not make up their minds between liberation and unification and if the latter was it to be monarchical, republican, or confederationist in nature.

Viewed in broad perspective, the results were not all negative and devoid of promise. The reduction of the divisions in Italy to three indicated that Italy was headed in the right direction. Many positive changes were introduced in the provinces annexed to France. Governmental subsidies encouraged salutary trends traceable to the reforms of the benevolent despots. Inter-regional cooperation was promoted. Moreover, Napoleon had not been ungenerous. He had bowed to patriotic fervor and permitted the term "Italy" to appear in official form, a magnanimity he did not extend to Polish nationalists who had to be satisfied with the Grand Duchy of Warsaw and not of Poland. The military force of the Kingdom of Italy was designated, "the Army of Italy." The Tolentino Agreement of February 19, 1797, between France and the Holy See, ceded the Romagna of the Papal States to the Kingdom of Italy. By May 1809, what remained of the Papal States, including Rome, became part of the French Empire, thus indicating that the temporal power of the church was not sacrosanct, but could, in fact, be abridged through negotiation or simply eliminated by superior force. Failure to have unified Italy compelled nationalists to struggle with the twin problems of liberation and unification. Italians had to think seriously on the means of achieving their goals, including such matters as foreign assistance and inter-Italian cooperation. Disappointment opened the door for Italy's most articulate writers and inspired poets who continued the tradition of the intellectuals' commitment to the national cause. They were singularly responsible for the growth of cultural nationalism and, with the possible exceptions of Foscolo and Leopardi, its escalation into political nationalism.

UGO FOSCOLO. Born in 1778 on the Venetian-held island of Zante, Foscolo, educated in the classics, gained a reputation in Greek and Latin above his colleagues in the literary profession. Foscolo observed Napoleon's campaigns in northern Italy at close range. His hopes for Italy were given expression in his ode to "Napoleon the Liberator." With his blunt approach and biting sarcasm, he reminded his audience of the Roman historian Tacitus. Foscolo was selected to be a deputy to the planned Cisalpine Republic, forerunner of the Kingdom of Italy, and to make the official presentation of the delegation at the inaugural convention, convoked by Napoleon at Lyons in 1801. Those in attendance expected Foscolo to offer praise and encouragement toward Napoleon's concern for Italy. With typical independence and solemn purpose, Foscolo surprised everyone by speaking instead of their grave obligations to Italy and history. Foscolo specifically warned his countrymen that their fractious attitude invited comparison to the factionalism which beset Rome, and which brought to Julius Caesar and his extreme measures: suspension of parties, cancellation of elections, and one-man rule backed by the unsuspecting masses. Disgust also brought forth the commemorative poem, "*Sepolcri* (Sepulchers)," (1804), which closed with the lines: "where the blood shed for the fatherland is holy water and mourned." Italy was the fatherland, the new divinity, and worthy of every personal sacrifice. Between 1804–06, Foscolo served in Cisalpine Republic's army, still believing that Napoleon would prove to be Italy's benefactor. Dejection led to the Wertherian epistolary novel, *Lettere di*

Jacopo Ortis (1802), and to the *Tieste Tragedies, Ajace (Ajax)* (1811), and *La Ricciarda* (1812). *Ajax* was an allegorical satire, in which the playwright used self-evident disguises to depict Napoleon, Pius VII, and local French generals as ruthless, untrustworthy individuals. Both ;*Ajax* and *La Ricciarda* were banned after their initial staging. Foscolo refused to renew his loyalty pledge to the Emperor and as a result was harassed by the police until he exiled himself to London, where he died in 1827.

It was independence Foscolo wanted and not unification. The Napoleon he invoked was the deliverer and not the maker of Italy. In opposition to Bettinelli, Foscolo acclaimed Italy's many cultural capitals because they made it impossible for any one city or region to dictate standards for the arts and the humanities. The more poles of attraction, the greater the difficulty, Foscolo maintained, for any city, as was the case with Paris and London, in France and Britain, to muster applause, contrive broad receptivity, and establish a monopoly. Like Machiavelli and his fellow-Florentine, Francesco Guicciardini, Foscolo related the splendid cultural achievements of the Renaissance to the peninsula's pluralistic political order, based on the liberty and autonomy of each state. It was the pain and sorrow Foscolo bore for his people, and his distancing himself to London, where he acquainted the English with Italy's plight, which endeared him to Italian nationalists.

VITTORIO ALFIERI (1749–1803). With Alfieri, nationalism became more coherent and substantive. Before him, nationalism was in the main a response mechanism to foreign intrusions. With Alfieri, it became a positive choice and a willful necessity. His personal odyssey telescoped several of the phases Italians experienced before they rallied to the fatherland. Inquisitive, by nature a lover of liberty, Alfieri expatriated himself from Piedmont in 1778, and made the rounds of several European countries. In his youth he learned English, French, Latin, and Greek but not Italian because it was despised in Piedmont. Exposed to alien ways while abroad, Alfieri discovered Italy as his motherland and the Italians as his compatriots. He resolved, as he informed posterity, to de-Europeanize and de-Piedmontese himself, so that he might become thoroughly Italian.

Alfieri's trademark was an abhorrence of tyranny. He sum-

marily rejected the Catholic Church because priests and ecclesiastics were the natural allies of autocrats. In the footsteps of
Italians from Dante to Petrarch, and from Machiavelli to Genovesi and Giannone, Alfieri scathingly denounced the temporal
power. It was an unspeakable offense to God and human dignity.
In the play, *Panegirico di Plinio a Traiano* (*Pliny's Panagyric to
Trajan*) (1776), Alfieri focused on the incompatibility between
dictatorial rule and progress. In a visit to Prussia in 1798, he
reproached Frederick II, the shrewd practitioner of enlightened
despotism, because his country resembled a giant encampment
rather than a civilized state. Revulsion against tyranny took its
most passionate form in the *Misogallo (The Anti-Gaul)* or
French Hater (1795–97). Having lived in France from 1786 to
1797, Alfieri had been an eyewitness to republican repression
and submitted there was no difference between it and divine-
right absolutism. It was not just a dislike of tyranny but also a
reaction against the moral and cultural ascendancy exercised by
the French over Italy. Alfieri's animus had an healthy aspect to it,
for it turned him, and those Italians who read the *Misogallo*,
inward, to themselves, essential to the development of a nationalist mentality.

Oppression was not to be tolerated but to be fought in the
name of liberty and freedom. *Della tirannide (On Tyranny)*, a
massive attack on the scourge, written in 1777, was also an
exaltation of "Liberty, Divine Liberty." *Bruto primo (The First
Brutus)*, a tragedy of 1788, highlighted the patriotic bravery of
the earlier Lucius Brutus who did not hesitate to order the
execution of his sons, Titus and Tiberius, because they had
conspired with the deposed King Tarquin of the Etruscans
against the infant Roman republic. Also significant was its
dedication to "George Washington, *Liberatore Americano*."
Washington was the incarnation of Brutus, determined to rid his
people of the odious British domination. In *Bruto secondo (The
Second Brutus)* (1789), Alfieri rehabilitated the much-maligned
Marcus Brutus, whose unquenchable thirst for liberty motivated
him to plot the assassination of the Julius Caesar who had
overthrown the republic.

Alfieri came to the idea of unification through culture. There
is no mention of Gioja or any political thinker who may have
been a proponent of a unitary state. Alfieri detected the conge-

nial relationship between cultural and political nationalism. Artistry and free government were inter-related and inseparable. *(See Reading No. 12.)* History proved that royal patronage and state handouts sapped moral faculties, deflected intellectual abilities, impaired objectivity, and undermined credibility. If Alfieri recalled "the great father—[Dante] Alighieri," "the famous Petrarch," "the unique thinker Machiavelli," "the divine Michelangelo," it was not a mere function of memory but to strike communion with past Italian immortals and to prod his contemporaries to ethnic pride and to action. There was a preview of the Mazzinian and Giobertian notion of an Italian mission, since Europe, the world, civilization, Alfieri reasoned, were in dire need of an Italian rebirth. Alfieri's nationalist presuppositions and intense love for Italy were such that they prompted him to offer his *Second Brutus* "to the future Italian people . . . to the generous and free Italians." Alfieri, the dramatist, could not predict how unity would come about, whether through Piedmont's leadership, or that of Naples, or by means of dynastic marriages, "but it will not be long." He dared to dream that his verses of hatred against foreign aggression, personified by "the Gaul," would agitate in the Italian breast and move Italians to their collective emancipation. *(See Reading No. 13.)*

Alfieri elevated the Italian theater with twenty-four dramas and tragedies. He deliberately employed the stage as the medium of communication with his people on the crucially important issues concerning their future. More than any other writer, Alfieri consciously placed literature in the forefront of the national cause. Through his tireless efforts, Piedmont ceased to be culturally and politically isolated from the rest of Italy. Carducci credited Alfieri with having provided much of the idealistic strain and moral zeal behind the *Risorgimento* as is targeted on unification. The unitary and federalist republicans, represented by Mazzini and Carlo Cattaneo respectively, the liberal, monarchical constitutionalists of the D'Azeglian-Cavourian school, and the Neo-Guelphs of the Giobertian persuasion found legitimate reason to hail Alfieri as the precursor of unification nationalism. To Foscolo, Alfieri was "the first Italian."

GIACOMO LEOPARDI (1798–1837). He was the Jeremiah, the weeping prophet, of Italian liberation. Not gifted with robust health, the many hours spent in teaching himself, poring over books and manuscripts, and worrying over Italy's fate, twisted his body and tormented his soul. He became a hunchback, which, as he confessed, matched the dark despair he suffered over Italy in particular and humanity in general. Leopardi's melancholic mood was admitted by the German Friedrich Nietzsche, who died insane, to have profoundly influenced him. *Canzoni (Songs)* (1818–22) amounted to a romantic defense of the world of illusions and the subjective against the cold and impersonal claims of early nineteenth century realism. Leopardi's *Operette morali (Moral Studies)* (1821–28) underscored the unremitting gloom that is man's lot. Leopardi did not seek the consolation of religion because Christianity in its purest form taught that happiness could only be attained in heaven. The Calvinist tenet of the total and natural depravity of man only added to his inner turmoil. The meaning of *Zibaldone (Miscellany)* (2 vols., 1817–32), a hodge-podge collection of 3,019 pages of musings on an amazing array of subjects, was that the search for truth, like life itself, delivered far less than originally promised. With certainty unattainable, Leopardi slumped into brooding skepticism.

Given his pessimistic and lugubrious nature, it would have been incongruous had Leopardi not ruminated over the Italian scene. Attachment to Italy only added to his sorrow and brought forth the poem, "*All'Italia (To Italy,)*" published in 1818 in Rome. It mirrors the patriot's soul in extreme grief, as it weeps over the misfortunes which have befallen his fatherland. Even if there was no evident projection toward unification, the sincerity of Leopardi's protests, together with his commemoration of Italy's glorious past, left an indelible mark on nationalists. Many recruits to the uprisings connected with liberation and unification committed passages of "To Italy" to memory and stormed the enemy's barricades with his words on their lips. (*See Reading No. 14.*) Through the very force of his expressions, personality, and spirit, Leopardi compelled Italians to suffer together the extended shame and anguish of their Italy and to commit themselves to its resurgence.

VINCENZO CUOCO (1770–1823). Born in Molise, near Naples, Cuoco, trained in law, became political advisor to the constituent body which formulated the constitution of the Parthenopean Republic of January 1799. Following the republic's collapse and the restoration of the Bourbon Ferdinand I, April 1799, Cuoco's holdings were confiscated and he was banned from Naples for twenty years. Exile took him to Paris, Marseilles, Piedmont, and Milan, capital of the Cisalpine Republic. Once Napoleon established the Kingdom of Naples (1804), Cuoco thought it safe to return to Naples, capital of the kingdom, where he served in state government from 1806 until the overthrow of the Napoleonic Order in 1815. The importance of the southerner to the nationalist movement rests with his *Saggio (Essay) storico sulla rivoluzione napoletana* (1801), and *Plato in Italy* (1804), already discussed. Both were published in Milan, a mecca for patriots. Equipped with a superb historical sense, Cuoco placed the Neapolitan revolution under intensive analysis. He lifted several lessons which applied to the Italian situation and to all subject people aspiring to self-determination.

To begin with, the republicans who masterminded the coup erroneously believed that France's 1789 was exportable. The ease with which insurrectionists shouted both for the monarchy and the republic indicated that nothing had been done to educate the masses. The wisdom of proposing rapid and unilateral reforms for an apathetic people and a static society was seriously questioned. Lacking a sturdy foundation, it was no mystery why the republic disintegrated at the appearance of the slightest difficulty and the people in short order welcomed the former regime back. Another fatal flaw in the revolutionary rationale was that French help had been sought for the grand objective of Italian unification, but no similar effort had been undertaken toward formal contacts with like-minded Italians elsewhere in the peninsula. In training his sights on unification, Cuoco underlined the need to rekindle the public spirit Italians had enjoyed of old and which transcended political and regional barriers. To recreate and fortify this national conscience, Italians were to look within themselves, study their history, become proficient in Italian as the mother tongue, and await fortuitous international circumstances and the promise they held for their nationalist vision. It is with Cuoco that we discern most clearly the progression of cultural nationalism to political nationalism. The Neapolitan ended his *Essay* on a magisterial note, deferring to faith, hope, and final victory. (*See Reading No. 15.*)

CHAPTER 5

NATIONALISM AND THE MAKING
OF ITALY

THE VIENNA SETTLEMENT AND THE METTER-NICHEAN SYSTEM. Having failed to obtain Italy's liberation and unification through the good offices of Napoleon and the French, Italian nationalists retained a flicker of hope that the delegates at the Congress of Vienna (1815) would be responsive to the principle of nationality as the new norm for the post-Napoleonic Europe, and grant the peninsula its unity. Because Italy was to Klemens von Metternich, the minister of state and mentor of the peace conference, nothing more than "a geographical expression," Italy was left divided. With compensation as a guiding precept, the Congress handsomely rewarded Austria for her struggles and sacrifices against 1789 and Napoleon. Lombardy was annexed, while Tuscany, Modena, and Parma, reorganized as duchies, became dependencies, governed by members of the Hapsburg ruling house. Based on legitimacy, the other operational concept, all new rulers who had come to the fore since 1789 were declared fraudulent and were dismissed. The Spanish Bourbon King Ferdinand I took back the throne he had vacated in Naples to Joachim Murat, the French general and brother-in-law to Napoleon. To strengthen his control, Ferdinand quickly obtained Austrian protection in the form of an alliance. The Papal States were reconstituted under the sovereignty of Pius VII. Piedmont remained unharmed. It came out of Vienna enlarged with the addition of Genoa, designed to strengthen northern Italy against French attack from the northeast.

Metternich's objective was to build a structure of peace which would avoid war and prevent revolution. War from without threatened the political survival of the state; revolution from within placed in jeopardy the social order. Each interfaced with the other, witness 1789 and its tumultuous aftermath. Local princes, monitored by Austria's watchful eyes, attempted to reverse whatever degree of opening had occurred in the peninsula. Any public servant thought to have been connected to

progressive and nationalist sympathies, was cashiered and replaced by loyal defenders of the former ways. Censorship was
everywhere. Metternich's efficient police developed a network
of surveillance that extended into the peninsula. Books or manuscripts considered anti-Austrian were confiscated. Pius VII
marked his return to Rome and the Papal States by admonishing
his constituents to be on the guard against ideologies that "are as
smooth as butter and as slippery as oil." Obviously, he had
constitutionalism, individual rights, liberation, and unification
in mind. The re-introduction of the Society of Jesus on July 7,
1814 did not augur well for progress. The final ingredient in the
Metternichean system was big power intervention, carried out in
several forms, from the diplomatic, to the economic, and the
military.

REVOLUTIONS OF 1820–21. Denied the opportunity to air
their grievances, patriots went underground, where they nourished
themselves on the memories and teachings of the prophets of a
free society and of liberation and unification. The *Carboneria*
was the most important of the secret societies. So-named because the members burned charcoal at their meetings for light
and warmth, the movement may have been a continuation of the
clandestine organizations which had cropped up since the sixteenth century against foreign usurpers. It also may have come
about through separation from Freemasonry, the latter having
acquired by the eighteenth century an unsavory reputation for
being elitist, agnostic in matters of faith, nonviolent in approach, and altogether accommodating to the officialdom in the
various states. The *Carboneria* swore perpetual hatred for the
foreigner and his accomplices in Italy, and pledged to exert
themselves to the maximum for the unification of all Italians. It
would be an error to ascribe the uprisings of 1820–21 to an
unsuppressible desire to free and unite Italy. It was too soon after
the disheartening defeats of the end-century to resume on that
score. The revolutions that exploded in successive order in
Naples, Sicily, Turin, and Milan have been correctly described
as liberal in nature. Democracy and a republic had few adherents. The promoters of the Neapolitan upheavals were the *Car-
bonari* and junior army officers, veterans of Napoleon's campaigns, who had not forgotten the shibboleths of 1789. They

protested the restoration of princely absolutism and the institutional trappings of the Bourbon regime. Specifically, Neapolitans demanded the re-establishment of the Constitution of 1812. At bay, Ferdinand reinstated the constitution, while awaiting Austrian military assistance. It arrived in time, and Neapolitan and Sicilian efforts at liberalizing political life were crushed.

Constitutional government and civil liberties were also the main concerns in Milan, where the participants represented broad cross sections of the intelligentsia, business classes, and the aristocracy. Austria put down the conspirators with typical savagery. Arrests were numerous. The noted philosopher Gian Domenico Romagnosi was confined to his house, while others were shipped to the notorious Spielberg fortress, Austria's Bastille, in present-day Czechoslovakia. Among them were Federico Confalonieri, patrician and patriotic leader of the uprising, and Silvio Pellico, editor of *Il Conciliatore*, a political weekly whose publication had been suspended in 1819. He wrote of his ten years of sufferings in *Le mie prigioni (My Imprisonment)* (1832), an indictment of Austrian cruelty which infuriated Italian nationalists. Others of the Milanese revolutionaries sought refuge in exile.

The independent state of Piedmont was not immune to revolutionary shock waves. In Turin, deep-seated aversion to the arch conservative policies and high-handed methods of King Victor Emmanuel I also provoked insurrections, led by the same socioeconomic groups which had figured prominently in Milan. They were also dismayed by the thought of having the heir apparent Charles Felix assume the throne rather than the young Charles Albert of Savoy, who was known for his liberal predilections. Victor Emmanuel abdicated as a result of the revolution, and Charles Albert acted as regent while Felix was absent from the capital. A constitution was hastily granted. All seemed to be moving in the right direction when Charles Albert categorically refused to join in the attempt to bar Charles Felix from the throne. Charles Albert's break with the proponents was adjudged a betrayal by the Turinese Liberals. Upon his return, Charles Felix abrogated the constitution, called on Austria to crush the insurgents, persecuted them, and required personal loyalty oaths and periodic checks.

Prospects for the future were bleak. Failure, nevertheless, led to the questioning of the reliance of the *Carboneria* and liberals on direct action, the reluctance to combine forces, the lack of emphasis on unification, the absence of the people, and the insufficient preparation. Those who had been involved learned the truth of Cuoco's scheme for a successful revolution. Defeats brought the end of the *Carboneria* as a vehicle for change, most of those enrolled going over to become the nucleus of Mazzini's *Giovine Italia (Young Italy)*, which was in operation by 1831. Unforgettably impressed on Mazzini's mind was the exodus of disaffected liberals from his home city of Genoa. The fact the heterogeneous elements in Naples, Sicily, Milan, and Turin were focusing on representative government and personal guarantees tended to create a public opinion of peninsula-wide proportions, indispensable for the fostering of a nationalist outlook. Austria was again seen as the main enemy.

THE REVOLUTIONARY TIDE OF 1831. Insurrectionary fever erupted with delayed action in the ducies of Modena, Parma, and the Papal States. The outbreaks were not planned. They were a spontaneous response to the rulers' unrelenting efforts to return to pre-1789 arbitrary government, aggravated by the economic depression that gripped sections of the peninsula as a result of the unwise and disruptive practices chargeable to the reactionary regimes. The goals were the same as 1821, with the addition, in the Papal States, of the end of temporal power and the total abolition of clerical privileges. There was also an initial cry for land redistribution and careers open to talent and not subject to the restrictions dating back to the medieval guilds. Involved were liberals, who were in commerce, the professions, and a few in agriculture. An unprecedented phenomenon was the presence of artisans and a small number of peasants. The center of the revolt in the Papal States was Bologna, where a provisional government was set up and a constitution promised. The same occurred in Modena and Parma. Soundings were taken aimed at unifying the endeavors, with the Modenese and Parma considering joining the two duchies into the United Italian Provinces. The plans fell through. Localism triumphed over collaboration. Fear of impending Austrian intervention crippled the revolutionary movements in Modena and

Parma, and Francis IV and Marie Louise, Napoleon's widow, immediately regained total control of their principalities. In the Papal States, appeal to Austria was just as readily honored, and Austrian troops smashed all resistance at Ancona in March 1831. Reprisals followed and the former ways reestablished.

ASSOCIATION. Much to Metternich's displeasure and that of his princely colleagues, the pendulum of history was not returning to royal absolutism, and multiracial empires, but was moving forward toward participatory government, individual liberties, and the self-determination of people. In Italy, as elsewhere, in spite of archaic laws, anachronistic institutions, and repressive measures, economics was transforming areas of the peninsula at a quickened pace. A middle class was emerging which by the decade of the 1840s was becoming aware of its opportunities and responsibilities. Immensely practical, the business class understood the benefits to be reaped from operating within one political-economic framework embracing the Italian states, to which Genovesi and Pietro Verri had alluded. Coinciding with the rise of the middle class was the emergence of the people. Although the process would take many years to be completed, it was discernible by the 1840s. The associative principle was coming into vogue and staking its claims to respectability. The movement was continental in scope. Consumer cooperatives, mutual aid societies, self-educational facilities, houses of commerce, technical institutes, professional societies, employment informational circles, even pro-worker organizations blossomed. As the associative idea advanced in Italy, particularly in parts of Piedmont, Lombardy, Tuscany, and the Romagna, urban and rural intellectuals, tradesmen and workers, formed their own organizations and began to speak of anarchy, social democracy, and socialism as terms of reference and for recruitment purposes. The *Communist Manifesto* (1848), of Karl Marx and Friedrich Engels was waiting in the wings. There were also mixed associations in which professors, teachers, lawyers, physicians, journalists, bankers, and manufacturers were prominent, and undifferentiated workers and a sprinkling of peasant proprietors also enrolled. Although the leadership and guidance were primarily middle class, objectives and activities were determined by majority rule, another novelty. To fill out the picture, a decided minority of the nobility was making its peace with the new world coming into view. This economic upliftment, social mobilization, and political modernization became suffused with the ideas which had been disseminated by universalists, regionalists, patriots, pre-nationalists, and authentic nationalists, from Dante and Machiavelli, to Genovesi, Gioja, Alfieri, and Cuoco.

MAZZINI BETWEEN NATIONALISM AND INTERNATIONALISM. Mazzini's thinking was undoubtedly encouraged by his appreciation of the association principle. Having accepted the inevitable elevation of the submerged portions of society as historical and rightful, Mazzini submitted that it was the responsibility of the aristocracy and the bourgeoisie to reach out and introduce these masses to public life. Without organization and leadership, the people would remain amorphous, at the mercy of self-serving demagogues, as had happened recently in France. Out of confidence in the capacity of people for self-rule, Mazzini opted for a democratic, unitary, not federal, republic, sponsored by popular action, and carried on through broad participation. Only the unitary republic could check the divisive effects of *campanilismo*.

Mazzini saw his unitary, democratic republic as a viable alternative to Gioberti's Neo-Guelph Confederationist approach. A new Catholic universalism under the guise and spur of a united Italy blessed by the pope would aggravate old wounds and provoke unremitting opposition from democrats, liberals, anticlericals, Freemasons, Protestants, and also lay Catholics. Moreover, a confederation given life by papal initiative and princely negotiations, supported by Catholic clericals and moderates, would intercept the rise of the masses to respectability. A confessional order of society was intolerable. Besides, as Gioja had convincingly pointed out, a confederative polity, like a federal republic, in contrast to the unitary state, would perpetuate and exacerbate inter-regional tensions, and eventually result in dismemberment.

Mazzini and his democratic republicans did not take any more kindly to the Cavourian state-inspired liberal, monarchical conception of liberation and unification nationalism, although they later begrudgingly accepted it as a transitory and intermediate stage. A unification which owed its success to the enlightened aristocracy and the upper bourgeoisie, to crafty diplomatic maneuvers, and to foreign assistance, however, well-intentioned, was a sham unification. It would leave the people out, unwanted, with no place in the new Italy. It would also weaken whatever resolve the ruling classes had for reform and leave the country unprepared to embark on the Mission of the Third Rome. Mazzini and his cohorts repeatedly believed they had reason to question the sincerity behind Piedmont's participation and to be outraged by the double game Cavour at times appeared to be playing, aiding and abetting Mazzini and Garibaldi, while simultaneously ready and eager to disown them and curb their activities.

The key was to persuade all elements of Italian society to work together for liberation and unification. Mazzini broke with the *Carboneria* in 1830, charging that the society had become sectarian, inbred, and unwilling to broadcast the message of national liberation far and wide. From his exile in Marseilles Mazzini, in July 1831, organized Young Italy, which immediately opened chapters where allowed in the peninsula. It probably was the first genuine Italian nationalist enterprise, aimed at the unification of the peninsula and a democratic republican government, for which goals no sacrifice was too demanding. (*See Reading No. 16.*) Several premature and imprudent tries at revolution occurred, with the attempt in Savoy, 1833, forcing Mazzini's exile to England, where he wrote, raised funds, and plotted additional insurrections for the national cause. The newspaper, *Young Italy* (1831–34), and later *L'Italia del Popolo (Italy of the People)* endeavored to indoctrinate all Italians on the virtues of Democratic and Republican Nationalism. Faithful to his vision of a new international order, Mazzini formed Young Germany, Young Hungary, Young Poland, Young Serbia, and Young Ireland. He undertook regular correspondence with nationalist leaders of Austria's and Turkey's minorities, looking toward imminent uprisings and joint action, which would free the subject nationalities to create their own state. The ultimate intention, as previously suggested in Chapter 2, was the voluntary union of all peoples in a world political structure based, as we would declare today, on the Fatherhood of God and the Brotherhood of Man. In 1848, Mazzini organized the *Asso-*

ciazione Nazionale Italiana, in the image of Young Italy but with greater driving force. Following a series of unsuccessful coups, the overthrow of the Roman Republic in 1849, and the abortive rebellion, scheduled for Milan, February 6, 1853, the Italian National Association gave way to the *Partito d'Azione (Action Party)*. It was designed to improve morale, tighten discipline, clarify objectives, and coordinate functions and all endeavors. Although Mazzini was defeated by general apathy as much as by the alarm his radical outlook spread among the middle and upper classes, his faith in the people never wavered.

GIOBERTI BETWEEN NATIONALISM AND NEO-GUELPHISM. Neo-Guelphs were also known as *Moderati (Moderates)*, to distinguish them from the arch conservative Catholics or clericals, and the Christian democrats, who appeared early in this century with Don Romolo Murri and later through Don Luigi Sturzo in the form of the *Partito Popolare Italiano*, 1919. Gioberti and the Neo-Guelphs sought liberation and unification by means of a confederation of three states, north, central, and south, under the nominal presidency of the pope. It was to be brought about by papal initiative and negotiations among the princes. Each of the three kingdoms was to retain its autonomy. Gioberti strongly recommended his confederation because its tripartite political system intelligently deferred to regional sensibilities. Italy simply had too many centers and too many local attachments to have its inhabitants enrolled in a uniform state desired by Mazzini and the democratic republicans and the monarchical polity advocated by the liberals. It was also realistic because it would solve the problems posed by the papacy's and the church's temporal power and millennial presence in the peninsula. The integrated involvement of the church would reinforce the role of hierarchy in Italian society. Moderate, liberal, and conservative unificationists could use the church as a stabilizing factor, to keep in check the democratic republicans, "Jacobins," "egalitarians," in the suspicious eyes of the Neo-Guelphs. Staunch Catholics and temporalists would be reassured against the inroads they feared anticlericalism and Freemasonry had made into Italian institutions.

A confederation realized through a high level agreement

among pope and princes would effectively control the state bureaucrats, the *municipalisti (municipalists)* Gioberti tagged them in derision. They were the most strident exponents of *campanilismo,* and determined to hold on to their status even at the cost of liberation and unification. The Catholic moderate prospectus also had the merits of gaining Piedmont's adherence. No more would the Savoy Dynasty and her civil servants be exclusively committed to Piedmont's interests at a loss to the peninsula's over-riding needs. Not the least of the assets offered by the Moderate program was the good will it was bound to promote among European traditionalists, mild progressiveness, and statesmen because of its friendly disposition toward the papacy and the church. Finally, as another Neo-Guelph personality, the historian and political figure Cesare Balbo (1789–1853) was to explain, a Neo-Guelph confederation would heal Italy's many wounds and anoint Italians with evangelical zeal for Europe's and the world's upliftment.

The Neo-Guelph plan took on distinct possibilities as the decade of the 1840s wore on. In one of those rare combinations of personal initiative, common sense, propitious external factors, and mobilized hope, it seemed as if Gioberti's confederation could be brought to fruition. In December 1847, Balbo became editor of *Il Rinascimento (The Rebirth),* Cavour's dynamic and progressivist newspaper, and later Piedmont's first minister under the grant of the *Statuto (Constitution)* in 1848. Gioberti succeeded him in the premier's chair. As Deputies and as prime ministers, Balbo and Gioberti favored a conservative or qualified type of liberalism, which ingratiated them with many Catholics and liberals alike. Their parliamentary and ministerial stances proved that Neo-Guelphs were anxious for internal progress.

Elected pope, June 16, 1846, Pius IX, born Giovanni Maria Mastai-Ferretti, quickly won a place in the nationalists' hearts through the constructive changes he encouraged in the Papal States. The reformer, Pasquale Gozzi was appointed internal minister. A council of state and a cabinet system of government were created. The regular police were replaced by a civic guard and arbitrary interference in private life ended. On October 16, 1847, Queen Maria Adelaide of Piedmont gave birth to a second daughter. The future King Victor Emmanuel II (1820–78) immediately inquired in Rome about having the supreme pontiff be the child's godfather. Pius accepted with delight and advised that the feminine form of his name-title, Pia, be given the offspring. Italians could not be chided if they surmised that Princess Maria Pia would have special meaning for Italy's future. Indeed, Pius IX had barely ascended the papal throne when, in his declaration of February 10, 1848, he closed with the dramatic call, "Oh great God, bless Italy."

Apparently, the savior and liberator Italians had sought from Machiavelli to Gioberti was on the scene. Italians seemed to close ranks. Idealists, liberal realists, conservative Catholics, even stalwart clericals, intransigent temporalists, and Mazzinian and Garibaldian democratic republicans, and socialist sympathizers like Carlo Pisacane and Giuseppe Ferrari were willing to grant Neo-Guelphism the opportunity to prove itself. All the teachings imparted by past masters were urging the adoption of Mazzini's call for God and the people, thought and action, in one giant synthesis of liberation and unification under the pope-prince. Giuseppe Verdi's *Nabucco* (1842), a popular opera which reviewed the Jews' subjugation by the Babylonian Nebuchadnezzar, represented the Italian plight in disguise. The voice of the participants resounded through oratorical efforts, manifestos, theatrical presentations, flag displays, female veils, processions, and torch light parades. In Vienna, Chancellor Metternich dreaded the implications for Austria and Europe of this Neo-Guelphist turn toward activism.

1848. The year opened with revolution in Palermo, followed in February with outbursts in Naples, Rome, Turin, and in March in Milan and Venice, where, on the 22nd, the Venetian Republic was proclaimed with Daniele Manin as president. Added to these was the February revolution in Paris, the Viennese liberals' insurrection, the Berlin uprising, and the Magyar revolt in Hungary, all in March. They seemed to give credence to the Mazzinian thesis that the hour of liberation, unification, and a new democratic republican world had struck. The upheavals in Italy were not concerted but were the agitation of the lower middle class and worker elements, along with a number of progressive nobles demanding, along with liberation and unification, constitutional government, majority rule, and civil liberties. The more radical called for the elimination of social inequality, economic inequities, and the cancellation of clerical dues. In the south the grievances were translated into one word: land.

The internal, uncontrollable contradictions soon became evident. The Neo-Guelphs had not expected such misdirected upheavals. Confusion on objectives, lack of cooperation and preparation, the very things Cuoco had warned against, hovered over proceedings. Naples was granted a constitution on February 10, Tuscany the 11th, Piedmont on March 4, and the Papal States on the 14th. If the charters were meant to appease, the more popular groups thought otherwise. The disinherited wanted political transformation and also social and economic reforms, which neither the opponents nor the middle and upper classes who had participated in the rebellions were willing to concede. They would not because of class interests and also because the Catholic moderates and liberals among them conceived of liberation and unification as the real and indispensable concerns. There was a kernel of truth in the allegation of the underprivileged that the Moderate-Liberal coalition had assumed that the desires of the people could be contained and perhaps instrumentalized on behalf of the more compelling issues of liberation and unification. Things became particularly tense in the Papal States, where a clash was provoked between demonstrators and the army, causing the pope to flee to Gaeta. As Mazzini and other notable democratic, unitary republicans returned to take personal command, the Roman revolution entered its most critical phase. A republic was announced, on February 9, 1849, featuring manhood suffrage, personal guarantees, the abolition of temporal power, and separation of church and state. Due to ideological convictions, strategic location, and its becoming increasingly isolated, the Roman Republic sent appeals to all the Italian states for the calling of a constituent assembly, which would declare Italy liberated, and would draft the constitution of the democratic, unitary republic.

One wonders whether bold creative statesmanship, calculated audacity, and defiance, even against all odds, would have carried the field. As might have been foreseen, state princes and regional governments had many reasons to turn a deaf ear to the cries of the Roman Republic for help. Liberal nationalists likewise. A democratic and unitary republic was too extreme for the bulk of the aristocracy and the bourgeoisie. Gioberti, who had become premier on December 26, 1848 and remained until February 21, 1849, was frightened by the probability of foreign intervention, especially in defense of the temporal power. Valuable time and priceless resources were being dissipated, energies that Moderates and Liberals had planned were to be directed to liberation and unification. On July 2, 1849, the Roman Republic capitulated, as President Louis Napoleon of France dispatched troops, who overthrew the defenders gallantly led by Garibaldi and Pisacane. Pius IX returned to his realm, the constitution was revoked, those arrested were numerous, and the sentences merciless.

Italy's cause was also lost in Piedmont. There the sense of impending events, generated by the grant of the *Statuto*, reached a crescendo with Piedmont's declaration of war on Austria, March 22, 1848. Petitions circulated throughout the peninsula for arms and men to aid Piedmont in what has been called the First War for Italian Independence. The Kingdom of Naples sent a detachment of civic guards, untrained to the onerous burden of soldiering. To the dismay of the unificationists, Pius explained, on April 29, 1848, that he was just a simple priest and not a conquering Napoleon and that he could not commit so unchristian an act and declare war against Catholic Austria. As the Roman Republic became radicalized, the pope was cured of any nationalist sympathies he may have had. In spite of the unrest Austria had to contend with in Vienna, rebellions in Milan, Venice, and Hungary, Austria was able to crush the revolts. Austrian forces under Field Marshall Joseph Radetzky defeated the Piedmontese at Custozza, July 5, 1848, and Novara, March 23, 1849. Piedmont sued for peace. Defeat resulted in the abdication of King Charles Albert in favor of his son, Victor Emmanuel II. Thus, Neo-Guelph unification nationalism was vanquished, externally in battle by the Austrians and as decisively internally by the Italians' misperceptions and failure to make common cause.

RE-EVALUATION. In the wake of the Neo-Guelph debacle, Gioberti, Balbo, and other Catholic moderate spokesmen engaged in a summary reconsideration of what had transpired and submitted recommendations for the future. Gioberti's observations comprised the second of his massive works, *Del rinnova-mento civile d'Italia (Italy's Civil Renewal)* (3 vols., 1851). Having blasted the reactionaries for refusing to enlarge the base of the state to accommodate the people and their legitimate demands, Gioberti scolded the bureaucrats, particularly Piedmontese administrators, who were more concerned with safeguarding their positions than in the prosecution of the war against Austria. Self-centered, Piedmont's municipalists had prevented the full mobilization and use of reserves at the crucial battle of Novara. The war was winnable. Pius IX was also castigated. He had surrounded himself with the Jesuits, who convinced him to remain extraneous from the conflict and to concentrate his energies on the preservation of the temporal power. France came in for her share of rebuke, although her reluctance to be drawn into the Italian struggle was understandable in the light of the Italian princes' refusal to rally around Piedmont. Gioberti would have been less than human had he not vented his fury on the Mazzinians, "the puritans." They had persisted in their doctrinaire belief that the only way one could be for liberty, unification, and progress was by subscribing to a radical republic achieved through revolution. Puritanism represented the degeneration of democracy, the rage of methedical equality, at the expense of moral and spiritual equivalents. Still, the Italian conscience had been profoundly stirred and the *Risorgimento* was an undeniable fact. The task which now lay before Italians was one of liberation. (*See Reading No. 17.*)

Democratic nationalists undertook their own review. Had they pressed too hard and prematurely? Were Mazzini's violent methods outdated and self-defeating? The most harrowing disappointment was the refusal of the people, notably the peasantry, to respond. Failure to deliver on the promise of land left the rural masses all the more in the grip of the clericals. True to form, they interpreted the goals and action of the Roman Republic to be anti-God, antichurch, antipope, and, therefore, in league with the devil. A rankling indictment stemmed from the schisms which had occurred in the ranks, undoubtedly, in part, the work of the moderates and liberals. To prevent further secessions, repeated efforts were set afoot after 1849 to fuse all the democratic and republican factions: anticlericals, Freemasons, internationalists, professional societies, worker brotherhoods, and peasant groups into one mammoth movement. Except, perhaps, during the 1850s, attempts ran afoul of the dogmatists and theoreticians. A chronic weakness of the Italian left, this inability to bury differences in favor of a unified stand, was carried over into postunification Italy and was a detriment to the survival of the liberal parliamentary regime. Its only redeeming value for the mid-nineteenth century was that its defeat cleared the decks for Cavour's statecraft.

CAVOUR BETWEEN NATIONALISM AND STA-TISM. Cavour became a member of Piedmont's Chamber of Deputies in June 1848. Between 1850–52, he held successive cabinet posts in trade, finance, and agriculture, and saw four tours of service both as premier and foreign minister from 1852 to 1861. Cavour continued Piedmont's modernization, which had been resumed by his predecessors, Balbo, Gioberti, and D'Azeglio, the work having been interrupted by the regressive policies of the Restoration rulers. Cavour had a marvelous and expansive understanding of the state. His use of state power was not paternalistic, mechanical, and self-perpetuating. It was intended to foster free capitalism and stimulate production. Since Piedmont lagged behind the more advanced countries of the West, economic power under state supervision would result in a more rapid and balanced growth. Under Cavour, Piedmont became a show case of moderate progressivism. It radiated vigor and optimism in all directions. Scientific farming was urged. Communication facilities and transportation networks were updated; road construction was promoted and railway lines were laid across Piedmont. Instruction and training of the army were also revamped, transforming it into an efficient and formidable organ, under the overall command of the king, general staff, and government. There was to be no repetition of the inertia and disarray which crippled the war effort in 1848–49.

Cavour's expanded deployment of state power is revealed in the changing relationship between church and state. The full weight of the government was marshaled for the adoption of civil marriage in August 1852, the withdrawal of the Jesuit monopoly over education, the secularization of hundreds of covenants and monasteries, and the confiscation of their wealth. With his superb grasp of the state, Cavour was bent on elevating the state and diminishing the stature of any institution, the church not excepted, which sought to interpose itself between the citizen and the state. Temporal power was condemned as reprehensible, a religious, moral, and civil outrage. Cavour summarized the latest reality in his famous deathbed dictum, "A Free Church in A Free State."

Operations of Piedmont's bureaucracy were tightened and the civil functionaries won over. They were reassured, a most important matter since their morale had been shattered because of the accusations lodged against them. Through burgeoning state responsibilities, Cavour convinced the Piedmontese operatives that they were not to be squeezed out or relegated to secondary chores. Cavour dispatched these *municipalisti*, whom Italians resented as die-hard Savoyards and self-serving provincials, to Naples, Sicily, the Papal States, and elsewhere, for their immediate incorporation within the developmental Kingdom of Italy and the extension of Piedmont's administrative system to the entire peninsula. The decision was a reasoned one, even if unpopular, and open to censure by historians. A major consideration why Gioberti from France exhorted his Neo-Guelph remnants to rally behind Cavour was because he knew that Cavour had captured the loyalty of Piedmont's civil cadres on behalf of unification, something he as prime minister had signally not been able to do.

On January 26, 1855, Cavour had Piedmont enter the Crimean War on the side of Britain, France, and Turkey, even though it was neither requested nor required, and the king, the military, and parliament were against involvement. There were many reasons why Cavour favored the move: prestige, experience, put neutral Austria in a bad light, and gain admission to the peace table where he might argue Italy's case. It allowed Cavour to boast that Piedmont had a state equal to all emergencies, a capable and disciplined array, and that Piedmont had catapulted itself to the vortex of continental affairs. The splendid performance of the 10,000 man expeditionary force under General Alfonso La Marmora made hearts throughout the peninsula glow with pride and glory. The daring policy, combined with the premier's striking stance at the Paris peace conference, had European statesmen, particularly Emperor Louis Napoleon III of France, take notice.

When Cavour became a nationalist is a matter of conjecture. He approached the peninsula as composed of "nations," yet was enough of an Italian and patriot to desire it freed from outside interference. He was sufficiently ambitious so that in the 1830s he admitted that he frequently dreamt waking up and finding himself prime minister of the kingdom of Italy. If he did not indicate the geographic reach of the kingdom, we can surmise it was an entity larger than Piedmont. Cavour established formal and informal contacts with nationalists of different ideological orientations. He knew personally several leaders of the *Carboneria*. In his travels abroad in 1835, he made the acquaintance of liberal and democratic republican refugees. He met the Catholic moderate Gioberti while he was in exile in Brussels. On July 20, 1858, the Plombières Agreement was negotiated with Emperor Napoleon, sealed by an alliance, the Treaty of Turin, signed December 10. The pact called for an Italian federation of four states with the pope as titular president: Upper Italy, Central Italy, the Papal States, and the Kingdom of Naples including Sicily. A unitary state was out of the question. It is probably correct to say that Cavour originally took to unification out of political necessity, to protect Piedmont's future. If he manifested regional outcroppings, Cavour imaginatively adjusted to unfolding events. As the unification drama proceeded and good fortune appeared, Cavour seized the current for the liberation and unification of the entire peninsula. Cavour read the defeats of 1848–49 to mean that nothing could be accomplished which threatened the class structure. Liberation and unification could not be attained through Gioberti-papal-princely energies, or by a Mazzinian popular uprising, nor by a sheer Garibaldian feat of arms. Neither a confederation nor a unitary democratic republic stood to gain the backing of crucial sectors of the middle classes. Only a liberal, monarchical state had a chance to succeed.

Cavour adhered to a state-sponsored campaign for unification. A superior instrument was needed to bring together, coordinate, and direct the nationalist sentiment that was scattered among disparate groups. Intellectuals of various genre over the centuries had laid the groundwork, but the climactic phase required centralized management of the unification forces. Confederate and unitary, democratic republican nationalists were indispensable for manpower. Only liberal Piedmont could provide the leadership and controls. If critics would label the effort and result the Piedmontization of Italy, so be it. Through all the turmoil and difficulties Cavour faced, he never yielded on state-directed nationalism. At Plombières, Napoleon decided to involve France in a war against Austria for an Italy of four states, provided the conflict could be justified as defensive and Italian public opinion was favorable. In exchange for France's help, France was to be ceded, assuming plebescitary endorsement, Nice and Savoy, and Princess Clotilde, Victor Emmanuel's fifteen year-old daughter, was to marry Prince Jerome Charles Bonaparte, the emperor's cousin. Since Nice was Garibaldi's birthplace, and Savoy the ancestral haunt of the Piedmontese royal family, and Jerome was shockingly obese, more than twice Clotilde's age, and a notorious rake to boot, only a minister in possession of himself, and in charge of his state, and confident of his people could have accepted the conditions and insure their implementation.

The avoidance of social upheaval and the fomenting of a premature and wider war against Austria were Cavour's constant worries. In 1854, an abortive Mazzini-inspired insurrection was set off in Genoa and the Lunigiana, the same in 1857 in Milan. Cavour assailed Mazzini, borrowing Gioberti's reproofs, as a vain utopian, whose senseless forays at revolution would neither foster liberation nor unification, but generate a backlash of uncontrollable proportions and possibly result in civil and class strife. Cavour was no less severe toward Garibaldi, branding him a fanatic, and a demagogue, who was incorrigibly blind to the diplomatic and international context in which unification was cast. Since Mazzini and Garibaldi were mainly responsible for the democratic element behind unification, Cavour found it necessary to use them and to exploit their rapport with the people, while prepared, at a moment's notice, to block their activities and also repudiate them should they prove embarrassing or detrimental to his plans. After Genoa, Cavour ordered the arrest of the fugitive Mazzini and had standby orders for Garibaldi's capture if the Sicilian invasion in May 1860 did not proceed according to his expectations.

Of significant help to Cavour in co-opting or opposing Mazzini and Garibaldi was his increasing ability to attract different factions to the national cause. By 1856, a number of liberal monarchists, confederationalist moderates, and also unitary, and federalist republicans were given reason to believe that Cavour and Piedmont were for parliamentary government, the free development of institutions, individual rights, and some type of a laic state comprising sizeable portions of the peninsula. Convinced that conspiracies and uprisings were counterproductive, Manin, a Venetian exile in France since August 1849, advised, like Gioberti had done with the Neo-Guelphs, all democrats and republicans to seek an understanding with Cavour. Another illustration of what was occurring was the transformation of the *Piccolo Corriere (Little Courier)*, a modest political weekly published in Turin, into a militant nationalist voice. This occurred in 1857. It was able to send correspondents to many Italian regions who sent back to Turin accounts of atrocities and misrule, laid at the door of the unrepresentative and foreign-supported states. Were Italy to unite, the *Little Courier* argued, and adopt Piedmont's liberal political structures, autocracy and oppression would disappear. By the fall of '58, it was predicting another war of liberation, and counting on Mazzini's Young Europe, Germany, Hungary, and Young Poland to threaten the Hapsburg Empire with a war on several fronts. When German nationalists organized the *Deutsche Nationalverein (German National Society)*, modeled after the *Società Nazionale Italiana (Italian National Society)*, the Turinese sheet immediately established cordial relations. It held out the hope of mutual understanding, possible joint tactics against the common enemy, Austria, in the name of similar objectives, and the unification of all the Italian and German states.

The founding of the Italian National Society in July 1857, was another salient indication of the distinctly nationalist temper permeating sections of society. It also vindicated Cavour's faith in state-chartered nationalism. The Society was the most visible and effective political organization of the *Risorgimento*. At its peak in 1860–61, the Society had 450 units or committees and 2,500 local officers or commissioners. Most of the 100,000 refugees in Piedmont were members. Where elsewhere proscribed, it functioned in secret. The organization did yeoman service in recruiting volunteers, obtaining munitions, supplies, shipping, and financial assistance for Garibaldi's Sicilian invasion. It drew liberals from the nobility and the bourgeoisie, radicals from the lower middle class, and former revolutionaries. It reflected the shift in mood and change of means, for some even objectives, that were taking place. Realism and experience had taught them that a mass, spontaneous uprising was naive and ruinous. They saw in Cavourian reformism the pathway to peaceful change. If members were diffident to Cavour's commitment to all Italy, they concluded that their pressure, combined with the logic of an unravelling situation, would compel Cavour and every nationalist to struggle for one, indivisible Italy. (*See Reading No. 18.*) When Garibaldi, as the price for his collaboration, devised the standard "Italy and King Victor Emmanuel," and the Piedmontese king, with Cavour's endorsement, accepted, it signified the maximum relevance of the Savoys and the unconditional acceptance of a liberated and unified peninsula.

After Plombières, Cavour extended relations with the Society to include regular exchange of information through intermediaries. According to the accord with Napoleon, Cavour was to promote the issue of war. He proceeded to encourage the National Society to stage revolts, which he hoped to control while forcing Austria's client regimes in the peninsula to appeal for help and invite her intervention. Outbreaks would convince the emperor that there was wide-spread backing for Cavour's policies, another proviso Napoleon had insisted upon. Several of the Society's attempts to instigate open unrest succeeded and others failed because the aristocratic and bourgeois liberals had little contact with the masses. Cavour was driven to rely on Mazzinian ventures and Garibaldian exploits to excite an adequate degree of popular support. As for the suitable pretext, the indomitable Cavour manufactured that also, Again, it was state power. In March 1859, Cavour ordered extensive military preparations and called up the reserves. The premier next enrolled young men from Lombardy as volunteers. They preferred to escape and serve in the Piedmontese army than be conscripted for Austrian military service. Cavour instructed his ambassadors to explain to the officials of the countries where they were stationed that it was Austrian provocations that were responsible for such extreme measures. Always searching for an excuse for a preemptive strike against Piedmont, as she was later against Serbia, Austria, on April 23, 1859, delivered an ultimatum, requiring Piedmontese demobilization within three days. Austria's demand provided Cavour with the hostile act needed to call on France for compliance with the Plombières pact.

With the rejection of the Austrian ultimatum and Cavour's unfailing efforts to impede European mediation, the Second War for Italian Independence ensued. The conflict itself was an example of state-dominated nationalism. No sooner had the war begun in earnest late in April, with the French and Piedmontese armies engaging the Austrians, than Cavour maneuvered the National Society into inciting minimal or qualified uprisings. The Society obliged, with insurgences erupting in Tuscany and Parma, June 10, Modena the next day, and in the Papal States except Rome, June 13–15. The insurrections in the Papal States were put down by papal troops, while in the other states they succeeded in overthrowing the foreign puppet regimes. The National Society and the *Unione Liberale* cooperated for an overwhelming Cavourian victory in the parliamentary elections of March 1860, conducted on the basis of limited suffrage, thus enhancing the prime minister's power and prestige. At his insistence, provisional governments were organized, and plebescites held between March 13–15, 1860, resulting in Parma, Modena, Romagna, and Tuscany requesting annexation to Piedmont. The National Society mobilized annexationist sentiment and had the plebescites based on universal manhood suffrage. Lombardy was secured by Austria's cession to France, July 11, which in turn handed it over to Piedmont.

Garibaldi and his Thousand Redshirts set sail from Quarto, near Genoa, on May 5, to aid the Sicilians who had rebelled against the Bourbons, April 4, 1860. The insurrection in the Papal States of September 8 gave Cavour the excuse he sought to head off Garibaldi. Within two days, the Piedmontese army marched into papal territory. On the 18th, it vanquished the papal army at Castelfidaro. It then ventured into the Neapolitan kingdom and joined forces with Garibaldi, who had liberated Sicily. It crossed the Messina Straits, fought and defeated the Neapolitans at the Volturno River on October 26, and had eyes fixed on Naples and, ultimately, Rome. On the same day, Garibaldi met Victor Emmanuel at Teano, just south of Naples, and hailed him as King of Italy. Naples and Sicily voted, October 21–22, for union with Piedmont and the other northern regions. The Marches and Umbria followed on November 4, 5, respectively.

On March 17, 1861, the Kingdom of Italy was proclaimed by the first Italian parliament, with Victor Emmanuel II as king, the *Statuto* as the constitution, Turin as the capital, with Cavour the prime minister. On June 6, Cavour died at the age of fifty-one.

Cavour harnessed state faculties, ministerial leadership, diplomacy, war, favorable European opinion, and restrained popular agitation for unification. His formula was sanctified by history. The Minister-President Otto von Bismarck adhered to Cavour's prescription. He used Prussia as the mainstay and bellwether for German unification. Serbia, on the morrow of its independence, in 1878, adopted the self-image of "the Piedmont" of the South Slavs. The organ of the *CRNA RUKA (Blackhand)* of the youthful revolutionaries was entitled, *PIJEMONT (Piedmont)*. It was Serbia that assembled the Southern Slavs into the post–World War I Kingdom of Slavs, Croats, and Slovenes (1919), renamed Yugoslavia in 1929.

Cavour was not spared stern criticism by historians and scholars from broad cross sections of Italian society. It was alleged that there was no authentic test of fire, no blood and iron in the unification process, as had occurred with Bismarck and German unification. Italian unification had depended excessively on Cavour's political sagacity and diplomatic astuteness, and not enough on Garibaldi's flaming sword. Italians remained divided in spirit. Cavour's unrelenting opposition to republican nationalism and to democratic revolution had gained the strategically important support of the middle and a segment of the upper classes, but rank-and-file Italians had not been brought to the liberal parliamentary regime. Individuals could participate in the annexationist plebescites who failed to qualify for parliamentary elections due to the property test. The exclusion of the lower orders became a facet of the theory of the *Risorgimento* as *una rivoluzione mancata* (a revolution that never took place). The current Italian republic is perhaps evidence that Cavour may have defaulted on genuine statesmanship. Another grievance was that Italy had forsaken her eternal mission. There were various aspects to this complaint, the more immediate, authored by Mazzini and Garibaldi and their intimate associates, was that Italy had refused to transform her unification struggles into a crusade for the emancipation, self-determination, and union of all free peoples. Worse, her leaders were sending confused signals to their own people and the waiting world. (*See Reading No. 19.*)

Cavour has not been without his admirers who have insisted that he should be judged within the framework of his time. Pragmatic and wise, Cavour did not, dared not, thrust beyond reach, toward the unattainable, and prejudice the future. The Kingdom of Italy was his monument and that of all his conationals, past and present. Cavour stoutly maintained that the centralistic pressures exerted by administration, economics, country-wide system of communication and transportation, pride, education, and general reform would insure the nationalization of culture and the socialization of all the people. (*See Reading No. 20.*)

Without disputing the intrinsic, inspirational impact of Mazzini's "mission" and Gioberti's "primacy," they left, on balance, an uncertain and disturbing patrimony. Dissension over the means and ends of unification cast an ugly shadow on subsequent Italian history. The resentment, the guilt each faction experienced for having betrayed what it accepted as the ideal Italy, proved impossible to eradicate or to submerge, especially when united Italy faced pivotal crossroads. There was a division of the soul which persisted through the liberal and fascist periods. Aside from the contrasting projections about what constituted Italy's singular destiny, Mazzini's and Gioberti's extreme formulations represented high callings nonetheless. Inherent in the attitude of many of their political and spiritual descendants was the tendency to distort the visions of the masters into a lust for power, for action, and adventurism, a turning away from the unromantic chores of state-building and economic reconstruction. The frustration inevitably resulting from unfulfilled grandiose dreams and the continued longing for some exceptional undertaking became a potent force within an important segment of the intellectuals. (*See Reading No. 21.*) It was a major factor in laying the seedbed for the authoritarian and aggressive nationalist movement of the twentieth century.

PART II

PROLETARIAN AND IMPERIALIST NATIONALISM

CHAPTER 6

IMPERIALISM IN THE SERVICE OF NATIONALISM

FORGING A NATIONAL CONSCIENCE Foremost in the list of problems confronting united Italy was the creation of a public spirit. A narrow and regional outlook, with its immediate nexus of loyalties, had to give way to a kingdom-wide pattern of attachments. Without moral cohesion, Italians would slip again into factionalism, into servility and bondage to foreign powers. How to educate a people with a literacy rate of twenty-two percent on the ways and responsibilities of independence and nationhood undoubtedly staggered the imagination and dampened the mood of exaltation generated by unification.

ESTABLISHING STATE AUTHORITY. Nothing was more critical than the buttressing of the state and the individual's cheerful submission to its mandates. Cavour was certain that the erection of a national bureaucratic apparatus, with an interlocking infrastructure, backed by economic growth, would, in time, convince all Italians of the legitimacy of the new order. He relentlessly pressed for placing all the peninsula under the Piedmontese system of administration because it was politically prudent and also because it was thought to be the only available means by which to mitigate sectional rivalries and to enforce a degree of uniformity.

STRENGTHENING THE PARLIAMENTARY REGIME. An effective and viable governmental order was another high priority item. Cavour's great ambition had been the introduction into Italy of the British liberal parliamentary system. He was a great admirer of British constitutionalism and political institutions, featuring up front a liberal and a conservative party, one, the majority party that ruled, and the other, the minority, the loyal opposition. Contrary to his political opponents and later to historians, Cavour saw nothing unethical or shameful in coalitions which transcended party lines when necessitated by national emergencies. In fact, early in 1852, he joined his mildly liberal center-right forces with Urbano Rattazzi's democratic left-center opposition. The alliance raised Cavour into the premier's seat; Rattazzi and his chief associates were rewarded with cabinet posts. Cavour's *Connubio* (hybrid and cynical political marriage), it was alleged, confounded political developments and distorted the premier's role. No sound two-party system was worked out, charges that reverberated into the next century.

Two major political groupings emerged from the unification era. Cavour's following was called the *Destra* (Right), later the *Destra Storica* (historic Right), also the Liberal Right, and, in the twentieth century, Right or Conservative Liberals, to distinguish it from the *Sinistra* (Left), also to be known as the *Sinistra Storica* (historic Left). From Cavour until 1876, Italy was ruled by a succession of Right prime ministers, eight to be exact. Ministerial turnovers became a characteristic of parliamentary life. The Historic Right was composed of liberals of every shade of opinion, progressive conservatives and former republicans who had accepted the kingdom and monarchy. All had been members of the Italian National Society. Their parliamentary origins went back to the late 1850s and early 1860s, firmly prompted by Cavour. The Historic Right always claimed it was in the footsteps of the immortal Cavour. It was dedicated to constitutional government, administrative centralization, social conservatism, limited suffrage, individual rights, balanced budgets, and the laic state. Persuaded perhaps to a fault on the merits of fiscal restraint, the *Destra* pushed through, on July 7, 1868, the *Macinato*, a heavy grist tax on all grains. Highly unpopular, it engendered disturbances, especially in Emilia, Romagna, and Tuscany. Some 250 of the demonstrators were killed in confrontations with soldiers. This tragedy, and the refusal to enlarge the suffrage, brought the *Destra*'s downfall, in 1876.

The incoming *Sinistra*, like the Historic Right, was a loose assemblage but of former Democratic and Republican factions. Since it faced off the Historic Right, it was labelled the Historic Left or the Liberal Left. The more radical and vocal gravitated towards the *Sinistra Democratica* (democratic left) under the liberal left umbrella, while those who held out for a republic and a social revolution were to comprise by the end of the century the *Sinistra Estrema* (Extreme Left): Anarchists, Radicals, Republicans, and Socialists. The year 1876 was a major watershed not only because it marked the end of the Historic Right's dominance, but also because a smooth transition of power was effected, proof that the liberal parliamentary regime worked. Once in power, the Liberal Left, headed by Premier Agostino Depretis, enacted moderate suffrage extension, educational reforms, tax abatement measures, and the gradual abolition of the *Macinato*. Such modest and deliberate changes enlisted Liberal Right collaboration. Party distinctions were virtually extinct. Reminiscent of Cavour's *Connubio*, the realignment, known as *Trasformismo* (Transformism), produced a break in the Left Liberals' ranks. Five of its more outstanding political personalities formed a parliamentary alliance, the *Pentarchia* (Pentarchy: rule by five). It was rabidly anticlerical, pro-irredentist, favored strong, basic legislation for the south's upliftment, and, most importantly, wanted the Liberal Left to remain independent as the best means of advancing the two-party ideal. Francesco Crispi's willingness to serve as minister of interior in Depretis' seventh ministry in April 1887 brought the collapse of the pentarchical experiment.

Italy's parliamentary waters tended to be muddied by the drift to machine politics. The phenomenon was not uniquely Italian, although critics, Italian and foreign, supposed as much. The restricted franchise, the single member constituency, combined with patronage and other types of inducements and forms of coercion radiated from Rome, resulted in clientalistic politics, frequently of the crudest sort, especially where the absence of modern culture rendered any other approach impossible. Through the ministry of the interior, the party in power mobilized the enormous influence of the local prefects, to have them return ministerial candidates to the Chamber of Deputies. Often, when confronted by deadlocks on crucial issues, governments avoided direct consultation with the electorate out of fear of being overturned. Parliament was dissolved and elections ordered so that the majority party could take advantage of a promising and tempting opportunity to increase its margin in the Chamber.

THE SOUTHERN PROBLEM. Although feudalism had been legally outlawed in the south by the opening decades of the nineteenth century, it continued to flourish openly and in secret. A sustained and comprehensive effort was needed to educate the southerners in personal initiative, communal pride, and for the creation of jobs, land redistribution, and mechanization of agriculture. This required commitment and huge sums of money, which did not exist. Cavour had unilaterally rejected any special arrangement for the south. Any form of interim regional autonomy, as advised by Garibaldi and the Sicilian revolutionary Crispi, was dismissed as a thinly veiled perpetuation of Neapolitan and Sicilian separatism. The sending of a swarm of Piedmontese officials wounded the southerners' sensitivity. Ignorant of the general situation, many northern bureaucrats believed southerners were biologically inferior. Denied compassion and relief, the peasant did not gain a stake in Italian society. The Camorra in Naples and the Mafia in western Sicily may have been conceived as local vigilante organizations against foreign usurpers. Steadily, they wormed their way into the intricate web of southern life with a labyrinth of patronage and retainership which has resisted extinction until our day.

If backwardness and lack of capital made it very difficult for an industrial or middle class to rise, the plight of the south was aggravated by the fact that noble proprietors and bourgeois capitalists who leased the land joined in an agrarian bloc. By the latter part of the century, this coalition sent over 100 Deputies to the Chamber. Proministerial, this interest group exercised tight control over the south. Under the circumstances, revolts, outbursts of violence, and vandalism were common. By official count, brigands in Naples and Sicily numbered 80,000 in 1862. Condemned to abject poverty or targeted as brigands, many southerners were driven deeper into a life of crime. In December 1865, at the height of the campaign for law and order, the state had 120,000 soldiers engaged in the south. Southern intellectuals were themselves at odds over how best to proceed toward improvements. Abandoned, a victim of the government, the underworld, and the ruling classes, many southerners sought seasonal employment in neighboring countries. Others added to the emigrant exodus, 119,806 in 1861, 533,245 by 1901, and a staggering 872,598 Italians leaving in 1912. The latter represented over two percent of a population of 32,475,253. A parliamentary study of 1863, the first of many such studies, revealed the depths of southern misery and the alarming loss of life which the struggle against brigandage was costing the country. (*See Reading No. 22.*)

CHURCH-STATE RELATIONS. Having excommunicated the *Risorgimento* and its main votaries, Pius IX, with the Syllabus of Errors, appended to the encyclical, "*Quanta Cura (So Much Concern),*" December 6, 1864, unequivocally placed the Catholics Church in opposition to liberalism and secularism. If the ultra-Catholics embraced the papal statement, the Catholic moderates interpreted it as dealing a fatal blow to their efforts at reconciling religious belief with liberal government. Similarly, the dogma of papal infallibility, announced on July 18, 1870, a date almost coinciding with Italy's taking of Rome, September 22, was designated to lift the church and the papacy above earthly states and worldly potentates. The final part of the papal triune attack came the following year, 1871, given more forceful expression in 1874, with the *Non Expedit (Not Expedient)*. This had a direct and immediate bearing on Italian Catholics, since the pronouncement declared it was "not expedient" to the church to allow Catholics to become involved in the political life of a state which had robbed the church of its ancient jewel, Rome, and with it the Papal States and the temporal power. The Roman Question, a term which referred to the loss of Rome, further exacerbated the tensions which had existed between Italy and the church.

Confronted by this new turn in hostility, the Italian parliament attempted on its own to regularize church-state relations through the Law of Papal Guarantees, passed on May 13, 1871. The person of the pope was held to be inviolate, as that of the king, while the church was declared to be an independent entity with exclusive jurisdiction over religious matters. The law recognized the pope's incontestable right to discharge his duties as the spiritual, administrative, and diplomatic head of the Roman Catholic Church. Officials of the church could meet their responsibilities without state infringement except in clear violation of Italian law. The financial clauses allowed for an annual payment of 3,225,000 lire, ostensibly as an indemnity for the decline in papal income due to the capture of the Papal States. Extraterritoriality was conferred on the Vatican and church edifices, ranging from church buildings, residences, monasteries, apostolic palaces, museums, and libraries.

Pio Nono refused to acknowledge the guarantees. Catholic apologists complained they were unworkable even though the commemoration of Pius's death, February 7, 1878, and the election, on February 20, of Gioacchino Pecci as Leo XIII, proceeded smoothly and proved otherwise. The pontiff considered himself "the prisoner of the Vatican." Church antagonism was partly accountable for popular apathy toward the Kingdom of Italy. Nationalists were scandalized by what they claimed was the provocative behavior of ecclesiastics, who prohibited Catholic institutions, from schools to charitable agencies, from displaying the Italian flag on national holidays. Slowly but surely, however, a *modus vivendi* was unofficially taking place. Increasingly, from the late 1880s on, Catholics took part in communal and provincial elections, activity not disallowed by the *Non Expedit*. Catholic money was valuable for the creation of an industrial base and a growing number of lay Catholics participated in business and commercial enterprises, banking and shipping, and also secured prominent positions in industrial and financial institutions, and in public utilities. As they took their place in the evolving public life of the nation, the Italian Catholic industrial, mercantile, and financial bourgeoisie were encouraged by the Catholic moderates, rich in the Neo-Guelph tradition of selective compromise. These conciliationists fought the clerical intransigents over the prospects of a new era in church-state relations. They were convinced that Catholic absenteeism from the national political scene seriously injured the liberal state and only benefitted the extreme Left, its ranks rife with anticlericals and Freemasons.

ECONOMIC NATIONALISM. The paramount issue was how best to foster and facilitate the industrial revolution then in full swing in the western world. In 1861, Piedmont's moderate tariff, a favorite of Cavour, was extended to the entire kingdom. A reversal occurred in 1878 and the country turned toward protectionism. Rates were gradually raised until by the end of the 1880s they were rather steep. Protectionism was no easy decision. Italy had little choice. All major powers were abandoning tariff reduction and leaning toward outright protection. The fact that protectionism was an integral part of the Liberal Left Premier Depretis's search for revenue to offset the easing of the grist tax and not of the Liberal Right should alert students on the complexities of the subject. Had Italy not adopted protectionism and not industrialized, she would have been condemned to be a dumping ground for the advanced industrial states, Britain, Germany, and France. Neither can defense considerations be ignored. Protection was a legitimate form of economic nationalism. Involved was Italy's survival as an independent state. Had Italian statesmen kept with a quasi-free trade policy, and not reduced the country's dependence on foreign supplies of steel, chemicals, heavy equipment, and capital, Italy would have been deprived of a valuable margin of safety. The recourse to protection may have resulted in distortions and imbalances, monopolies in steel, chemicals, machinery, shipbuilding, metallurgical industries, cereals, and also led to governmental handouts, vociferously deplored by the *liberisti* (free traders). The fault was not inherent in the protectionist principle but in the application.

During the third and fourth quarters of the nineteenth century, Italy experienced the beginnings of an industrial revolution. It was sizeable even if understandably spotty. Protection put Italy in the position where commercial treaties with other countries modified tariff rates on a mutual basis, stabilized external markets, and opened outlets for Italian farm products as well as manufactured goods. If France retaliated, and Italy's trade war with France between 1888 and 1898 was immediately disastrous for the Italian economy, its long term effects were salutary. Italy diversified, sought additional markets, and redoubled its efforts to work out more satisfactory trade arrangements. With the incidence of higher prices it connoted, economic nationalism was viewed by public-minded Italians as another means of implanting within the citizenry the instinct to sacrifice for the peace and prosperity, prestige and safety of the Fatherland.

ITALY'S PLACE IN THE WORLD. Economic nationalism was part of a comprehensive program by which Italy would enter the Concert of Europe as an equal partner. The more realistic trade accords negotiated signified economic and interstate reciprocity. In spite of the inimicable attitude of the papacy and prelates, all important states extended diplomatic recognition. Italians learned to use the European power balance to their advantage. Italy gained Venetia, July 3, 1866, following Austria's cession to France, as a result of the Seven Weeks War, Italy and Prussia having joined, on May 12, in an alliance against Austria. On August 19, 1870, France completed the withdrawal of the military force protecting papal Rome. On the morrow of

France's defeat at Sedan by Prussia, the Italians, on September 20, after a brief bombardment, occupied Rome. After a plebescite, the city was annexed. On October 2nd, it became the capital. Foreign monarchs and high governmental personalities were reluctant to undertake state visits to Rome out of respect for papal sentiment. German Emperor William II was the first foreign head of state to visit Rome. He undertook the trip in 1888, Humbert I greeting him at the railroad station. As a result of the solution of the trade war and the Franco-Italian Agreement of December 14, 1900, which exchanged a free hand for France in Morocco for similar liberty for Italy in Tripoli, French President Émile Loubet and Foreign Minister Théophile Delcassé ventured to the Italian capital in April 1904. That gesture succeeded in removing nearly all inhibitions against world dignitaries journeying to Rome.

Italy was invited to participate at the Congress of Berlin, which met June 13–July 13, 1878. It was called to settle their problems arising from the national liberation uprisings in the Balkans against the Ottoman Empire and from Russia's exorbitant demands following her victory in the Russo-Turkish War of 1877–78. Once underway, the Congress, with the shrewd guidance of Bismarck, the German chancellor, became a clearing house for the big powers' imperialist ambitions in Africa. Italy had several objectives in mind: gain pride in having a voice in the conclave of states, mingled with the hope that Austria could be persuaded to relinquish either the Trentino or Trieste, two areas of Italian-speaking people left under alien rule. There was the desire to have the scramble for African colonies work out for an Italian protectorate over Tunis. Directly across the Mediterranean from Sicily, Tunis was rapidly becoming a haven for the poor peasants of the south. Count Luigi Corti, who headed the Italian delegation, evaluated his people's expectations as purely fanciful, and disclaimed Italian aspirations in advance. The fact that Austria, Italy's arch enemy, was mandated the occupation of Bosnia-Herzegovina on the Adriatic only poured salt in Italy's wounds. Britain's invitation in the 1870s for a possible joint move on Egypt was summarily rejected to avoid becoming entrapped in Africa while animosity with Austria was at a high pitch.

Disappointments in foreign policy, France's registration of a protectorate over Tunis, May 12, 1881, together with the wave of Francophobia stemming from the breakdown in trade negotiations, and the fear that Austrian and Italian tensions over Trent and Trieste might erupt into open conflict, are the major reasons behind Italy's entrance into the alliance system. On May 20, 1882, Italy, Austria, and Germany signed the Triple Alliance. It was for a five-year term and was renewed and in force until May 3, 1915, when Italy renounced it in preparation for involvement in the First World War on the Allied side.

Italy also indicated an African presence with the purchase in 1869 of the port of Assab on the Red Sea from the Rubattino Shipping Company. The firm had engaged in economic projects of a dubious nature and had threatened to sell out to other interested European states. Feeling more secure, and to prevent other European countries from taking possession, Italy acquired Massoua in 1890, and then incorporated Assab and Massoua into the colony of Eritrea. Italy also took ownership of a stretch of coastal territory fronting on the Red Sea and Indian Ocean renamed Italian Somaliland. Italy proceeded into its designs over Ethiopia, climaxed by the Treaty of Uccialli, May 2, 1889, which established an Italian protectorate over the ancient kingdom. The campaign was not without its comic-tragic aspects. Italy's advance was achieved more by stealth than by force of arms, by generous bribing of Menelik II, King of Shoa, against the sovereign, Emperor John, the king of kings, who was succeeded in the imperial throne upon his death by Menelik. On January 26, 1887, two regiments of 7,000 Abyssinian soldiers ambushed a column of 500 Italians at Dogali, Eritrea, later in Ethiopia, carrying food and supplies to the main body of Italian troops. Few Italians escaped death. As for Uccialli, Menelik soon disputed the Italian version, from which Italy's right to a protectorate was derived. In 1891, he abrogated Uccialli. Unable to solve the problem amicably, Crispi decided in 1893 to resume hostilities.

CONFUSED AND CONFLICTING IDENTITIES. In the face of political inexperience, the debilitating church-state feud, and Italy's limited natural resources, achievements were substantial. Illiteracy declined to 49 percent by 1901 and to 38 percent in 1913. The statistics of economic growth were equally impressive. Real annual per capita income, 1,331 lire in 1872, rose to 1,906 in 1895, and to 2,539 by 1913. Within the ten-year period of 1872–82, savings doubled from 500,000,000 to 1,000,000,000 lire. The gross net product, 6,142,300,000 lire in 1895, climbed to 9,460,800,000 as of 1913. Between 1890–1907, Italy's foreign trade soared by 118 percent; a thumping 87 percent increase in industrial production was registered from 1901 to 1913. Not all Italians shared proportionately and the south lagged woefully behind. Many sober and patriotic Italians, in public and private circles, were satisfied that a modern state was painstakingly evolving, that Italy was finding her proper place in world affairs, and was responding positively to historical forces, to the point of embracing economic nationalism, becoming an integral cog in the European alliance system, and establishing colonies in Africa.

This tempered judgment was increasingly challenged by other currents of opinion, particularly by the objections which emanated primarily from a sector of the literary intelligentsia. The contagion eventually built up was insidious and affected elements of the Historic Right and Left. There were many strains of idealism and of genuine care in the effusions, mingled with overtones of the bombastic and the irrational. One can sympathize with the *literati*'s discontent since their cultural forbearers had been for centuries in the forefront of the liberation and unification struggles. It was natural for them to post themselves as the anointed custodians of the *Risorgimento* heritage. It functioned to filter and evaluate postunification experiences. It is no surprise that liberal Italy always ended up a distant second.

The humanistic bourgeoisie was upset over the lack of social cohesion and emotional unity. The people remained isolated. Emigration was tearing families and communities apart. Localism prevailed as never before. As industrialization spread, the bourgeoisie may have appreciated the statewide gambit of economic activity while their own enterprises and political outlook did not comparably expand, as with their British, French, and German counterparts. They remained regional. Commentators regretted the absence of two distinct parties as had become the custom in Britain and the United States. The Liberal Left was simply another edition of the Liberal Right, only many times more decadent and vulgar, as political pundits decried. An embarrassing similarity was sketched between Cavour's *Connubio* and Depretis' *Trasformismo*, and both were condemned as combinations put together for sake of political expediency and the lure of personal profit. The parliament was neither national nor representative but oligarchical. To make matters worse, it was drab; deputies were unusually wordy, and Montecitorio, the building which housed parliament, was "a mud hole," where all sorts of horrible cliques congregated to despoil the country.

Republicans charged that the sluggish conditions of public life were because Italy was a kingdom, artificially imposed by Cavour, with an aloof and retiring sovereign, instead of a grassroots republic, whose presidents vibrantly related to the citizenry. Italy had just barely been united and already in the mid-70s three outspoken young men, Errico Malatesta, Carmelo Palladino, and Carlo Cafiero, university trained and from landowning families, were championing anarchist communism, to be realized by "propaganda of deeds," meaning insurrections, later replaced by the instrument of assassination. By the next decade, Andrea Costa, Filippo Turati, Arcangelo Ghisleri, Anna Kuliscioff, Antonio Labriola, and Claudio Treves were laying the local and national foundations of a workers' movement. Their efforts came to fruition in 1892, with the Italian Socialist party, which from its inception included proponents, like Arturo Labriola, of revolutionary syndicalism. Patriotism and nationalism, if mentioned at all, were terms of opprobrium. To the doleful professionals, the introduction of labor agitation and the class struggle combined with the tumults they presaged to make Italy's general position even more precarious and perhaps untenable.

In the approach, and also in the conduct of foreign policy, ambitions were not adequately weighed by a realistic evaluation of national energies and the world situation. They were nearly always considered in terms of Italy's divinely ordained role as the revitalizing nation of mankind. Particularly galling to Italian pride was that Italy had not been completed and that she had not sealed her unification with the liberation of all subject nationalities. Remnants of Garibaldians and Mazzinians, still entranced by the old myths and holding Victor Emmanuel to his pledge, were restless, eager to incite uprisings, coupled with invasions, to wrest Austria's Italian-speaking provinces and to free Rome from the pope. It was Renato Imbriani, a Mazzinian Republican, who in 1876 coined the designation, *Fratelli Irredenti* (Irredentist Brethren), to refer to the Italians disgracefully left to Austrian rule and who needed to be rescued. Such treachery convinced the former Republican Carducci, who was to win the Nobel Prize in literature in 1907, that "our fatherland is depraved."

If Garibaldi offered the public oath, "Rome or Death," to the unreconstructed Republicans the choice was between "Rome or Revolution." Rome's liberation was to be timed with the tumults of Austrian and Ottoman Empire minorities. At the battle of Aspromonte, August 29, 1862, Garibaldi and his band of irregulars were thwarted in their resolve to secure Rome by a Franco-Italian force. Papal troops, reinforced by French contingents, did the same at Mentana, November 3, 1867. In both encounters, Garibaldi was captured and amnestied to his island home of Caprera. At Aspromonte, he suffered the supreme insult of being wounded "by an Italian bullet," he disdainfully remarked. Periodically, he attempted to break out of his self-imposed inactivity, to head crusades for the liberation of Trent, Trieste, and Dalmatia, the latter by appeal of the Slavs, as he had tried for Venetia and Rome. Official support was denied in advance of the contemplated undertakings. Italy's refusal to give tangible assistance to the Polish revolt of 1863 was attacked in the Chamber by the former Sicilian revolutionary Crispi as dishonorable and a betrayal of *Risorgimento* values. (*See Reading No. 23.*)

Added to these disquieting events was the second defeat at Custozza, inflicted by the Austrian army, on June 24, 1866, and the shattering naval losses near Lissa, July 20. Italy's acquiring of Venetia by way of France, as she had Lombardy in 1859, was another irritating indignity. The War of 1866, also called the Third War for Italian Independence, brought little consolation to those Italians who sought for Italy military glory and psychological oneness via war. Rome's annexation, October 2, 1871, following a favorable plebescite, and its becoming the nation's capital, counted for nought. Italians were not entering Rome like Julius Caesar, as mighty conquerors, but like a rabble of disarmed soldiers undeservedly smiled upon by the fates. Italy's pitiful performance at the Berlin Congress of 1878, from which her commissioners returned, as it was explained in derision, "with hands that were clean but also empty," was evidence that Italy commanded no respect in the councils of foreign states. The sparse territories Italy picked up in East Africa were mere desert scraps, with the choice morsels already gobbled up by "lesser people." The extension of the franchise in 1880, from 600,000 to 2,000,000 males, was not hailed as an advance but was dismissed as an unworkable form of appeasement. Stymied and depressed, Garibaldi, who had been repeatedly elected to parliament and had refused to serve, withdrew to the sidelines. Mazzini also turned his back on the Italian state he had labored to create. He repaired to Genoa and fulminated against the Italy which was not Italy. (*See Reading No. 24.*)

The more the years between them and the *Risorgimento*, the more unworthy these Italian men of letters considered their founding fathers. From the long range point of view, a massive revolt was gathering against the liberal order by ideologues who misapplied the teachings and spiritual force of *Risorgimento* luminaries. In many instances, love for Italy and moral fervor masked the search for self-clarification; attachment to the glamor and excitement inherent in the lofty destiny bequeathed to Italy became a substitute for the humanitarian service Mazzini and Gioberti had articulated. If anything, the outcries against the political system which tolerated the mediocrities responsible for the repeal of Italy's world mission became more insistent as European culture experienced an upheaval of mammoth proportions. Impersonal, one-sided, and predictable theories, from Marx's dialectical materialism and Charles Darwin's evolution, and Auguste Comte's sociological positivism to Sigmund Freud's discovery of man's incorrigible tendency for self-destruction, stirred minds to the utmost.

In Italy, as elsewhere, there was acceptance, by extreme Left factions and their intellectual sympathizers, and, in the main, rejection by Liberals and Moderates. Although many of the disgruntled professionals under review disputed the hypotheses' claims to irresistible validity, they extracted from the schematics scientific verification for their belief in the inseparable connection between force and progress, implicitly or explicitly underlying the various determinisms. They had added incentive to publicize their notion that Italy alone could rescue civilization from the lies and strange doctrines being circulated. But first an Italian empire and revival. (*See Reading No. 25.*) If the same individuals seriously questioned the reliability of Marx's, Comte's, and Freud's thinking, they were inclined to believe that the flight of many Italians to foreign shores endowed Darwinism with a remarkable and foreboding accuracy. Depopulation, and with it, third class status appeared to be Italy's lot. Colonies, for the conservation of Italy's surplus population and to confirm the Italians as destiny's chosen people, thus became a must for the Garibaldian and imperialist exponent, Pasquale Turiello. One can detect a tinge or two of racialism in such expostulations. (*See Reading No. 26.*) Rather than stampede for empire, the garrulous Right Liberal Deputy Rocco de Zerbi pleaded for a gruelling war, preferably of a civil variety, "a second test of arms and blood" was how he described it, which would rid the country of mundane preoccupations and divisive endeavors. Apparently, the *Risorgimento* had been flagrantly insufficient.

Many youths in search of themselves, Italy, the world, and rewarding careers, found reason to be impressed by the exhortations of the prodigious literary figure from the Abruzzi, Gabriele D'Annunzio (1863–1938). He reports that in his opening days he was captivated by "a desire for glory" which, "sometimes," he confessed, "made for a tormented melancholy." Soured and dismayed by the monotonous pace of life. D'Annunzio advised youthful artists and writers to follow his example and shun politics and public life, and to concentrate their strivings on the exaltation of beauty, the sole unfailing goddess. Because he was too much of an activist and he was instinctively drawn to violence, D'Annunzio's posture of frivolous disinterest proved to be short-lived. Sensing, like Alfieri, the close inter-relationship between politics and literature, D'Annunzio, unlike Alfieri, implored "*la straga più vasta* (the vastest massacres)" as the only remedy for the stifling cultural climate which had paralyzed civilization. Whether it was the *Armata d'Italia* (*Italy's Navy*) (1888), *Le Laudi* (*The Canticles*) (1903), or *Canzoni delle gesta d'oltremare* (*Songs from the Overseas' Action*) (1911), the latter lyrical verses of praise to Italy's Libyan invasion, D'Annunzio's new-found passion for Italy was mortgaged, as Italy's foremost philosopher-historian Benedetto Croce expressed, "to a spirit of adventure and thrill of combat." Such was the spell he cast that many of the professional bourgeoisie originally adhered to the same unconcern.

ITALY TURNS TO CRISPI. A deteriorating situation, punctuated by demoralization, estrangement of many intellectuals, the accelerating peasant unrest in the south, which entered its critical phase with the spontaneous outbursts of the *Fasci Siciliani* (Sicilian Bands) in late autumn, 1894, the tariff war with France, and the deadlock over interpretation of Uccialli, demanded a leader of vision and patriotic devotion. On December 10, 1893, Italy recalled Crispi to the premiership. His many qualifications made Crispi a logical choice. Crispi was the lone distinguished survivor of the nationalist movement who represented continuity between the *Risorgimento* and the end of the century. Veteran conspirator, a refugee in France and Britain, in close collaboration with Mazzini, Crispi had served as Garibaldi's chief of staff in the 1860 campaigns in Sicily and Naples. Elected to parliament the following year, Crispi, by example and appeal, prevailed on many of his Republican colleagues to accept the Savoy monarchy and to join him in the ranks of the Liberal Left. Crispi's reputation as a selfless nationalist and a wise statesman stood to rise or fall on the outcome of the Ethiopian War, the conflict re-opened in December 1893. Although he was not responsible for initiating the overseas undertaking, any more than he was responsible for the deplorable conditions in the south, Crispi, nevertheless, made both his own. Crispi presented the program of his second ministry to the Chamber, on December 15, 1893. He indicated that the *Risorgimento* nationalists had formed the unitary state and that it was the assignment of the current generation "to give the country a consciousness of itself" and "to make Italy equal among equals," which, in his estimation, was "the most difficult task since unification."

Repeatedly, Crispi lectured his countrymen that whatever the motives behind Italy's original commitment, and however haphazardly conceived, Italy's belief in self and her sense of future were inseparably linked with the war. Italians simply could not pull out without inflicting on themselves an incalculable moral and psychological defeat. The premier argued that any course short of total victory would be a stain on the country's honor, impossible to remove, resulting in pervasive self-doubt, lowered international esteem, and inevitably, to domestic disorders. The country could not afford another Custozza or Lissa. Were Italy to persevere and see the imperialist struggle through to success, there would be colonies, markets, raw materials. Victory would lift the eyes of all Italians from the improvident nature of daily life to a reawakened sentiment of patriotic fulfillment. Crispi may have become so obsessed with the war's many rewards for Italy that he may have forced the issue on Menelik by deliberately or unwittingly misinterpreting Uccialli to signify Ethiopia's acquiescence to an Italian protectorate. Italy will have vindicated to herself and the world her right to independence and have the Italians greeted as worthy successors of their *Risorgimento* patriarchs. The solemn sight of the Italian soldier fighting in distant lands and unfamiliar climes for the Fatherland would gain for the country the elusive morale and élan derived from arms.

Errors in assumptions, leadership, execution, political controversies, and Crispi's own shortcomings came together with cumulative effect at the slightest appearance of difficulty. Crispi did not have Cavour's uncanny ability to size up goals with available opportunities. The larger ministerial majority obtained in the general elections of May 1895 convinced him that the African expedition had strong popular support. He did not foresee the likelihood that political groups from the right and even from the left would immediately back the new campaign and that they would just as readily oppose it and make him the scapegoat as soon as obstacles surfaced. Italy was veering in many directions and taking on an excessive number of problems: Ethiopia, France, the deficit, the economy, the *Fasci Siciliani*. Crispi misunderstood his people and the moment. The cutting edge in society was represented by Sicilian peasants crying for bread, land, social justice, and by industrial workers, and businessmen clamoring for relief from the ill effects of the recession, worsened by the commercial war with France. The louder the criticism, the more beleaguered Crispi felt, and the more certain he became that victory was the indispensable cure. Crispi and the framers of Italian policy did not concede the possibility that France would help equip Menelik's army.

Nothing reveals the state of disorganization and mental disarray more than the contradictory instructions Crispi sent to the field commander, General Oreste Baratieri. Having advised the general that nothing but a decisive military triumph would suffice, the premier also admonished him that Italy's budgetary crunch required a swift ending of the war. Given the choice, Baratieri naturally opted for the former. He marched deep into Ethiopian territory, extending his lines of communication. To compound the mistakes, Italians thought they could buy the loyalty of Menelik's vassals without being suspicious of their prompt willingness to accept the bribes. Lulled into overconfidence, the Italians were no match for the Ethiopians' combined forces, which sprung a surprise attack at Adowa, a town in Tigre province, on March 1, 1896. Menelik's army of 100,000 men clashed with Baratieri's Italian force of 17,000 and 10,000 Eritrean colonial troops. Italians suffered 5,500 soldiers and officers killed, and 1,500 Italians and 800 Ascari (Eritreans) taken prisoners. Italy sued for peace. The Treaty of Addis Ababa was negotiated and signed October 26, 1896, by which Italy acknowledged Ethiopia's independence. Crispi, meanwhile, resigned on March 5. It became the fashion of the Nationalists and Fascists of later years to revere Crispi as a forerunner of Mussolini. Nothing is further from the truth. Crispi was an authoritarian Left Liberal, or democrat, an anticlerical, and a Freemason. His questionable policies were imposed upon him by circumstances and were not the designs of the born despot.

POST-ADOWA SYNDROME. The period between March 1, 1896, the date on which Adowa occurred, and February 1901, the formation of the Left Liberal ministry of Giuseppe Zanardelli and Giovanni Giolitti, when the full and open practices of parliamentary government were restored, was one of extreme tensions. Italian society was polarized almost to the breaking point. Led by Socialists, Republicans, and a number of Radicals, a chorus of "Long Live Menelik," "Away from Africa," "Down with the Monarchy," and "Up with the Republic" echoed throughout the halls of parliament. Servicemen returning from Ethiopia slipped quietly into Italy lest a commemorative reception provoke retaliatory violence. Premier Antonio S. Di Rudinì, Crispi's successor of the Liberal Right, succinctly and quaintly expressed Italy's new foreign policy as that of

"*Piedi in Casa* (*Feet Indoors; Stay-at-Home*)." He withdrew as a result of the *Fatti di Maggio* (*Incidents of May 3–8, 1898*). Bread riots were triggered in many parts of the peninsula, culminating in scuffles between demonstrators and soldiers in Milan. Order was only reinstated after martial law had been declared and at the cost of 100 civilian fatalities. Apprehensive and unconvinced of their loyalty, Rudinì, before retiring, temporarily loosed the socialist and Catholic lay organizations and briefly imprisoned several of their respective leaders. When King Humbert I brazenly bestowed the nation's highest military decoration on General Fiorenzo Bava-Beccaris, who had quelled the disorders, he became the target of several anarchist plots. On July 29, 1900, Humbert was assassinated by Gaetano Bresci, an anarchist from the United States.

General Luigi Pelloux became premier on June 28, 1898, and remained until June 18, 1900. He attempted to rule by executive fiat and royal decree. He presented a drastic Public Safety Law and planned to change the Chamber's standing orders. His actions provoked an epidemic of strikes and an informal coalition of Left Liberals and the Extreme Left for the defense of constitutional procedures. Filibusters, overthrow of ballot boxes, and heated exchanges between the right and left were common. Thinkers had a field day. The political scientist Gaetano Mosca and the sociologist-economist Vilfredo Pareto wove theories about the hypocritical nature of parliamentary institutions. Government was not by the people but by elites, based on birth, wealth, or traditions of public service. The criminologists and anthropologists Cesare Lombroso and Alfredo Nicefero proceeded with scientific precision to isolate the delinquent type and to identify him with the southern Italian. To the sociologist Giuseppe Sergi, the signs of the times, from banking scandals, political and social unrest, emigration, Adowa, to regicide, conclusively proved that "Italy is the most wretched of all nations," "rotten to the bones," and, in conformity with the Darwinian script, doomed to "final collapse." Public figures wondered what the future held in store. (*See Reading No. 27.*)

CHAPTER 7

ENRICO CORRADINI AND PROLETARIAN AND IMPERIALIST NATIONALISM

AN ALIENATED YOUTH. Corradini was born on July 20, 1865, in the town of Samminiatello di Montelupo, Florence province. Upon graduation from the University of Florence, he became a high school teacher of Italian literature. Under D'Annunzio's influence, Corradini drove hard for a culture divorced from political and social content and anchored in estheticism. The Tuscan was also drawn to esthetics because the reaction against positivist culture was in high gear. Positivists were determined to introduce in the arts and the humanities the methods and approaches of the natural sciences. Corradini joined in the counterattack unleashed by several Florentine periodicals of art and literature, criticizing positivism's system of thought, its claims to precision, its predictive arrogance, and the drab features it paraded as art. The key to cultural renewal and intellectual refinement was the banishment of positivism and the elevation of beauty as the artist's and thinker's yardstick and guide.

Try as he might, Corradini did not experience the ecstasy contemplation of the beautiful was supposed to induce. His plays, novels, short stories, essays, and review articles illustrate preoccupation with estheticism, flirtation with realism, together with a contempt for the middle and upper classes, and a shocking submission to the fatalistic nature of human existence in a world in which impersonal powers reigned supreme. One also meets an early instance of Corradini's appreciation of literature's potential for public discourse. The melange he composed of his gropings did not lead to fame or applause.

CONVERSION TO NATIONALISM. By Corradini's admission, Italy's defeat in Ethiopia jolted him into the discovery of the fatherland and of himself. (*See Reading No. 28.*) Given the background, it was logical for Corradini to believe he had been ordained to bring nationalism, "the religion of the fatherland" as he defined it, to the Italian rank-and-file. It was also normal for Corradini to have an overwhelming sense of guilt for his past indifference and that of business, culture, and politics. In *La guerra lontana* (*The Faraway War*), a doctrinal novel of 1911, Corradini lashed out at the ruling classes and the intellectuals who had betrayed Crispi and the soldiers, and subordinated the country's safety to their crass political fortunes and sordid individual interests. Since he intuitively surmised that Adowa would be the directing force of his life, Corradini was sure that a triumphant Italy would have found and placed herself on the road to messianic fulfillment. That made his grief more poignant. *Gioia* (*Joy*) (1897), and *Verginità* (*Virginity*) (1898), two novels, reiterate the unavoidable disappointment awaiting individuals who strive to keep their honor and integrity in a day of rapidly dissolving moral truths. Sorrow was not relieved by religion. Corradini spurned Christianity as an anthropological relic at best and a psychological aberration at the worst. It made Italians gullible and numbed them into passive subjection to foreign invaders.

The divisions which cropped up on the *Marzocco* compelled Corradini to take a stand. The weekly review of art, literature, and sculpture was cofounded by Corradini on February 12, 1896, just five weeks prior to Adowa. Corradini's collaborators were all his senior. Besides taking their place in the fight against positivist culture, and searching for another form of art, possibly realism or classicism, since estheticism was not proving satisfactory, the review's writers shared apprehension over emigration and an aversion for the inequities and environmental ugliness chargeable to capitalism and industrialization. They also abhorred socialism, not because they despised the working masses, but due to its positivist-materialist philosophy. This blurred distinction between socialism and the people it spoke for was carried by the literary Corradini into the nationalist movement he was to head. As he learned from Mario Morasso, who lay bare the modern world to him, from the clanging machine to the publicly engaged man of letters civil society now required, Corradini saw war as conceptually beautiful, as well as politically rewarding. War was in close harmony with the deeper impulses of the opening century.

As Corradini continued to fathom art-literature as a medium

of communication and change, antipathies between him and his *Marzocco* colleagues came to the fore. A basic incompatibility was surfacing between Corradini's initial acceptance of the Darwinian biological struggle for survival and its application to peoples, races, and states, and their trust in the lingering principle of peaceful competition and their faith in the Tolstoyan ideal of Christian brotherhood. That the distempers were cathartic is demonstrated by the shift in themes and moods. *Gloria (Glory)*, a D'Annunzian drama of 1899, in which he posited the legitimacy of revolution, and his references elsewhere to the mighty Roman Empire and the sprawling Venetian Republic, assisted Corradini in overcoming any feeling of inadequacy toward history and politics. The drama, *La leonessa (The Lioness)* (1899), was a transitional milestone. In bold relief was an iron will, a capacity to surmount impossible circumstances, and a sturdy confidence over the future. The drama *Giulio Cesare* (1902) offered solid evidence that Corradini was being liberated from self-doubt and that he had begun to formulate a political ideology. He did not shrink from disagreeing with Alfieri who had rebuked Caesar for having conspired to set himself up as dictator. Corradini's Caesar, instead, was an epic giant, the embodiment of the Roman spirit. Caesar showed that the Florentine had high regard for the strategic importance Thomas Carlyle assigned great men in the unfolding of history. Classicism's merits were also reappraised. It was viewed as an imperialism of style, as natural and distinctly Italian as the Roman Empire.

GIOLITTI AND GIOLITTISMO. With few exceptions, Giovanni Giolitti was the statesman who guided Italy between 1901 and 1914. From the Liberal Right, he gradually went over to the Liberal Left, and thence to democratic liberalism. The larger meaning of Giolitti's rule has been locked in controversy, although a consensus appears to be emerging which interprets his years as a period of liberal-democratic transformation, however haltingly and insufficient it turned out to be to ward off the tremors set off by the Great War and the rise of Fascism. Giolitti unveiled a new approach. Giolitti, like Cavour, hailed from Piedmont, and like Cavour he believed that the most effective way to achieve the moral unity of the country was through the centripetal impact of economic developments. A corollary to this premise was greater state involvement in the people's welfare.

A basic antagonism toward Giolitti was always present within citizens' groups, particularly rife among the intellectuals. The charge was that Giolitti maintained himself in power through an efficient political machine which thrived on intimidation and rewards and contrived electoral victories, bedubbed *Giolittismo*. The system did not originate with Giolitti. No one, however, carried on with such flagrant impudence and premeditated results as he. Intellectuals saw political blocs, secret electoral understandings with Catholics, connivance between government and big business, and concluded that practices represented the degeneration of the liberal parliamentary regime. Tariffs, reform enactments, were a form of class legislation, favoritism for one socio-economic caste at the expense of the majority. The liberty given to workers to unionize and to strike was not extended to the southern peasantry, Giolitti fearing landowner-peasantry confrontations would trigger social wars. It was rumored that Giolitti engineered universal manhood suffrage in 1912 as a pay-off for Socialist acquiescence, if not support, in the War for Libya. Compromise politics still prevented the formation of a genuine two-party government. *Giolittismo* was reviled as the most pejorative type of Cavour's *Connubio* and Depretis' Transformism. The bureaucracy, even by Giolitti's standard, monstrous in numbers and shockingly incompetent, interfered intolerably with the citizen's private life.

There was an undercurrent of complaint that economic strength had not manifestly reinforced cohesion and interclass harmony, nor had it enhanced Italy's prestige. This hurt the most, because many of the professionals had been reared on the universalist pulls of the Italian people. Custozza, Lissa, and Adowa had not been avenged. Italy's membership in the Triple Alliance had not freed a single Italian among the many who groaned under the Austrian yoke. In fact, it had not even been able to stop the Austrian students' periodic attacks on Italians attending Austrian universities. Confident that the Giolittian government had resigned itself to the permanent loss of her Italian minority, Austria saw no reason to establish an Italian university at Trent or Trieste, periodically demanded by her Italian subjects and irredentists in Italy.

IL REGNO *(THE KINGDOM).* Corradini's Florentine weekly review of politics, issued its first number on November 29, 1903. In terms of possibilities, the *Regno* was one of the foremost periodicals of modern Italy. It marked Corradini's debut as a national spokesman. With it, the Tuscan began the composition and articulation of his nationalist credo. By its very appearance, the *Regno* fulfilled a valuable function. As the title suggested, Corradini intended to deploy "the Kingdom," "Italy," as the first and ultimate reality. Above and beyond the disorganizing activities of the ruling elite and social classes, alleged scientific theories preaching irreversible Italian decline, Corradini was out to emphasize the nation, its flag, institutions, traditions, and aspirations. Neither the Extreme Left's narrow, partisan goals nor the bourgeoisie's sectarian interests but Italy's security and prosperity comprised the new criteria. In the opening article, "Per coloro che risorgono (For Those Who are Resurgent)," Corradini lifted the word *risorgono* from the *Risorgimento* to provide continuity, seriousness, purpose, and optimism. Although Corradini did not verbalize the hope, the times he may have sensed were premature, there seems to be no doubt that he conceived of what he was about as a possible sequel to liberation and unification nationalism. An additional inference is that the metamorphosis Italy was undergoing during the inauguration of Giolitti's ministry was not as devoid of promise and expectations as Corradini's fellow-intellectuals were wont to think. *(See Reading No. 29.)*

During the three years it held forth, the *Regno* discussed and debated anticlericalism, the cumbersome and overextended bureaucracy, the dwindling authority of the state, emigration, the reduction of irredentism to rhetorical exercises, the ruling classes' unconcern, the injuries inflicted by Socialists and the class struggle, the need to revamp education, the absence of ethnic pride and demonstrative patriotism, the possibility of bourgeois renascence, the claims of economic and territorial expansion, the deplorable state of the armed forces, Italy's low standing abroad, blamed on the failure to have drawn all Italians together and for having reneged on Italy's "superior birthright." Even if the collaborators only touched on these central issues, they set the agenda for the subsequent nationalist movement and for fascism. Nationalism was mentioned once or twice, and

Corradini preferred the term "expansion" to "imperialism," most likely for prudence's sake than lack of convictions. The doctrine of Italian nationalism when complete was, by and large, studied elaborations of what the *Regno* had introduced in embryonic form.

The *Regno* left the scene all too soon. It was in financial trouble from the start. Most of the 400 subscribers were chronically behind in their subscription fees. The review was also crippled by dissension. Such youthful and highly individualistic personalities like G. A. Borgese, Giovanni Papini, and Giuseppe Prezzolini resented Corradini's insistence on explicitness and the desire to remain within the political parameters detailed from the start. Public indifference was also a factor. Observers praised the *Regno*'s public concern and Corradini's moral courage in tackling the country's critical problems but still declared aggressive patriotism, expansionism or imperialism counterproductive distractions, witness Crispi and his ill-fated campaign in Abyssinia. Interestingly enough, if Corradini was reluctant, the opponents were not, to identify the undertaking with nationalism. The *Regno* ceased publication on December 25, 1906.

Corradini's review was not the total failure initially thought. It created an incipient stir among the National Young Liberals and a sector of the revolutionary Socialists and Syndicalists, illustrating from the beginning Corradini's ability to woo disparate elements. Scattered throughout the peninsula, youthful readers styled themselves "Friends of the *Regno*," and eventually became Corradini's followers and then leading Fascists. Corradini's associates who became estranged, returned through intervention in the First World War and, with the exception of Borgese, also by way of Fascism. The *Regno*'s demise vindicated Corradini's wisdom in not headlining his effort as a nationalist venture. Momentarily discouraged, Corradini had to await a major crisis in foreign relations to give him credibility and his protests relevance.

AUSTRIA'S SEIZURE OF BOSNIA-HERZEGOVINA.

To head off the Greater Serbia movement and block Serbian-South Slavic expansion to the Adriatic, Austria annexed both provinces, October 6, 1908. On the same day, Foreign Minister

Tommaso Tittoni spoke at Carate-Brianza and assured his countrymen that Italian diplomacy was fully prepared for any eventuality. It is understandable if Italians seized on Tittoni's statements and outdid one another in predicting the territorial compensations due Italy. Italy's right to reparations, were the *status quo* in the Balkans to be upset, had been incorporated in Article VII of the Triple Alliance's renewal in 1891. Italians conjured Trent, Trieste, or both as indemnities. In short order, Italians realized that Austria had no intention of meeting Italian objections with sizeable concessions. Austria's official position was that she had, in effect, annexed the two provinces as of 1878, when the Berlin Congress had authorized her to occupy and pacify them.

Bosnia was as devastating an experience for many Italians across the political spectrum as Adowa had been for Corradini. It was another Adowa, in Europe, on the Adriatic, across from Italy. Italian diplomats had been hoodwinked. From a psychological point of view, the Triplice became a dead letter, then and there. Every newspaper, with the exception of the Milanese *Corriere della Sera* (*Evening Courier*), denounced Premier Giolitti and demanded that Foreign Minister Tittoni be fired. Sidney Sonnino's Conservative Liberal, *Giornale d'Italia* of Rome was sharply anti-Giolittian while the *Stampa* (*Press*), a Left Liberal daily of Turin, which had underscored Giolitti's program of internal reform, interpreted the Austrian maneuver as proof that the Triplice had little practical value. That Austria could act as she had with punity also suggested that Giolitti was notoriously uninformed and uncomfortable with foreign policy. An important number of Republicans and Socialists were won over to the fatherland over Bosnia. Self-appointed custodians of the Mazzinian principle of national self-determination, the Republicans were morally outraged over Italy's apparent complicity in the absorption of another segment of the South Slavs within the Austro-Hungarian Empire.

The convulsive atmosphere traceable to Bosnia engendered an upsurge of patriotism. Veteran commentators reported that they had never seen such spontaneous outbursts of patriotic indignation. There was a sudden influx of members into the two main irredentist organizations, *the Lega Nazionale* (National League), established in 1889, and the more numerous Trent and

Trieste Society, set up in 1903. Deputy after Deputy in the Chamber spoke out for national honor and for supplementary appropriations to complete Italy's fortifications against Austria and her revised naval construction program ahead of schedule. Italians worried, believing that Austria might be tempted to take advantage of Italy's sorrow over the earthquake-tidal wave disaster at Reggio-Messina, December 28, and loose a preventive war against her nominal ally. High school and college students rushed to organize volunteer military battalions, called *Sursum Corda* (Lift Up Your Hearts), in defiance, for defense, and to take the war to Austria for the freeing of Trent and Trieste. The number of shrill political sheets founded on the morrow of Bosnia indicated that something of an ultrapatriotic or nationalist cast was brewing in the Italian conscience. (*See Reading No. 30.*)

A contribution toward the reawakening of patriotism was the change taking place in the public perception of emigration. Corradini was partly responsible. Commissioned by the *Corriere della Sera*, Corradini spent the summer and autumn of 1908 surveying the South American immigration scene. Corradini's reports, serialized in the Milan daily, countered the long-standing belief that emigration was primarily a positive force, sparing Italy insurrections, alleviating misery by means of the remittances emigrants sent to relatives in Italy, which also helped to finance industrialization, and by creating markets for Italian products. Corradini had it that emigration, as Turiello had pointed out, was a national disgrace, the depletion of racial resources. The fact that between 1902–08, 1,382,863 emigrants had returned was evidence that they had not left Italy except under severe economic duress. Having heard of the Austrian strike, Corradini skillfully referred to the loss of Italians to Austria and to overseas countries as a mortifying symptom of an unconcerned government and an uncaring society.

THE TURIN NATIONALIST CLUB. The initiative arose from Mario Viana and his group of "Friends of the *Regno*," centered in industrial Turin, who were responsible for the political weekly, *Il Tricolore*, founded in April 1909. They were impressed by the conceptual mutuality Corradini had begun to draw between nationalism and syndicalism and, as a result, wanted, if possible, to combine the French Syndicalist Albert Sorel's idea of the general strike with the Corradinian nationalist precept of the victorious war. When informed of the undertaking, Corradini expressed in private strong reservations due to the inconsistency he espied in his Turinese supporters. He had met similar personalities on the *Regno*. Obviously unable to disown the effort, he gave it his blessings and offered advice. The intent was to capitalize on the wave of Irredentist popularity for nationalist purposes and then, if the response warranted, proceed to an organized movement. Nationalism, Corradini cautioned, was not to be highlighted, but was to take second place to irredentism. The approach was to be low-keyed throughout in order not to scandalize those who were groping toward some form of nationalism. Socialism, the Florentine admonished, was not to be criticized any longer because it, like Nationalism, endorsed the idea of life as a collective and relentless struggle.

The club was constituted in July 1909. Corradini's diffidence was proven correct. The statement of beliefs, given subsequent elucidation by the *Tricolore* staff, angered many and pleased few. Nationalism was both irredentist and imperialist; it preached social solidarity and acknowledged the class struggle. It favored national unanimity and urged that all shackles be removed from the exercise of individual liberties. War was zealously advocated. (*See Reading No. 31.*) To make matters worse, the *Tricolore* published a number of vicious, thinly veiled accusations against the king, who was caricatured as a lazy, do-nothing monarch. Viana, the editor, was held responsible by the authorities, and he was forced to leave the weekly in August. By September, the *Tricolore* had closed down. The Turin Nationalist Club sputtered and then disappeared.

CORRADINI TAKES CHARGE. To repair the damage inflicted by the Turinese Nationalists and to facilitate nationalism's practical development, Corradini went on the offensive. He travelled, observed, wrote many explanatory newspaper articles, composed doctrinal treatises, and held numerous conferences throughout the peninsula. True to his word to Viana, he announced that he was lifting irredentism to the forefront of his developmental nationalist creed. It was, however, an Irredentism stripped of liberal flourishes and democratic romantic display. It was steeped in militancy. Supple and astute, Corradini utilized Marxian and Sorelian terminology to clarify and to disseminate what he held were collateral facets of nationalism and syndicalism. This would also balance out his irredentist predilections and neutralize the antidemocratic outlook his opponents had been exposing in nationalism. The nationalist theorist contended that the twentieth century state had to be broadly based. Both nationalism and syndicalism were schools for mass organization, mass mobilization, and mass heroism. For survival sake, Italy had to achieve the national integration which had eluded her. Nationalism's "victorious war" was extolled as the highest, most expansive, and most magnificent manifestation of syndicalism's "general strike." Only a new and robust nationalism could finish the work begun by the *Risorgimento*. It alone could transcend class barriers and *campanilismo* and concentrate energies on the conquests of "fields of wealth," that is farm lands, raw materials, markets, and living space for the Italian people. Only nationalism could transform irredentism into an operational state program and it alone could unfold an imperialist policy, as Crispi had imagined, for the harnessing of the country's teeming population on behalf of Italy's power, prestige, for empire. (*See Reading No. 32.*)

Based on press accounts and prefectural reports, Corradini aroused wide attention. Among those who were in turmoil over Bosnia, irredentism, emigration, political corruption, social unrest, and worker agitation, there were those who now admired and respected him as a seer and teacher. Accordingly, in March 1910, the desire took root in Corradini to meet supporters and sympathizers, and, if feasible, establish an organization for common action. The idea was greeted with such enthusiasm that Corradini and his intimate associates decided to go for an enlarged national conference, scheduled for Florence, December 3–5.

THE ITALIAN NATIONALIST ASSOCIATION. Qualifications for admission were acceptance of the kingdom's plebiscitary nature and rejection of any confessional attempt to infringe upon the full exercise of state sovereignty. A number among the 300 or so who assembled in Florence were from emigrant colonies in Africa and South America. Those in attendance ran the gamut from Syndicalists, Socialists, and Republicans, to conservative Liberals. Few of the adherents shared Corradini's comprehensive type of nationalism. Their brand was cultural, economic, financial, or political. Irrendentism was probably the major connecting link. In his keynote address, Corradini argued for a populist nationalism, based on the theme he had been circulating recently concerning the complementary affinity existing between nationalism and syndicalism. Italy's population bulge was proof of the unparalleled virility of the Italian people, which, in turn, underlined Italy's call to a mission of civilization. The solution of problems lay in the adoption of proletarian nationalism, the nationalism of the destitute and the downtrodden. It was not the expansion of class but of an entire people, national imperialism. Corradini urged the conventioneers to study Japan's response. Like Italy, a youthful, populous, and deprived state, Japan acquired valuable living room and mineral resources by projecting herself onto the Asiatic mainland. (*See Reading No. 33.*)

A companion piece, on the internal level, was Filippo Carli's report on "The Economic Policy of Greater Italy." The Brescian chamber of commerce economist spoke for a "bourgeois syndicalism," which would push for an expanded and disciplined industrial order. Such an order would create many employment opportunities, thus easing the problem of emigration. Although Carli's "bourgeois syndicalism" was vague and lacking in depth, its airing indicates that the subject of a possible conservative syndical reorganization of the Italian economy was introduced at the first convention of Italian nationalism. Because of the nature of the subjects, neither Corradini nor Carli submitted resolutions.

The other speakers and reports, Giulio de Frenzi (acronym of Luigi Federzoni), "The Policy of Alliances," Scipio Sighele, "Irrendentism and Nationalism," Senator Luigi Villari, "Nationalism and Emigration," and Maurizio Maraviglia, "The Nationalist Movement and Political Parties," were delivered and corresponding resolutions adopted almost routinely. The heterogenous background of the participants and Corradini gracious restraint insured an accommodating attitude. In view of the uproar over Bosnia, criticism of Giolitti and his stewardship of foreign policy was surprisingly mild. To be sure, there were those who wanted Italy to leave the Triplice. They were placated by the acceptance of a more watchful Italian presence in the alliance. The question of protectionism was too difficult to resolve; consideration was deferred for future conventions. An associational form of organization was assumed early in the proceedings, one which permitted members to remain in other political parties. A tense moment occurred on the last day when Viana and Riego Girola from Turin and Gino del Lago from Venice impulsively and spiritedly advised that the designation "Imperialist" be included in the title to read, the Italian Nationalist Imperialist Association. Because Corradini refused to budge, the move failed. Nationalists then drafted a constitution, selected a central committee as the governing body, and an executive board, the *Giunta*. Members were encouraged to establish local Nationalist clubs, of which there were forty-six by the end of 1912.

Public reaction was sharply divided. Scoffers took a wry delight in reminding Corradini that the only glories Italy could claim were poverty, illiteracy, slothfulness, scandal, and emigration. Borgese and Prezzolini taunted Corradini for his refusal to fight for his nationalist-syndicalist-imperialist faith. The more favorable comment maintained that a sturdy nationalist enterprise was long overdue and that nothing but good would result from an affiliation that intended to speak to all Italians. Others were of a mind to wait-and-see. The undeniable fact was that a nationalist congress had been held and that an Italian Nationalist Association had been born. Pietro Foscari, the Right or conservative Liberal Deputy from Mirano, and Romeo Gallenga-Stuart, a Young Liberal Deputy from Perugia, and Luigi Siciliani, professor of Italian literature at the University of Catania and future Nationalist Deputy from Catanzaro, were sufficiently impressed and became charter members. Maraviglia, on the agenda, had been won by Corradini from revolutionary Socialism, and Roberto Forges-Davanzati from Syndicalism.

THE WAR FOR LIBYA. The Nationalist campaign for Libya went into high gear with the appearance of *L'Idea Nazionale* in Rome, on March 1, 1911, the fifteenth anniversary of Adowa. The founders and collaborators, Corradini, Forges, Federzoni,

Maraviglia, and Francesco Coppola accepted Tripoli at face value and for the leavening effect it would have on the infant nationalist movement. The Association's central committee soon joined the bandwagon, and advised all clubs and concerned citizens to lobby hard for Libya. Several authoritative nationalists, led by Corradini, went to Libya to survey its possibilities. Their accounts were carried in many of the country's dailies as gospel truth. National security—Libya was ninety miles from Sicily—pride, raw materials, trade, a colony for emigrants, Italy's civilizing mission—all these assets and arguments were extensively used. About 600,000 square miles of desert sand did not detain the Nationalists from praising Tripoli as a veritable Garden of Eden, reserved by God for a deserving Italy. Mazzini's mission and Gioberti's primacy were summoned to get leftist and Catholic elements behind the venture. Notoriously tied to high Vatican circles, the Banco di Roma had fallen on evil days due to excessive speculation in Libya and other areas of the Ottoman Empire. Its petitions for a rescue may not have fallen on deaf ears. Nationalists participated at the meetings of civic organizations and insisted that resolutions in favor of Libya be adopted. Demonstrations were organized in cooperation with liberal groups, which frequently provoked clashes with opponents, mainly the Socialists.

Historical opinion is divided over whether the anticolonialist Giolitti was stirred primarily because standing diplomatic preparations had reached maturity or whether he succumbed to the intensive propaganda drive mounted by the nationalists. Most Italians connected Libya with an active nationalist movement. Giuseppe Bevione and Giuseppe Piazza, war correspondents of the proministerial *Stampa* and the *Tribuna* of Rome, respectively, joined the Association over Libya. Many Nationalists and their supporters at large stoutly believed that the mass rallies had lighted a fire under a reluctant prime minister and government. This was to be vividly recalled in 1914–15, over the battle for intervention, and again in 1922, with the Fascist March on Rome.

Nationalists embarked for the war zone when hostilities with Turkey commenced on September 30, 1911, and relayed articles on the progress of the Italian armed forces. The imperialist venture was utilized to validate major aspects of nationalist doctrine. War had a subtle way of inducing people to close ranks and sacrifice for the fatherland. Almost unnoticeably, and to Corradini's satisfaction, the Association's irredentists took a back seat to the imperialists. The Socialist party's attempt, captained by Pietro Nenni and Benito Mussolini, to stage a general strike and cripple the war effort failed, as much due to defections, as to public indignation. Observers noted that many Catholic moderates, also strict clericals, as well as significant numbers of Republicans and Socialists, were assuming a positive posture toward the war. Notable syndicalist theorists, such as Arturo Labriola, Angelo Olivetti, Paolo Orano, and Libero Tancredi, spoke and wrote in the language of Corradini and proletarian nationalism. The war represented a despised people's aroused fury, determined to fight for its rightful share of the world. Commentators, including those who had unilaterally dismissed as foolhardy any thought of an attack on Libya, and foreign reporters described the country's new-found sense of unity and self-esteem in glowing words. In such a hypnotic atmosphere, another myth was propagated, that of "the Fourth Italy," to supersede or update Mazzini's "Third Rome."

After the initial euphoria, Nationalists had reason to doubt the ministry's handling of the military situation. The conflict was fast becoming a stalemate. Anxiety was only momentarily relieved when the government, November 5, 1911, promulgated an annexationist decree. What the Association wanted was offensive action into Libya's interior and blows at vulnerable spots of the tottering Ottoman Empire. There was cause for jubilation when Italy seized the Dodecanese Islands in the Aegean Sea between April 20 and May 21, 1912. An empire was in the making. Actually, the capture was dictated by the need to control the sea lanes between Turkey and Libya and for leverage at the peace table. The Treaty of Ouchy, October 18, 1912, acknowledged Italy's sovereignty over Libya and her occupation of the Dodecanese until the completion of Turkish evacuation of Libya. Although the peace met with general approval, it caused a letdown among the Nationalists, conservative Liberals, Catholic moderates, and a small but distinct number of Left Liberals and Radicals. As the Balkan Wars broke out on the same day Ouchy was signed, these groups regretted that Italy had not continued the war to extract another colony or two from Turkey. Ouchy was lampooned and stylized "the mediocre peace," the forerunner of D'Annunzio's "mutilated peace" of 1919.

A swashbuckling nationalist movement bent on a decisive field victory and empire threatened the delicate internal political situation. Giolitti's radical-socialist backing, upon which he had leaned for his fourth ministry, was unable to withstand the shocks of nationalism and the war. Anger generated by Libya provoked schisms and ousters in the Socialist and Republican parties, and left the Left liberal and Radical affiliations precariously divided. The war's cost, estimated at 1,750,000,000 lire, translated into less funds for home improvements. Cutbacks in defense spending following the war's end contributed to the bleak employment picture. Universal manhood suffrage, a reality in August 1912, added 5,000,000 to the electoral rolls, and politicians braced themselves for the onslaught of new voters. Unable to contain the splintering effects, Giolitti resigned on March 31, 1914.

ROME NATIONALIST CONGRESS. It was held, December 20–22, 1912, against the background of the Tripolitan War and the general elections, set for October–November 1913. Nationalists clubs prepared for Rome by grappling with the issue of political involvement. The majority of Nationalists, especially in the Rome, Milan, Turin, and Venice clubs, favored a modest but effective presence in the Chamber. It would forestall another Bosnia or Ouchy. The problem was one of ideological orientation. The Milan club and the *Grande Italia e Carroccio*, two political weeklies which had merged after the Florence conference, believed Nationalism was to be democratic, sincerely working for the upliftment of the lower orders. Nationalism's duty was to combat all antinational factions, the Moderates and Clericals, no less than the Socialists, Republicans, and Radicals. Theodore Roosevelt's America was the model the democratic Nationalists desired to copy. It was intensely nationalist, imperialist, and avowedly democratic.

Opposed were the authoritarian nationalists of the Corradinian stamp, who manned the *Idea Nazionale* and were entrenched in the central committee. The Association, they countered, had no choice but to be conservative and seek electoral support among the conservative Liberals and the Catholic

groups, particularly among the moderates, the heirs of the Giobertian tradition. In spite of differences over the Roman Question and state supremacy, these Nationalists wanted all Catholics
to participate in the nation's public and political life. Logic
would have them vote for law-and-order candidates, meaning
Nationalists and conservative Liberals. Catholics had shown
their patriotism over Libya and deserved to be rewarded. The
votes of the democratically politicized masses had already been
preempted by the extreme Left. Any gesture toward the Catholic
moderates was sure to attract sizeable numbers of the Catholic
rank-and-file to the kingdom of Italy, to the Nationalists' credit.
The situation in Rome, where the commune and four of the five
electoral districts were bastions of the Extreme Left, tended to
encourage mutual respect between Nationalists and Catholics of
every political persuasion. Industrial and commercial conglom-
erates had begun to take notice, as had the military, and the
intellectual community. Nationalists could not fail to recipro-
cate. Corradini took a hard line because he wanted to achieve a
degree of doctrinal uniformity not permitted at Florence. Irren-
dentists sided with the Democrats because their irrendentism
was related to the democratic conception of auto-decision and
because they feared that the conservatives wanted to focus the
Association's attention exclusively on imperialism. Liberal Nationalists, proud that they were antidemocratic, strongly and
ingenuously accepted the conservative thinking.

As befitted his stature, Corradini delivered the opening address at Rome, entitled, "The Prosecution of the Libyan War." It
was nothing less than a scathing indictment of Italian democracy's incorrigible incapacity to wage the all-out war Nationalists had expected. Parliamentary democracy had been tried and
found sadly wanting. There was no deference to Giolitti's statesmanship, nor did Corradini make any concession to the diplomatic skill and technical ability with which Italy had conquered
Tripoli, in contrast to Crispi's bungling over Ethiopia. Indeed,
the same political manipulations, behind-the-scene chicanery,
personal self-interests, and internal considerations which had
frustrated the Crispian effort had re-appeared and thwarted
Italy's imperialist designs. Socialist internationalist pacifism
had pervaded Italian democracy. Corradini's speech perpetrated
acrimonious debate on internal policy. The crux of the contro-

versy was they rejected anticlericalism since the papacy was resigning itself to the loss of the temporal power and was relaxing its injunction against political-electoral activity. The upshot was that at least 200 of the Democrats resigned from the Association.

The central committee did not become alarmed. The Association had chosen its course. That was a plus. Personal loyalty to Corradini prevailed over other democrats who wanted to bolt. Corradini's continued invitation to the Syndicalists by way of proletarian nationalism was proof that he was not philosophically against the principle of democracy nor unconditionally adverse to the Extreme Left as the Rome deliberations may have suggested. The broad attack against Freemasonry, launched by Federzoni on the *Idea Nazionale*, reached its peak during the first half of 1913, and was a prelude to the elections. Since most public figures registered their displeasure with Freemasonry, assailing it as secretive and of foreign origins, the Association immediately recouped whatever prestige, numbers, and momentum it may have lost due to the exodus of the Democrats. Ironically, most of the schismatics also returned to nationalism in 1914.

GENERAL ELECTIONS OF 1913. The anti-Masonic crusade gave the Association visibility and convinced many, from the conservative Liberals to Catholic moderates and clericals, as well as segments of the military-industrial complex, that the Association was a vanguard institution speaking for the public interest. Most Nationalist clubs had only recently come to life and were too modest in size to tackle the electoral process. Rome was the major exception. Based on negotiations with the local Constitutional Electoral Union, the Rome club's Luigi Medici, a Liberal and wealthy industrialist, opposed the anti-Libyan, Radical incumbent, Leone Caetani, in the I electoral district. In district IV, vigorous efforts to select an individual with strong moderate and clerical appeal to square off against the anti-Libyan, Official Socialist, Antonio Camponozzi forced the withdrawal of Sonnino's conservative liberals, who went over to the Rome Radical Association, which was backing the Radical Scipione Borghese, scion of a Roman patrician family. When the Union decided to go with Domenico Oliva, the president of the capital's flourishing Nationalist club and a literary critic of the *Giornale d'Italia*, Sonnino's newspaper took offense and compelled Oliva to choose between his candidacy and his job. As Oliva capitulated, revulsion occurred over the immense pressure used against him. Federzoni resigned from the newspaper's staff and accepted the Union's draft.

In hotly contested frays, Federzoni deposed Camponozzi and Medici bested Caetani. A total of six Nationalist entries were victors. The results of the general elections added to the unsettling effects of the Libyan War. The Popular bloc, composed of Radicals and Freemasons, which ruled the Rome Commune, resigned in consternation on November 7, and a royal commission took over. Mussolini and the Official Socialists assumed Italy was entering a revolutionary situation. They would speed it on. Republicans were of a mind to boycott parliament, politics, and to take the battle to the streets, as Mazzini would have done. Excited by the impact Catholic votes had in the elections, youthful Catholic moderates founded the *Torre* (*Tower*), a Sienese weekly, November 6, 1913, through which they advertized their hopes for an Italian empire, sponsored and sanctified by state and church, political and Catholic Rome. Although subsidies from the world of big business were never bountiful, it is nonetheless true that when in May 1914 the *Idea Nazionale* searched for money to transform it into a daily, it eventually found 135,000 of the total capitalization of 700,000 lire in a Turinese munition firm.

MILAN NATIONALIST CONVENTION. At Milan, May 15–18, 1914, the Nationalists achieved differentiation from other political organizations and took a giant toward building and consolidating their thought. It marked the entrance into high Nationalist deliberations of Alfredo Rocco (1875–1935), former Radical and presently professor of law at the University of Padua and a formidable theoretical and managerial brain. The Association's Political Secretariat, run by Federzoni and Maraviglia, successfully recommended single party membership and the facilitation of a nationalist-conservative liberal-moderate regrouping. The coalition would hope to unite and reinvigorate the Liberal Party and keep the more reactionary clericals and the emergent Christian democrats in line. It would bring the democratic or Giolittian Liberals back into the traditional fold. Such a realignment toward the right would bring about the idealistic revolt previewed by the dour Oriani in *La rivolta ideale* (1906). If the end of dual allegiance was an ill omen for the Liberal Nationalists, worse was in store when the convention acted on the Report of the Special Commission on Economic Nationalism. Guided by Rocco, the Milan adherents examined economic and political liberalism, exposed the flaws, and rejected it for a program of national integrated economics. In an age of mass society, Nationalists desired to mobilize and control the emancipation of the people, achieve political stability, spiritual oneness, economic unity, and social harmony. That was the organic state in full operation. (See "Nationalist Ideology and Policy," *Reading No. 43*.) All these indispensable goals rendered Italian Nationalism remarkably different from other nationalisms. (*See Reading No. 34*.)

Liberal Nationalists defended liberalism and multiparty affiliation in vain. As best as could be certified, twenty-two Liberals left the Association, including Deputies Gallenga-Stuart, Medici, and Camillo Ruspoli. If the attitude of the Rome Nationalist club was any indication, the club endorsing the Milan decisions by a vote of 594 to 6, there was overwhelming support in the Association for the new directives. No sooner had the convention adjourned than the central committee became the impetus behind the fusion tickets of Nationalists, conservative Liberals, and where possible, contingents of Catholic moderates. The combination helped to defeat the popular blocs in the administrative elections of June and July, 1914, in Rome, Florence, Siena, Padua, Ferrara, Modena, Venice, Brescia, Turin, and elsewhere. The strategy of electoral cooperation and political collaboration, selective as it was, was reinforced in the Chamber, where the Nationalist Deputies backed the conservative Liberal prime minister, Antonio Salandra, who succeeded Giolitti in April.

CHAPTER 8

NATIONALISM AND THE GREAT WAR

TAKING SIDES. The coming of the war in 1914, was a golden opportunity for the Nationalists. They were determined to make the most of it. To remain spectators was an impossibility. Immediately, they called for war on the side of the Central Powers, Germany and Austria-Hungary, Italy's allies in the Triple Alliance against the Entente Powers, Britain, France, and Russia. With dazzling speed, the Nationalists backtracked and changed their preference. Italy's declaration of neutrality on August 3 convinced them that there was no secret clause in the Triplice which obligated Italy to fight alongside Germany and Austria. When it became known that Austria had drafted and dispatched her ultimatum to Serbia without prior consultation with Italy, memories of Bosnia and 1908 resurfaced. Since Austria did nothing to appease Italian anger, Nationalists had additional reason to steer Italy away from the Central Powers. What sealed the Association's conviction on the necessity of a pro-Allied position was the pact concluded among Britain, France, and Russia, on September 5, 1914, which pledged the warring states to a fight to the finish. There was to be no separate peace. That did it. It was not idealism but realistic calculation. As the influential *Idea Nazionale* put it, the combination of Britain, France, and Russia had money, material, and manpower, assets which Germany and Austria simply could not match. Having become identified in the public mind with the national interest, the Association's switch from a pro-Central Powers stance to the Entente, without suffering qualms, set a precedent for other political parties to follow.

THE MANY FACES OF INTERVENTION. Because Nationalists were prone to believe that Italian participation would be decisive, they expected maximum returns for Italy's troubles. Nationalists were gratified that the opening battles indicated a gruelling struggle, requiring the total mobilization of the citizenry and resources of the country. Such a war was exactly what Italians needed, as Zerbi and Crispi had urged. It would complete Italy's territorial unification, achieve economic independence, realize the country's imperial aspirations, and vindicate the faith that her visionaries had nourished. A heightened fighting spirit and material compensation would make up for the despicable insufficiencies of "the mediocre peace" of Ouchy. The economist Carli, in his tract, *L'Altra guerra* (*The Other War*) (1916), reminded Italians that among the wars Italy was engaged in none was more crucial than the one to eradicate German influence over the Italian economy through the *Banca Commerciale Italiana*. (*See Reading No. 35.*)

SALANDRA AND THE NATIONALISTS. The premier's views coincided with those of the Nationalists. He, too, was furious over Ouchy and also blamed the slow, tantalizing tempo of the Libyan war on internal politics. Salandra carefully weighed the options available to Italy. No ministry or the monarchy could survive were the liberation and annexation of *Italia Irredenta* and the gaining of a colony or two lost by inactivity. Through the bold plans and unavoidable misgivings Salandra shared with Foreign Minister Antonio di San Giuliano and his successor Sonnino, it is clear that he and his subordinates were of a mind to enjoin the conflict for purely foreign policy goals and morale purposes. The prime minister also had a sturdy grasp of possible domestic repercussions. He had condemned the Giolittian decade as an unmitigated disaster. Giolitti's reforms produced a sprawling, costly, and inefficient bureaucracy, and Red Week. The lower classes had neither been satisfied nor won over but incited to revolt. War would impose conformity, obedience, sacrifice, and patriotic service. The economic bourgeoisie, like Salandra, also understood the dualistic nature of the war. Through his main conservative Liberal support, Salandra hoped he could use the war to unify the Liberal party and enlarge it by courting the Nationalists and the Catholic moderates on the right and favorable elements from the Radicals and Reformist Socialists on the left. A revitalized Liberal party would then be able to present itself to the voters as a compact unit, without resorting to Giolitti's scandalous coalitions.

In his memoirs, Salandra described the Association as an impetuous interventionist front. He had cause to be irritated by the irrepressible Nationalists. The armed forces, recuperating from the Libyan War, could not be combat ready until spring 1915. Perfectural reports, personally ordered by the premier, revealed that public opinion, while staunchly patriotic, was divided over the wisdom and need of intervention. Diplomacy took patience and skill. Aware of the Nationalists' worth, because of their stirring campaign for Libya, Salandra maintained regular channels of communications with them. Nationalists reciprocated, knowing that Salandra was a better choice than the neutralist and reformist Giolitti. They backed Salandra, in and out of parliament. In order that Salandra might chart an independent course, which for them meant war, Nationalists, along with those of like mind in other parties, voiced opposition to any special session of parliament, and called for the dismissal of all governmental personnel who were friendly to Giolitti and shared his views. On October 2, Corradini addressed an open letter to the premier, in which the Florentine strove to summon the southerner Salandra to his historic and nationalist duty. Salandra was reminded that he was in select company with Cavour who had maneuvered tiny Piedmont into the Crimean War, thus setting in motion a chain of events which culminated in Italian unification.

On August 22, Salandra announced that no special session of parliament was required, even less contemplated. Major General Vittorio Zupelli was appointed war minister in September. An Istrian Italian, his selection was well received by Entente supporters, while disturbing to those who had remained triplicists or had become neutralists. Salandra, on October 19, addressed the foreign office functionaries to commemorate San Giuliano's decease. He chose to elevate *sacro egoismo* (sacred egoism) as the sole and highest criteria on which the issue of peace or war had to be resolved. A people with as honorable and serviceable a past as the Italian had the moral right and inescapable responsibility to consult itself alone and to pursue its own objectives and not someone else's. If Nationalists and their next of kin were ecstatic, sacred egoism did not disarm or lull them to sleep. They put themselves on guard lest sacred egoism become an empty formula or a beguiling abstraction. (*See Reading No. 36.*) Nationalists were confirmed in the pressure they helped to apply. In his December 3 speech to the Chamber, Salandra explained neutrality as not a permanent policy but an intermediate arrangement. Also distinctly reassuring was the follow up Bettolo Resolution, approved 413–19, which left the future of neutrality at the discretion of the ministry. The Chamber's decision of March 21, 1915 to recess until May 12 could only mean that a momentous event—war—was in the offing.

NATIONALISTS AND INTERVENTIONISTS. The latter divided themselves into right and left interventionists. In the former camp were the Nationalists, conservative Liberals, a number of Left or Giolittian Liberals, and self-styled constitutionalists or independents. Among the left were Radicals, Republicans, Reformist Socialists, the more forward looking of the Left Liberals, who were now comprising part of the democratic Left, Fascists, Freemasons, and Futurists. Left groups favored the completion of Italian unity and the creation of an industrial democracy. Many left interventionists approached the war in terms of the possibilities it held out for the continent's reorganization into the United States of Europe, a dream attributed to Mazzini. The Republican Party issued a manifesto, dated April 2, 1915, which denounced neutrality as "a disavowal of Italy's mission," and warned that Republicans would "not leave any betrayal unavenged."

Increasingly important for the future was the collaboration and rivalry which characterized relations between Nationalists and Fascists from the moment that Mussolini left the neutralist Socialists, founded his organ, *Il Popolo D'Italia* (*The People of Italy*), on October 8, 1914, organized his *Fascio d'azione rivoluzionario* (Revolutionary Action Bands), December 10, 1914, reorganized January 24, 1915, and began to campaign for intervention on the Allied side. Nationalist delight was understandable. Mussolini's abandonment of neutralism was proof that the neutralist forces were in disarray and that no segment of society could remain for long untouched by the war's centralizing effects. Because Mussolini and the bulk of the fascist hierarchs emanated from the ranks of revolutionary Socialism and had syndicalist leanings like key Nationalists, an informal party of interest was being established. From the outset, Mussolini and his daily newspaper may have assailed the Nationalists even more than the Socialists. He singled out the Association's war aims as "pernicious imperialist infatuations." Unruffled, sober

Nationalists maintained that neutralist animosity and the joint desire for involvement would draw nationalism and fascism closer together. As the period of neutrality appeared to them to be unnecessarily prolonged, Corradini and Mussolini candidly advertized the war as revolutionary and antimonarchical in nature. (*See Readings 37, 38.*)

Nationalism, official and unofficial, was the driving force behind the drive for intervention. Joint conferences of right and left partisans of involvement were organized. On occasion, left interventionists balked or bolted because of the nationalist presence. The need for unity against the neutralists frequently overcame distempers. As the former Republican and Reformist Socialist Gaetano Salvemini regretfully admitted, it was the nationalist conception of the war which became the prevailing public view. However excessive or extreme nationalist objectives were, non-Nationalists were placed in the uncomfortable position of having to choose between acceptance or rejection of the nationalist expectations. Rejection, they feared, would weaken the interventionist cause by dividing its spokesmen and leave those opposed to the Nationalists open to censure for their willingness to settle for less than Italy supposedly deserved. Left interventionists were not above accusing the Nationalists of chauvinism, while they themselves affected a big brother attitude toward the South Slavs, and trumpeted Italy's "natural rights" across the Adriatic.

GIOLITTI AND COMPENSATED NEUTRALITY. To Giolitti, there was nothing idealistic about the war. Both sets of belligerents were motivated by cynicism and greed. Unlike Salandra and the interventionists, Giolitti foresaw a long war, of at least three years' duration. Victory, he confided, was probably going to the Central Powers. They were better armed than the Entente Powers and more prepared to withstand the war's privations. Giolitti worried that intervention would be a devastating experience for the Italians. It would provoke agitation and most likely insurrections, especially in the south. When called upon by his many admirers and concerned citizens to advise what course of action Italy should take, Giolitti strongly recommended a negotiated settlement with Austria, one which would meet legitimate Irredentist hopes and preserve Italian neutrality.

He let his sentiment be known in a letter he inscribed to Camillo Peano, a Deputy and his former chief of cabinet. He used *parecchio* (much, quite a bit) to describe what Italy could obtain without war. He explained that his neutrality was conditional, in contrast to the absolute neutrality of the Official Socialists. (*See Reading No. 39.*)

The *parecchio* letter was handled clumsily and brought awkwardly to light. Many of Giolitti's closest followers thought it was a grave mistake. Using the most vituperative language, right and left interventionists seized on the statement to show that Giolitti had scorned the *Risorgimento*'s humane spirit and that he was shockingly unaware of the moment's historic possibilities. *Giolittismo*'s bankruptcy had now been fully exposed. Giolitti would barter Italy's future as a world power in the same manner in which he carried on and compromised state interests in parliament. Because he had led Italy to war on Turkey for Libya, few of the neutralists, if any, were convinced of Giolitti's sincerity. Neutralists were plagued by defections and ill will. Those Catholics who remained steadfastly for peace would never consort with the antichurch Socialists. As the campaign for entrance into the war escalated, Catholic, particularly moderate, public figures adopted a more open mind toward the war, demonstrating that the Catholics' move toward political responsibilities and the liberal regime was irreversible. Giolitti may have defeated himself and the neutralist cause by his adamant refusal to unseat the Salandra ministry by a vote of no confidence, take again the reins of government, and head negotiations with Austria. He had the backing, was urged to do so, but he did not budge.

NEGOTIATIONS. As Austria had not checked with Italy before forwarding her impossible demands to Serbia, Premier Salandra and Foreign Minister San Giuliano were convinced that Austria, with German complicity, had resolved to destroy Serbia and remove the threat which South Slav nationalism was to the multiracial Hapsburg Empire. Austria's refusal to acknowledge Italy's right to indemnification, combined with her preemptive blow against Austria, and her flat reluctance to accede to irredentist minimal wishes for an Italian university in Trent or Trieste, exacerbated feelings to a very serious low level. Italian government officials never fully believed that Austria could be prevailed upon to relinquish the Trentino and Trieste and agree to the Alpine Brenner frontier as the border between them. By approaching the Entente over inducements for intervention, Foreign Minister Sonnino, San Giuliano's successor, hoped to avoid Italy's isolation and to have a suitable alternative in the planning stage were talks between Italy and Austria to break down.

Soundings in London and Paris were encouraging. Sonnino, on March 3, 1915, sent instructions to Guglielmo Imperiali, the ambassador to Great Britain, to present Italy's terms for joining the Allies to British Foreign Secretary Sir Edward Grey. Six days later, on March 9, Austria consented in principle to Italy's right to territorial reparations. Was Austria persuaded because she had gotten wind of Italian approaches to the Entente or because of German pressure, or both, is impossible to say. No sooner had negotiations begun in earnest, as Giolitti had advised, than they bogged down over which territories were to be ceded and when, during or after the war. Salandra and Sonnino became daily more certain that Austria was procrastinating, hoping that a possible major victory on the battlefield would intimidate Italy and compel her to soften their demands. Italian diplomats were left with the impression that even if an agreement were reached and immediately implemented, a German-Austrian triumph would force the return of what had been received from Austria. Completion of discussions with the Allied Powers were hastened, with the result the Pact of London, concluded April 26, 1915.

The Treaty consisted of sixteen articles and was to be kept secret. Having specified provisions for joint military and naval action (Arts. 1–3), the majority of the remaining articles dealt with compensations due Italy. At the end of the conflict, Italy was to gain the South Tyrol and the Trentino, giving her the Brenner mountain frontier against Austria, and Trieste; Italy was to acquire the counties of Gorizia and Gradisca, the Istrian Peninsula, a considerable section of Dalmatia, excluding the city of Fiume. Valona was to be placed under full Italian sovereignty, with a protectorate over Albania. Italy's occupation of the Dodecanese was declared permanent. The Treaty accorded ample recognition to Italy's desire to extend her interests and influence into the Middle East in the event of a partitioning of Asiatic

Turkey. Were Germany's African colonies to be divided between Britain and France, the Italian colonies of Libya, Eritrea, and Somaliland were to be enlarged. Britain pledged to arrange for a 50,000,000 pound loan from the London financial market. The signatory powers also agreed that there was to be no separate peace and that the Holy See was not to be invited to the peace conference.

THE RADIANT DAYS OF MAY 1915. With the negotiations with the Allies safely in port by April 26, and the renunciation of the Triple Alliance on May 6, 1915, and military preparations completed, all appeared to be in place for the May 12th reopening of parliament, the awaited declaration of war, and Italy's entrance into the war by May 23, as stipulated by the London Accord. Things did not proceed as smoothly as expected. A frantic period ensued, precipitated by Giolitti's arrival in Rome on May 6. In spite of Italy's disavowal of the Triplice, Austria, probably due to Giolitti's informal insistence, advanced on May 10 more generous terms in exchange for Italian neutrality. Germany was to be the guarantor for the execution of any possible transaction. Giolitti met with Victor Emmanuel III, Salandra, and several prominent ministers. What precisely was conveyed to Giolitti is impossible to say. It is likely that Giolitti was made aware of the general nature of the London Pact, but not of its particulars nor of its binding character on the sovereign and state. Whether Salandra's decision to resign on May 13 was intended to force Giolitti's or the king's hand, or whether it was a signal for public rallies or both, is conjectural. Salandra had instructed his country's sixty-nine prefects to do their utmost to prevent public manifestations for war. Giolitti remained fixed in his reluctance to form a ministry and take personal charge of negotiations. Other possible candidates also discounted themselves. The Salandra ministry was reinstated on May 16. Neutralist opposition crumbled, and Giolitti repaired to Dronero, Piedmont. Four days later the Chamber, by a 407–74 vote, granted the government "full powers" for war.

During the interval between Giolitti's arrival in the capital, May 6, and the pro-war parliamentary decision of May 20, 1915, an apprehensive feeling spread about Giolitti's alleged backstage maneuvers. Many ugly scenarios were imagined, and reprehensible rumors circulated concerning his motives. Out of revulsion and fear of a last minute formation of a Giolittian neutralist ministry, interventionists, with Nationalists, Fascists, and Futurists in the forefront, assembled on the main streets of Rome, Milan, Genoa, Venice, Florence, and Naples. The struggle for involvement had spilled on to the public square. On the average, between 3,000 and 4,000 participated, including a strong representation of high school and university students. Nationalist clubs capitalized on the fervor to launch their youth affiliates. The demonstrations reached a feverish crescendo in Rome with D'Annunzio's incendiary rhetoric. On May 13, he delivered a virulent attack against Giolitti, labelling him a traitor, a swindler, the antithesis of what Italians had symbolized in history. With D'Annunzio's performance, political rhetoric in Italy took on a vulgar and theatrical tone. (*See Reading No. 40.*)

Interventionism was not only degenerating into an anti-Giolittian crusade but an anti-institutional one as well. Beginning with the opening phase of the debate over involvement, and on through its convulsive climax in May 1915, the war was increasingly seen by the Nationalists, Fascists, Futurists, and other partisans of intervention, and also by a large number of neutralists, as revolutionary in its internal implications. Respect for the monarchy as a stabilizing factor did not restrain Corradini, any more than it had Mussolini, as noted, from threatening the Savoy Dynasty with extinction unless it immediately pushed the Salandra ministry into war. When it became known that a majority of Deputies were eager to back, even at the last minute, a pro-peace Giolittian government, both Nationalists and Fascists sharply rebuked parliament and demanded its overthrow. (*See Readings Nos. 41, 42.*)

The "Radiant Days of May," as they were memorialized in interventionist folklore, bequeathed liberal Italy a doubtful legacy, distinct from the war. Esteem for the parliamentary regime sank to a new low and was never fully restored. Ingrained on the popular psyche, and in Mussolini's D'Annunzio's and Corradini's mentality, was that their organized forces and mobilized effort, projected onto the streets, had decisively turned the tide for war, against the unusual inertia and stupidity of the monarchy, government, parliament, and the ruling classes. This was the grand rally for Libya with a vengeance. May revealed the frivolous spirit with which the bulk of the right and left interventionists either joined in the arming of the public squares or watched from the sidelines. Many of them defended nationalist, fascist, and futurist antics as the righteous wrath of dedicated youths who were assuming direction of the country. This, too, was prophetic. The same passivity, even degree of connivance, over developments ultimately sinister to liberal Italy, were repeated and extended into the establishment of the fascist dictatorship.

WARTIME ACTIVITIES. The Association practiced what it preached. Many nationalists volunteered for military service and many times more were drafted. Members were awarded an extraordinary number of decorations for gallantry and heroism. Gualtiero Castellini and Vincenzo Picardi of the four-man preparatory committee for the Florence Convention were lost through battle, as was Emilio Vita Zellmann, head of the thriving Rome nationalist youth club. Since they were above service age, Corradini, Coppola, Forges, and Rocco maintained the nationalist witness at home. Using the Libyan War to advantage, they endeavored to encourage morale. As the war was longer and costlier than anticipated, Nationalists urged the state's total mobilization. They guarded against socialist antiwar manifestoes and the consequent spread of *disfattismo* (defeatism). Nationalists were gratified that parliament's role was drastically reduced. Always on the offensive, nationalist Deputies were zealous participants in the formation of coalitions to insure the war's aggressive prosecution and to present a solid front against a Giolittian return to power. In speeches and lectures throughout Italy, Corradini praised the sacrifices all Italians were making for the fatherland's greatness. A nation-in-arms had a special unifying appeal, which exposed the state democracy Giolitti desired to build as artificial and un-Italian. Attention was drawn to the workers' "high salaries" and the industrialists' "high profits" as twin fixtures of the producers' society nationalism was envisioning for postwar Italy.

CHAPTER 9

UNION WITH FASCISM

POSTWAR GROWTH. The Association experienced an outburst of activity and sizeable membership increase, up to 300,000 by the close of 1922. This is attributed to skillful leadership, broad interest in the movement resulting from the war and to the many crosscurrents set off by intervention. The Association gained a strategic number of university professors, teachers, lawyers, journalists, literary personalities, armed forces' officers, and entrepreneurs. They gave Nationalism high visibility and prestige. Professionals were attracted because the petite bourgeoisies' material fortunes and social status had declined considerably since the war. They saw the Association as an agency to recoup and safeguard their position in much the same manner unions represented worker concerns. Another sign of upsurgence was the founding of political organs and reviews. A Federation of Nationalist University Students was established, along with many social and cultural auxiliaries, to match or rival analogous Fascist, Communist, Socialist, and Catholic societies.

Nationalism had to address itself to new and old national problems. Sharp disagreement at the Paris Peace Conference between President Woodrow Wilson and the Italian delegation over compliance with the London Treaty caused great concern. The Bolshevist Revolution in Russia, October 1917, and the organization of the Italian Communist party, January 1921, engendered consternation. Additional cause for alarm was instigated by the formation of the Italian Popular (Christian Democratic) party, January 1919, Mussolini's *Fasci di combattimento* (Combat Bands), March 23, 1919, and the adoption of proportional representation, September 2, 1919. Political deadlock, social unrest, and extensive labor agitation worsened parliament's chronic malfunctioning. The situation confronting Italy was responsible for serious internal difficulties and also weakened her competitive place in the world economy.

The Association held its first postwar convention on March 16–18, 1919, in Rome. Over 200 clubs sent delegates. Having called on all parties in Paris to live up to the London Treaty,

Nationalists firmed up their ideological underpinnings and explicitly declared for the restructuring of Italy's political-social-economic system, based on their syndical-corporative ideal. The industrial democracy they were devising was hailed as a constructive cure and alternative to bourgeois pessimism and world revolution. (*See Reading No. 43.*) The seductive charm which proletarian nationalism and its producers' society might pose for the working classes was illustrated by the appearance in 1921 of the Association's National Labor Bureau, composed of the National Association of Postal-Telegraphic Operators, Railroad Workers, and Streetcar Conductors. The phenomenon was used by the Association to give lie to the charge that it was primarily proboss and antilabor. Although never conceived as an institution comparable to the fascist, communist, socialist, or Catholic trade unionism, the National Labor Bureau expanded to an enrollment of 75,000 by 1921. The Red Peril, exaggerated or overdrawn, induced the strengthening of whatever bonds existed between the Association and sectors of Italian industry. The Association sponsored several noteworthy regional and national business and commercial conventions.

A dramatic surprise development was *I Sempre Pronti per la Patria e per il Re* (The Minutemen for the Fatherland and the King), of 1920, who took an oath of allegiance "to the Fatherland and the King." It was another extra-legal law-and-order force, which the Liberal regime strangely encouraged and tolerated. Under the stalwart monarchist and war hero, Colonel Raffaele Paolucci, the Minutemen, who wore uniforms of blue, formed a parallel organization to that of the Fascist black shirts. Because blue shirts were dedicated to the defense of national institutions, Po Valley agrarians did not think them accommodating as the Fascist militia, and turned to the latter to put down farm labor uprisings and strikes. The camaraderie which developed between the Nationalists and Fascists over intervention tended to carry over into the postwar period. Contingents of black and blue shirts undertook joint raids on Communist and Socialist centers.

As a result of the general elections of May 15, 1921, the Association boosted its token parliamentary representation to twelve. Federzoni surpassed all winners in the Rome-Lazio constituency with 22,900 votes, followed by his fellow-Nationalist Gelasio Caetani with 21,119, with Rocco placing fifth, with

17,610 votes. Heading the victorious fascist list was the youthful intellectual, Giuseppe Bottai, who finished seventh, receiving 15,412 votes. Neither the order of the results nor the ballot count was lost on fascist politicians.

THE MUTILATED VICTORY. Italians were stunned when the nationalist Bevione revealed in the Chamber session of February 13, 1918 that the Pact of London had not awarded the port city of Fiume nor all of Dalmatia to Italy, as had been supposed. With 600,000 men killed and 1,000,000 wounded, and the country's economy severely strained, Italians, particularly the Nationalists, grieved because Italy had been short-changed. Fearing that a repetition of the "the mediocre Peace of Ouchy" was in the making, Nationalists were quick to pick up and endorse D'Annunzio's public pledge of October 8, 1918, *Vittoria Nostra Non Sarà Mutilata* (Our Victory Will Not Be Mutilated). If the London Treaty had not reserved Fiume for Italy, Nationalists claimed it on the basis of what they submitted was an Italian disproportionate share of the war effort. The last major battle of the war, they reminded their allies, that of Vittorio Veneto against Austria-Hungary, October 24-November 3, 1918, had been won exclusively by Italy.

The truth is that the loss of Fiume would have been a bitter defeat for all Italians. Individuals as diverse and as temperate as Giolitti and Salvemini believed in the Italian character of Fiume. According to the Austrian census of 1910, there were 22,488 Italians and 13,357 Slavs in the city proper. If the Susak suburb was included, the figures were 24,351 Slavs and 23,988 Italians. The fact that the vast majority of the middle classes and administrative personnel were Italian and that for several centuries Fiume had been part of the Venetian Republic reinforced the Italian position. In the supercharged nationalist climate of the day, Fiume became a symbol of Italy's valid rights at the peace table. The Allies, exhorted by Wilson, thought otherwise. Because Italy already had Venice and was about to gain Trieste, they reasoned that Italy did not need another Adriatic port. The new Slavic state of Yugoslavia did. Wilson remained immovable when warned by Premier Vittorio E. Orlando and Foreign Minister Sonnino that a hard line on Fiume would provoke a major political crisis. Determined to introduce a new standard of morality in diplomacy, Wilson privately accused the Italian statesmen of using Fiume as a ploy to extract unjustifiable concessions and to avoid basic internal social and economic reforms. On April 23, 1919, Wilson issued a manifesto directly to the Italian people. On the next day, the Italian delegation, headed by Orlando and Sonnino, left the Paris Peace Conference. Wilson had misjudged the Italian reaction. Wilson's reputation was finally destroyed in the eyes of the Italian people when it was realized that he appeared willing and eager to take on poor and proletarian Italy while acquiescing to the larger and more nakedly imperialistic designs of the more privileged powers, Britain and France.

The Association formed the cutting edge of Italian protests against the Paris proceedings. Under the guidance of the Association's executive secretary, the capable Umberto Guglielmotti, Nationalists arranged a mammoth loyalty parade to greet Orlando and Sonnino when they returned to Rome. They coined the expression, *Rinunciatori* (Renouncers, Supine Capitulators), to deride those Italians who did not speak out for Fiume's and Dalmatia's incorporation within the Kingdom of Italy, by force if necessary. The pledge, "Fiume or Death," was endlessly recited. When they learned that Sonnino had failed to hold out for Fiume's and Dalmatia's inclusion in the Treaty of London, Nationalists interpreted the omission as another disgusting example of the incompetence of the Liberal state's functionaries. Since he could not make any progress with Italy's allies, the new premier, Francesco S. Nitti, in June 1919, ordered the withdrawal of the Italian occupation units from Dalmatia. In line with what it believed had occurred in 1911 over Libya and in 1915 concerning intervention, the *Idea Nazionale*'s editorial of June 27, 1919, defiantly announced "the command is being transferred to the people." Nationalists serving as armed forces officers and personnel stationed in the Association's informational centers unleashed a volley of antistate criticism among soldiers and civilians which was avowedly seditious. By the Treaty of St. Germain, September 10, 1919, Austria ceded the Trentino, South Tyrol, Trieste and the Istrian Peninsula, but neither Fiume nor Dalmatia.

D'ANNUNZIO'S FIUMIAN EXPEDITION. Aroused Fiuman nationalists contacted D'Annunzio and found him eager to captain an armed intervention. Top-level Nationalists and Fascists were clearly involved in all phases of the action, which D'Annunzio undertook on September 12, 1919. They alerted public opinion, gained the moral support if not outright complicity of key military officers and government personnel, helped in the recruitment of volunteers, acquisition of supplies, and fundraising. Several of the more important of D'Annunzio's staff were either Nationalists or former Nationalists who had left the Association over tactics but still subscribed to most of its objectives. D'Annunzio's legionnaires were mainly Nationalists, Fascists, and Futurists, nearly all veterans of the World War.

Because of the apparent ease with which D'Annunzio broke through to Fiume, Nationalists and Fascists concluded that the Italian state was on the verge of collapse. Another attack would send it crashing to the ground. Although the record is not complete, it appears the D'Annunzio and the Nationalists and Fascists were concocting a plan pointed at Rome. The broader scheme quickly vanished. It was far-reaching and risky. Besides, there were suspicions between D'Annunzio and Mussolini, while nationalist notables were scandalized over the *Comandante*'s carefree mode of living and his disabilities as ruler. In short order, Fiume itself was in jeopardy, since neither the Italian government nor the Allies acknowledged the D'Annunzian regime. Having assumed the premiership, on June 9, 1920, Giolitti's firm resolve to end the breach compelled the Nationalists to reality. The Treaty of Sèvres, August 20, 1920, confirmed Italy in the possession of the Dodecanese and Rhodes. With the handwriting on the wall, Nationalists beat a hasty retreat, and virtually abandoned D'Annunzio as he became more uncompromising and truculent. The Treaty of Rapallo between Italy and Yugoslavia, signed November 12, 1920, confirmed the independent status just conferred on Fiume by the League of Nations. Zara and several smaller Adriatic islands became Italian, and Italy renounced claims to Dalmatia, which remained Yugoslavia's. Unresponsive to ministerial and extraministerial urgings, D'Annunzio surrendered, December 24, when General Enrico Caviglia attacked Fiume.

NATIONALIST-FASCIST RELATIONS. There were simultaneous sympathies and antipathies between Nationalists and Fascists. Both had cooperated over intervention. Neither was adverse to threatening violent means to attain its goal. Participation would not only gain foreign policy objectives but would give those who were in the vanguard for involvement the needed momentum for basic institutional revamping at home. There was a measure of collaboration in D'Annunzio's coup in Fiume. Squads of their militias acted together in assaulting opponents' headquarters. As the fears of a Sovietized Italy became a nightmare in agrarian and industrial circles, the conservative economic and social policies advocated by the Nationalists and Fascists solidified their public receptivity. This was particularly true of fascism following the 1919 electoral debacle and its consequent veering to the right.

As for misgivings, Nationalists were monarchical and against Freemasonry, while Fascists were outspoken republicans and Freemasons. Nationalists drew the bulk of their adherents and support from the middle and upper ranks of the bourgeoisie; the Fascists were mainly of lower and lower middle class provenance. If powerful currents in both enterprises favored a syndical-corporative reconstruction of society, Fascists, like Mussolini, Alceste De Ambris, Angelo O. Olivetti, and Edmondo Rossoni, criticized the nationalist initiative as too employer-oriented. Theirs was more original and revolutionary. Most distressing to the Nationalists was the network of shogunates fascist chieftains were establishing: Italo Balbo in Ferrara, Michele Bianchi in Calabria, Roberto Farinacci in Cremona, Dino Grandi in Bologna, and Aurelio Padovan in Naples. They were mortgaging, according to the Nationalists, the Fascist party to their petty fortunes. This made for a deplorable situation and, apparently, was the price Mussolini had to pay for his leadership role. The forces pushing nationalism and fascism together proved stronger than the antagonisms pulling them apart. Corradini, Coppola, and Rocco sensed that and emphasized what united the two movements. Nationalist strategy was to underline the similarities in the hope of strengthening the more moderate and rightist elements within fascism. Nationalism was never more astute than when it predicted that as fascism matured it would increasingly take on nationalist substance until major contrasting ideas would disappear. Nationalists noticed that Mussolini, understandably, stressed fascism's uniqueness and that he minimized its differences with nationalism. (*See Reading No. 44.*)

NATIONALISTS AND THE MARCH ON ROME. The situation just prior and during the March on Rome on October 28, 1922, offers a confused picture. There are many unanswered questions regarding official nationalist conduct. The concept of a March on Rome was not new. Beginning with the original drive of Julius Caesar in 33 B.C., Italians have periodically believed in the efficacy of a march to settle accounts and to right things gone wrong. They, like the Apostle Peter, saw Rome as Babylon, apostate, where spiritual and political wickedness prevailed in high places. Rome could also appear in the guise of the Apostle John's New Jerusalem, the very nerve center for a purified Italy and a reinvigorated humanity. What had transpired in Rome during the Radiant Days of May 1915, and the plans afoot during D'Annunzio's *putsch* in Fiume, encouraged Nationalists, Fascists, D'Annunzians, and affiliated spirits to think of extraordinary means pointed at Rome as the swiftest and most effective way to moral and civil redemption.

As 1922 unfolded, Nationalists appeared to shrink back from the high ground they had stormed. The Association adopted a two-track attitude. The crucial ingredient was the Minutemen's ambiguous position. Nationalists felt obliged to cultivate the cooperation they had been carefully encouraging with Fascists. Press reports during October spoke of confidential agreements between local commands of their respective militias. The blue shirts were also on special maneuvers in major areas of the country. On October 28, 1922, the central committee ordered general mobilization of its legions. As it seemed that Mussolini was determined to force the issue to the breaking point, Nationalists moved to avoid a potentially ruinous dilemma. The Association attempted to protect fascism, and also itself, by protesting against voices of a preventive army strike against the Fascists. Nationalists worked feverishly behind the scenes for the resolution of the parliamentary crisis by resurrecting old ideas: a coalition ministry embracing conservative Liberals, Nationalists, Catholic moderates, and the Fascists as the new element, with Salandra, Mussolini, and possibly Federzoni as the main protagonists. Although participants have their own particular version of the details, it has been generally believed that Rocco in Mussolini's Milan headquarters and Federzoni from the interior ministry in Rome warned Mussolini that intransigence would plunge Italy into civil war. Mussolini, Balbo, Bianchi, the last two having actually conceived and planned the March, and Cesare Rossi refused the nationalist counsel for moderation and compromise, in favor of fascist control of the government.

As the fascists' uncooperative comportment became ominous, the matter of martial law loomed larger. Premier Luigi Facta's martial law decision was posted on October 28, 1922, in anticipation of King Victor Emmanuel's verification. Was it Federzoni who secretly met with the king and dissuaded him from accepting the martial law decree? It is debatable. Since the king refused to endorse the order, Facta rescinded it. Different estimates have been advanced for the number of Fascists converging on the capital. Fascist apologists placed the number between 70,000 and 100,000. Military authorities used 70,000 as the maximum, which in itself may have conjured in the king's mind the specter of a general massacre were confrontation to occur. Mussolini, retrospectively, informed the king that 30,000 was more nearly correct. Antonio Répaci, a respected scholar of the episode, concluded that there were many thousands of fascist stragglers headed toward Rome but that Mussolini, on the critical day of October 28, had no more than 5,000 ill-equipped black shirts in Rome. Nationalist accounts tell of 4,000 Minutemen stationed in sensitive areas of the city and environs, furnished with army rifles. A clash did not take place and the Minutemen were spared a test of their loyalty oath. Summoned by the king to form a ministry, Mussolini hastened by train to Rome, arriving on October 30. The honor guard awaiting him was composed of fascist black shirts and nationalist blue shirts.

MERGER OF NATIONALISM AND FASCISM. Mussolini confided, in 1938, that it was indispensable for fascist fortunes. It probably was. It was the one and only attempt the Italian National Fascist Party undertook to absorb or completely win over another political group. The theoretical and programmatic community of interests existing between nationalism and fascism could be conducive to harmony but it could also provoke internecine rivalry. Much to the chagrin of the party, the Association was gaining many new members daily. One early error, and the Nationalists might resume their flirtation with D'Annunzio or go with their own Federzoni for the post of prime minister. Until they began to appropriate nationalist themes, Fascists were, to quote Mussolini, "the gypsies" of Italian politics. It took principles and resourceful governmental operatives to solidify Mussolini's control and to lead Italians in a new direction. Nationalism had doctrine and imaginative personnel to spare. In his cabinet Mussolini had included Federzoni as minister of colonies, Rocco as under secretary of the treasurer, and Siciliani the under secretary for cultural affairs. Another asset that union offered was the strengthening of fascism's contacts with conservative Liberals, the Catholic moderates, those friendly to fascism being called Clerical Fascists, and gain valuable respect at the monarchy, court, and within the armed forces. Joining of the two movements would service the relations initially established with big business, high finance, and with prominent church figures. Merger would undoubtedly assist Mussolini in organizing a united front against political detractors, Socialists, Communists, Radicals, and democratic Liberals.

A major source of worry were the awkward presence and illegalities committed by the militias. Italy, and least of all fascism, could ill afford them now that Mussolini was premier. Still, Mussolini could hardly have loosened the black shirts while the blue shirts remained intact. Tensions between them became particularly explosive in the south where a number of Fascists who felt socially superior had left fascism to become the nucleus of nationalist clubs. Such irritations made for deep antipathy. Among Mussolini's lieutenants, the conservative Fascists Emilio De Bono, Cesare Maria De Vecchi, Bottai, and Grandi, fusion was the only way to break the impasse. Radical Fascists, Balbo, Bianchi, and Farinacci, the party secretary, and the Futurist leader Filippo T. Marinetti, were decidedly against it. It was courting disaster to have an infant movement unsure of itself strike a deal with an established, unified, and experienced organization.

Amalgamation was a foregone conclusion for the Nationalists. All the dominant personalities were union-conscious. As Corradini explained it, the Nationalist Association was the elite and it had met the Fascist party, the mass, its following. Perhaps the lone exception was Federzoni, who may have harbored high political ambition and was inclined to adjudge any combining of nationalist and fascist forces as premature. He would have preferred to watch and wait, although he chose not to make an issue of the subject. Opinion within the Association at large preferred federation to outright fusion. With their checkered careers, Mussolini and the Fascists could not be trusted. It was imperative for the Association to maintain its freedom of action. Like the conservative Fascists, Nationalists were also concerned and vexed over the skirmishes occurring between black and blue shirts. In January 1923, an incident at Bernardi, in the Basilicata, left two Minutemen killed, fifteen wounded, and three Fascists wounded. The clash prompted the Nationalists Forges, Maraviglia, and Paolucci, all from the south, to second the advice of fusion-minded Fascists.

Mussolini took their word and cleverly had it appear that he was simply acceding to nationalist desires. The matter of nationalist-fascist relations was placed under official advisement by recommendation of the Association's central committee and the Fascist Grand Council, the highest ruling body of the Italian National Fascist Party. A joint commission was appointed. It immediately assumed that union was the only lasting solution to the inherent friction aroused by the two militias and by the existence of two compatible and ideologically connected institutions. A trade-off was effected. The commission granted "doctrinal precedence" to Nationalism while deferring to "the definite Fascist nature of the revolution" in progress. Process toward merger was greatly enhanced when the Association during the first week in February disbanded the *Sempre Pronti* and the Party, on February 15, proscribed Freemasonry. On February 27, the Pact of Fusion was signed by the negotiating team. (*See Reading No. 45.*) In anticipation of total compliance, the Association's central committee met with Premier Mussolini on March 8, and exchanged best wishes. (*See Reading No. 46.*) The *Idea Nazionale*), the mouthpiece of the most ardent fusionists, interpreted the merger as a signal victory for Italy and fascism, and saw nationalism's "reincarnation in fascism" (*See Reading No. 47.*) Nationalism-Fascism was born or, as the historian Salvatorelli expressed it at the time, *Nazionalfascismo* (National Fascism).

CHAPTER 10

NATIONALISM-FASCISM

COLLABORATORS. At the same time that nationalist and fascist organizations were being integrated, prominent Association members were elevated. As Mussolini had requested, the Association provided a pool of expert personnel. Fascism had just thirty-five Chamber seats when Mussolini became prime minister and neither Mussolini nor his closest colleagues had governmental experience. Federzoni and Rocco, to cite two examples, offered immediate indispensable assistance. Corradini, Foscari, and the renowned economist Maffeo Pantaleoni of the University of Rome, became Senators, with Corradini, Federzoni, Maraviglia, and Rocco entering the Fascist Grand Council in April 1923. Of the forty-two members of the Council in 1925, ten were Nationalists. Corradini, Coppola, and the Deputies Francesco Ercole from Catania and Fulvio Suvich from Trieste were appointed to the Commission of Eighteen for Constitutional Reform. Such nationalist personalities and others quickly gained for Mussolini and fascism a significant measure of strength and support within the monarchy, court, service establishment, industry, education, church, and the intellectuals, the molders of public opinion.

CONSOLIDATION OF POWER. Between June–December 1924, Mussolini, fascism, and Italy were rocked by a crisis, precipitated by the kidnapping and brutal slaying of Giacomo Matteotti by fascist thugs on June 10. Matteotti was secretary of the Unitary, formerly Official, Socialist Party, and had been outspoken in his Chamber exposé of Fascist atrocities, committed particularly during the April 1924 general elections. About 120 Deputies, primarily Socialists, Republicans, Radicals, democratic Liberals, and *Popolari*, withdrew from parliament and met on the Aventine Hill in Rome. Although it was unable to decide on concrete political action, the Aventine Secession succeeded in arousing moral indignation against the fascist regime. Mussolini's complicity, although suspected, has not been definitely established. At a time when his rule was hanging by a thread, Nationalists declared Mussolini clear of involvement and attacked the secessionists, charging that they were exploiting Fascist hierarchs' irresponsible acts to bring down the Mussolini government. On June 16, six days after the incident, Federzoni was transferred from the colonial post to the interior ministry. Historians date the fascist dictatorship's inauguration January 3, 1925, when Mussolini addressed the Chamber of Deputies and accepted full responsibility for the Matteotti assassination and dared the opposition to topple him. Two days after Mussolini's defiant performance, January 5, Rocco left the presidency of the Chamber and assumed the portfolio of minister of justice, which he retained until 1932. Simultaneously, at Mussolini's request, Forges, editor of the *Idea Nazionale*, undertook a rigorous review of the Fascist party's structure and practices and upon completion, joined the party directorate. Nationalists, known as law and order champions, were being used to pacify and convince the Italian people to stick with Mussolini and fascism. The stratagem worked as the Aventine Secession crumbled and on November 9, 1926 all the antifascist Deputies were deprived of their seats.

The Matteotti murder dramatized the interparty struggle over direction, the party's function, and the terrorism (*squadrismo*) of local fascist organizations. Three major tendencies came to the fore between 1922–26. One, represented by the right Fascists Grandi, De Bono, De Vecchi, and Massimo Rocco, were of the opinion that all party segments were to end their illegalities and come under the umbrella of state authority. At the other extreme were Balbo, Bianchi, and above all, Farinacci, vocal exponents of provincial fascism and *squadrismo*. They favored the extensive use of the Combat Bands to protect their leverage in the event Mussolini betrayed their brand of fascism or, as they feared, was co-opted by the Nationalists. Dubbed "the second wavers," they were eager to back up the political revolution in course with a social revolution. The Fascist party, according to their rationale, was to be superimposed on the state, with the locus of decision-making to be deposited neither with Mussolini nor with the administration but at party headquarters in close communications with local secretaries. The more intermediate position was that of Bottai and the intellectuals who flanked his celebrated review, *Critica Fascista* (*Fascist Criticism*). They, too, demanded an end to lawlessness. Their view of the party was one which was semiautonomous and made its own essential contribution. The party was to become the training and proving ground for the new principles and public servants who were to bring about the transformation of the Italian state and society. Nationalists, obviously, were unanimously hostile to the second option and could give selective and lukewarm support toward the third alternative. The first suited them very well.

These attitudes were impossible to reconcile. The Combat Bands were an institution of the Fascist party. They highlighted Fascism as a unique movement, close to the people. Yet, fascism was on trial. Confronted by the multitude of doubters, in and out of the party, Mussolini was compelled to move. During 1923–24, party leadership was shared by a four-man directorate, which included Forges. In February 1925, in the wake of Matteotti's murder and the initiation of the dictatorship, Mussolini appointed Farinacci as single secretary. Mussolini attempted to meet the more tolerable demands of the left Fascists because he could count on Federzoni and Rocco to thwart their efforts to lift the party and its Combat Bands above the government and state. Between June 1924 and November 1926, Minister of Interior Federzoni and Minister of Justice Rocco systematically proceeded to realize national order and party discipline through legislative enactments and decrees. The Fascist party, including local and country-wide officers, as well as the militia, were placed under state supervision. Farinacci, evidently grumbling, was relieved as party secretary, March 1926. A subsequent statute, first ardently backed by Corradini, Federzoni, Maraviglia, and Rocco in the Fascist Grand Council, abolished all the Council's elective offices.

Designated as "auxiliary bodies of the State," provincial and communal councils were placed under such tight national government regulations that the last shreds of autonomy were eliminated. Mayors were replaced by *podestà* (authority), nominated by the ministry; the communal secretaries were subject to extreme scrutiny of the interior ministry. A firmer grip on the localities would serve national uniformity interests. Individual liberties were curtailed, press censorship instituted, with antifascist newspapers suppressed, and passports cancelled. Due partly to the Vatican's hostility, the Christian Democrats had

ceased to exist as a political force by the end of 1925. By the time
Federzoni left the Interns in November 1926, the outlawing of
the Communist and Socialist parties had been decided. Following four attempts on Mussolini's life between 1924–26, the
secret police, *OVRA* (*Opera Vigilanza Repressione Antifascista*)
became operational in December 1926. As the army came under
fascist control, and the intimidating legal methods were proving
effective, *squadrismo* became untenable. Combat Bands were
absorbed into the newly-devised state militia. Looking ahead,
the penal code that Rocco designed and pushed through in 1931
also contributed toward making Italy into a police state. He
seized on unrevised and unprogressive features of Liberal Italy's
criminal procedures and expanded on the restrictions already
advanced by Federzoni and him in the mid-1920s. Protective
custody, house break-ins, arbitrary arrest and imprisonment,
confinement, and exile—all these were given statutory license.
Because all crimes, whether civil or political, resulted from
man's irreligious and antisocial instincts, prison wardens, male
and female, were to be religious personnel, specially instructed
by church and state to extract confessions and to reclaim the
fallen to the church and the state.

HISTORICAL LEGITIMIZATION. Through speeches,
books, and essays, Nationalists, along with mainline Fascists,
delineated the march of Italian history, with Fascism as the
climactic manifestation. To quote Rocco, Fascism was "the
integration of the *Risorgimento*" and "the resumption of the
mission of Italy." Fascism was restoring the Roman conception
of the nation as the extension of the family. Like Rome, Fascist
Italy embodied solidarity, obedience, purpose, sacrifice, empire. Corradini advanced two major observations which enjoyed
broad acceptance. The *Risorgimento*, he submitted, had nothing
at all to do with liberalism or democracy, but with liberation and
unification. Secondly, Corradini argued that the Italian tribes,
Roman Empire, Communal Era, Renaissance, *Risorgimento*,
and the many periods of foreign occupation were inseparable
phases of Italian history. The connecting link was supplied by
the omnipresent Italian *stirpe* (race). The interminable search for
Italy had been superfluous and ill-advised. All the celebrated

individuals who served valiantly in the peninsula deserved to be acknowledged as harbingers of Fascism. (*See Reading No. 48.*)

Nationalists invariably assigned fascist Italy a universal mission, although there was disagreement with left Fascists and radical Syndicalists over what the mission was all about. Left Fascists and radical Syndicalists Olivetti, Orano, Rossoni, Sergio Panunzio, and Curzio Suckert, clinging to their version of the Mazzinian vision, did not favor war for territorial aggrandizement, but for the general imposition of a democratic syndical state. In an article published in the *Popolo D'Italia*, February 18, 1923, Panunzio boasted that "Italy and Italy alone can give Europe the first example of a new organic, stable, and realistic political-national constitution on a syndical basis." To the Nationalists, it was war for civilization, empire, and for war's intrinsic psychological benefits. It was war for the refinement and perpetuation of the Italian species, to obtain raw materials, markets for a proletarian nation, and to rid culture of the deadening dross of crass materialism and individual egoism.

IDEOLOGICAL-POLITICAL ASSUMPTIONS. Nationalists and fascist thinkers approached the state as an absolute goal. The nation comprised the underlying moral and spiritual ethos, identified with the mysteries and instincts locked in the people. There was no theory of natural and inalienable rights. Rights were grants of the omnipotent, nationalist-fascist state, which could neither be grasped nor exercised apart from duties and obligations. Citizens were to be inextricably tied to the state. All privations were to be borne in the name of the state, including autarchical measures. Pacifism, internationalism, labor-management strife, political deadlock, and social tensions undermined the state. They were to be outlawed. Since politics was time-consuming and had divisive effects, parliament's functions were to be drastically reduced. The arena of combat was to be transferred from the state to the external world.

The fascist state which Nationalists conceived was imaginative and innovative. It would end the people's estrangement. The masses were to be organized and a degree of popular participation allowed. Populist means were to be utilized for conservative ends. A syndical-corporative order was preferred because it gave workers a sense of belonging, provided for the citizens' basic

health and well-being, and simultaneously monitored their behavior. The producer and not the politician or the labor leader
was the prototype of the fascist state. Nationalism's production-
ist principles automatically assigned a foremost place to the
upper bourgeoisie, called the "productive bourgeoisie" by Corradini, in contrast to the "political bourgeoisie," who spent or
wasted their time and energies in the political process. A new
ruling class was to be recruited from big business, and high
finance, and was to include the technocrats who would update
Italy's economic machine, and the bureaucrats who would serve
as the managers of the corporative state. This ruling class was to
have hereditary status and remain apolitical. If this revamped
system smacked of *gerarchia* (rank), no apologies were offered.
A stratified society discovered its *raison d' être* in the fact that all
Italians, according to their ability and calling, were voluntary
producers of wealth for the national community, of which each
citizen was a vital part.

To the extent that Corradini and his fellow-Nationalists and
also Fascists conceived the fascist regime to be power, production, population, growth, discipline, and war, to that extent they
helped to compose the structural foundations of the fascist state.
Through Rocco's conceptual and administrative ingenuity, Nationalists gave cardinal principles common to them and many
Fascists institutional life and convincing explanation and defense.

MUSSOLINI THE *DUCE* (LEADER). In the interests of
hierarchy and mass integration, Nationalists, as well as Fascists,
publicized Mussolini as the personification of the leadership
principle essential to a sound state and a well-ordered society.
Duce was first occasionally applied to Mussolini when he was
editor of the Socialist daily, *L'Avanti* (*Forward*)! It became the
premier's trademark. He was described as a man from the
people, instinctive and insightful, plain, even crude and rough,
revealing a sincerity without the sophisticated airs of upper-class
men. Mussolini was the self-made man who had overcome
numerous adversities. While liberal and democratic state leaders
had manipulated their way to the top, Mussolini had been catapulted to the premiership by the people like Julius Caesar. As a
charismatic and tireless ruler, the *Duce* drew his energies and

zeal from the Italians. He was the first soldier in the battle of wheat and in the reclamation of the Pontine Marshes near the capital. He epitomized respect for traditions, continuity, and institutionalized values: country, family, monarchy, armed forces, the work ethic. Together with King Victor Emmanuel, Mussolini offered his people a lively and robust emotional center. There was no conflict in authority or rivalry between them, only collaboration for the fatherland's greater good.

CHURCH-STATE CONCILIATION. Much of the credit for the climate of opinion from which there emanated the desire and the will to heal the breach in church-state relations belongs to the Nationalists. They had publicly anticipated, as they did regarding the Fascists, that the realities of Italian life and electoral politics would steer a major segment of the Catholic movement toward nationalism and the state. In fact, Rocco had been anxiously awaiting the day when the state could deal with the Vatican and enlist the Catholic Church's assistance for the promotion of Italy's imperialist aspirations. (*See Reading No. 49.*) The nationalist attitude was most persuasive to Mussolini. Resolution of the church-state impasse, which had eluded statesmen from Cavour to Crispi and Giolitti, would add immeasurably to his stature and win Catholic millions to the fascist side. Nationalists actually spearheaded the conciliation when Interior Minister Federzoni informed Mussolini that prominent ecclesiastical figures had indicated that the Holy See would welcome a high level agreement. A major reason why Rocco was brought into the justice ministry on January 5, 1925 was Mussolini's eagerness to have Federzoni's intimation explored by a nationalist who had been outspoken and optimistic over the prospects of working something out with the Catholic officialdom. Within six weeks, on February 12, 1925, Rocco installed the Mattei-Gentili Commission to examine the future of church-state relations. By May, Rocco and Federzoni in the Chamber were calling for compulsory Catholic religious instruction in the schools. Church-state discussions proceeded fruitfully, thanks to Mussolini's resolve and that of the papal secretary of state, Cardinal Pietro Gasparri, with the real work done by Domenico Barone, councillor of state, and Ernesto Francesco Pacelli, legal consultant to the Holy See and brother of Monsignor Eugenio Pacelli, later

Pope Pius XII. Barone died before the negotiations were brought to fruition and was replaced by Rocco. In his posthumous recognition of Rocco's distinguished service to the Fascist state, Mussolini underscored Rocco's contribution to the Lateran Accords and the sizeable body of legislation they generated.

The Lateran Accords of February 11, 1929 consisted of a Conciliation Treaty, a Concordat, and a Financial Convention. In the Conciliation Treaty, the fascist regime accepted Roman Catholicism as "the only religion of the State," while the Holy See declared the Roman Question permanently settled, recognized the Kingdom of Italy under the House of Savoy, and Rome as the capital. An area in Rome, of 109 square miles, and designated "Vatican City," was deeded in perpetuity to the church. It was to have the papal residences, the church's headquarters, and the facilities through which the pontiff could communicate freely with the Catholic world and maintain diplomatic relations with foreign states. Under the Concordat, Italy guaranteed the church the right to exercise its responsibility as a church and as a religion. All bishops were obligated to take an oath of loyalty to the head of the state. Provisions were incorporated for religious teaching in elementary and secondary schools. While the state acknowledged the subsidiary units of Italian Catholic Action, the church agreed to ban church officials from participating in political activities. The Financial Convention pledged payment of 750,000,000 lire in cash and 1,000,000,000 lire in government bonds as compensation for the papal territories and church properties seized since unification.

Before and after the Ethiopian conquest in 1935, Federzoni, as minister of colonies, and his successors in the colonial office, and undersecretaries of state for foreign affairs from De Bono to Grandi, made it increasingly difficult for Protestant missionary societies in Italian East Africa (Ethiopia, Eritrea, Italian Somaliland) and Libya to carry out their religious-educational-humanitarian functions. Officials hoped that the Catholic Church would welcome the opportunity to supplant Protestant efforts. They thought that the national church they contemplated for Italy would be extended to the empire as Rocco had dared to hope. Protestants were foreigners, sectarian, democratic, and individualist. Catholics stressed uniformity, hierarchical values, and they were Italian. This was a preliminary aspect of a new, comprehensive policy of settling Italy's African empire and attracting Italian business investments. The Catholic Church, because of its worldwide commitments, simply did not have the monetary means or the personnel to cover Italy's holdings in Africa. Where they made an effort, Fascists were insulted by what they perceived was a calculated policy of embarrassment and of insubordination. Interested in emphasizing the church's universal reach, the Vatican included a majority of non-Italian clerics and nuns in the enterprises set up.

THE SYNDICAL-CORPORATIVE STATE. Nationalism served itself and Fascism by assisting it in the formulation of a syndical-corporative substitute for the liberal parliamentary regime. The desire was first limited in reach, confined to the economic realm, encompassing labor-management relations, as Carli explained at the Florence convention. The Nationalists' nagging displeasure with parliament's performance, particularly during the crisis for intervention and postwar unrest, enlarged the scope to embrace the political sphere. Inability to cope with the Red Scare convinced Nationalists that the liberal order was in a state of dissolution. A replacement had to be found. The intent was far from a nationalist monopoly. Although many Fascists had exited from revolutionary Socialism and Syndicalism, they retained syndicalist predilections, vague and disparate as they were. The problems were means, orientation, and ends. Corradini, Coppola, Ercole, and Suvich on the Commission of Eighteen for Constitutional Reform instituted in September 1924 argued for a state-sponsored and state-controlled syndical-corporative arrangement, promoting limited mass involvement, productionism, and expansion, which Corradini had introduced in his *Patria lontana* in 1910. Guidance would be facilitated through consultation between state technocrats and the upper bourgeoisie. If this type was supported by right Fascists, it was opposed by the left Fascist representatives, Olivetti, Panunzio, Rossoni, and Agostino Lanzillo. They fought for a democratic syndical-corporative system, in which the driving force would not be from the state and industrial-commercial class, but from the party and the new labor aristocracy to arise from the fascist unions. In the background was Mussolini who was publicly approaching the subject from a nationalist perspective. Paralyzed from the outset by the ideological split, the Commission was reconstituted in January 1925, with no better results.

Deadlock paved the way for Rocco's intervention and his momentous contrivances in the Syndical Law of April 3, 1926. The first provision called for juridical recognition of labor unions. Parallel employer and employee organizations were to face off. Thirdly, nationwide contracts were to be negotiated for each category of occupation. Strikes and lockouts were banned. Finally, a labor magistracy was to arbitrate labor-management disputes. The Syndical Law met with the obvious approval of the Nationalists, conservative Fascists, and also of the radical syndicalist firebrands, Lanzillo, Olivetti, Orano, Panunzio, Bottai and Ugo Spirito, the latter two serious and sedate idealists. Congratulations were premature, for a serious difficulty arose over implementation. As minister of justice, Rocco interpreted the law within a statist, probusiness context. The labor syndicates were made submissive to the state and any hint of politicking was prohibited. Moreover, as a high state organ, the labor magistracy saw fit to impose its decision without appeal.

It might well be that Mussolini conceived of the *Carta del Lavoro* (Labor Charter) to soften the disappointing impact which Rocco's enforcement of the Syndical Law had on the more extreme fascist Syndicalists. Worked out by Rocco, the Labor Charter became effective in 1928. Acclaimed as another fundamental document of the Fascist regime, the Charter was a hodgepodge of compromises Rocco entered in order to satisfy dissident Fascists. The Syndical Law of 1926 was confirmed. Many social-welfare measures were provided, as well as protection against unfair employment practices. The Charter advised the creation of a joint management-labor board for production supervision. The expectation proved to be fallacious. If it sanctioned the inviolability of private property and capitalist enterprise, the Charter also stressed the state's right, indeed responsibility, to intervene in any facet of factory operation to insure the national interest.

As fascism appeared headed toward a syndical-corporative reorganization of the state, the basic incompatibility between divergent views became more divisive and troublesome. Because Mussolini had pledged to bring forth a new state worthy of

Fascism and the revitalized Italian people, he sought an accommodation to placate those on both sides of the issue. On July 2, 1926, the Ministry of Corporations was formed to monitor labor unions and employer organizations and to submit plans for the corporative state. Bottai was the ministry's undersecretary from 1926 to 1929, and minister between 1929 to July 1932. A cautious, serious, and inspired public servant, Bottai was open to many discordant outlooks. If Rocco banked on the state bureaucracy, Bottai's mainstay was the party. Bottai's initial blueprint satisfied the radical elements in the party and the labor syndicates but was strenuously criticized by the Nationalists, right Fascists, and employer associations. When Mussolini turned to Rocco and authorized him to rework Bottai's draft, Rocco's effort, predictably, leaned heavily toward capital. The final version, approved by the Fascist Grand Council in April 1927, represented a combination of both endeavors. Although it did not explicitly set up a corporative structure, the enabling legislation which followed reassured corporativists that Italy was making giant strides in that direction. In May 1929, the Chamber abolished the system of geographical representation for one based on vocation. Worker syndicates and boss organizations in the professional, social, and economic corporations were instructed to select parliamentary candidates whose names were to be submitted to the Grand Council for approval and presentation to the electorate. The corporativist idea was assuming political dimensions.

In March 1930, the National Council of Corporations was introduced as the umbrella institute and governing body for the employer and corresponding labor organizations, which were reduced to seven: industry, agriculture, banking, commerce, internal navigation, sea and air transport, and the arts and professions. Representatives chosen by the respective components were to meet in an assembly having a consultative role. It could not infringe on parliament's traditional competence. In February 1931, the number of corporations was increased to twenty-two. Essentially a Bottai creation, the National Council of Corporations also caused much consternation. As a prominent governmental official, Bottai could better appreciate the emphasis the nationalist Rocco had placed on state priorities. Complaints were voiced that the power of the original Fascist Labor

Corporations had been vitiated by their separation and subdivision into many economic classifications. Laborites grieved that the worker corporations did not have an authentic say in formulating contracts with the corollary managements units. Wages and employment conditions were not set by bargaining in good faith between capital and labor, but by tacit understanding between the government and employers' corporations. As a result, profits soared out of proportion to salaries.

The insistent desire to replace parliament and the need to silence critics and to convince skeptics motivated Bottai and his collaborators to propose sweeping institutional changes, climaxed, on January 19, 1933, with the Chamber of Deputies giving way to the Chamber of Fasces and Corporations. The new legislature was composed of the National Council of Corporations, assigned 525 members, the National Council of the Party, 139, and the Grand Council of Fascism with 18 seats. A major concession was made to the Fascist party, with which Rocco and the Nationalists would not have agreed. The corporative state institutions were now in place. Based on economic representation, the Chamber of Fasces' responsibility was theoretically extended to all areas, except for the military and foreign affairs, which were reserved for the king and the premier.

Most Italians hailed the corporative state as a historic achievement. Nationalists and Fascists believed that they had solved the basic problem of contemporary industrial society, that of providing mass participation within a state-controlled framework. They had corrected the distortions which had cropped up over the proper relationship among government, labor, management, and interest groups. Individual initiative and collective discipline had been effectively paired. (*See Reading No. 50.*) The corporate state also drew rare notices from foreign observers, who did not understand or evaluate its authoritarian cast and the ulterior motives which animated it. Scholars simply focused in amazement on the originality and ingenuity which eliminated parliament based on geographic representation for one founded on what was deemed the more salutary principle of occupational representation.

NATIONALISM IN EDUCATION. Nationalists had long contended that a reorganization of the country's educational establishment was overdue. The Liberal-Democratic school was for mere knowledge and accumulation and not for training the mind. It emphasized the intellect at the expense of character and traditional Italian mores. It ignored science and technical learning. The Gentile Reforms, July 16, 1923, was the first educational measure of the Fascist regime and for the revamping of the school since the Casati Law of 1859. The school was conceived as a state organ, designed to mold the student's spirit, underscoring order, obedience, patriotism, with no neglect of the thinking faculty. Core requirement became standard; academic specialization was postponed. Religious instruction was mandated on the primary level. The school was supposed to educate the new elite and be accessible to all who could meet qualifications. Nevertheless, a cap was placed on the number of students who could enter high school. Class distinctions were not erased but became more pronounced. An intensive university competitive state examination program was framed, which placed students from the lower middle classes and worker families at a disadvantage. Contrary to the nationalist avowed desire to stimulate technical learning for economic modernization, graduates of even the most prestigious technical institutes discovered that the universities were beyond their reach.

Between November 1926 and July 1932, the ministry of national education, the term public instruction giving way in November 1929, was headed successively by the Bolognese Nationalists Emilio Bodrero and Balbino Giuliano. Under their stewardship, but particularly with Giuliano, former professor of philosophy at the University of Bologna, the ministry embarked on an outright conversion of the schools to fascism. Texts, especially in history and political science, adhered to the fascist line exclusively, and were written by nationalist or fascist stalwarts. The ministry, on October 31, 1931, launched a loyalty check of full professors. The choice was between allegiance sworn to the regime and dismissal. The fact that only 11 of 1250 academicians refused was a source of immense satisfaction and given wide publicity as proof of fascism's intellectual support. The period was also marked by increasing tensions between church and state over youth. In his parliamentary justification of the Lateran Accords, Mussolini had acknowledged the indispensable role of religion in society but had unequivocally reserved for fascism the values to be incorporated in the school curriculum. In addition to civic awareness, Mussolini called for, and the ministry attempted to push, the ideas of will, power, dominion, war, preservation of the "race," the Corradinian requirements for a rejuvenated Italy. This attitude could stand on its own merits. It was also intended to break the hold it was thought Catholic teaching had on the youthful imagination. A crisis ensued, which was settled by compromise. Political activities were to be the state's prerogative, while spiritual preparation remained the church's preserve.

Bottai, the former minister of corporations, took over the ministry of national education in 1936 and remained until 1942. His purpose in assuming the top educational post was to restructure the teaching process to inculcate corporativist temperament within the student body. Through his tireless efforts, another educational charter was devised, which became effective in February 1939. Cooperation, mental toughness, self-esteem, ethnic pride, personal voluntarism, and industry were the qualities to be pursued. After the Ethiopian conquest Italy had become involved in the Spanish Civil War, and World War II would soon supervene, making for an added sense of urgency. All students had to submit to a stint of manual labor. Stipulations suffered from inconsistency. While the regime was anxious to speed the country's industrialization, the charter spoke in glowing terms of the virtuous and resourceful plebes as the finest example of the new breed of Italians. At the same time that administrative, cultural, economic, and social integration was ardently preferred, localities were offered many opportunities and channels by which to express their customs and conventions, even in dialectical form.

POLITICAL CULTURE. To encourage consensus and physical fitness, the Fascist regime introduced institutions and societies, catering to males and females of all ages, and covering a wide spectrum of activities. The *Opera Nazionale Balilla* (National Balilla Institution), which organized children up to eighteen years of age, became operational in 1924, and was managed by the Fascist Renato Ricci, one of the signers of the Pact of Fusion. On October 27, 1937, the *Gioventù Italiana del Littorio* (Italian Youth of the Littorio) absorbed the *Balilla* and the *Fasci Gioventù* (Youth Bands), a creation of the late twenties. The Balilla and the Italian Youth of the Littorio enrolled millions, who took the pledge, "In the name of God and of Italy I swear to execute the rules of the *Duce* and to serve with all my strength and, if necessary, with my blood, the cause of the Fascist Revolution." Impressed on their minds was respect for authority, sympathy for the poor, and compassion for the indigent and the jobless. Another highly visible agency was the *Gioventù Universitaria Fascista* (Fascist University Youths), organized in 1923. Initiated in 1926, the *Opera Nazionale Dopolavoro* (National Afterwork Institute) was the single, largest, peacetime, public organization of Fascist Italy. At its peak in 1935, it boasted of 2,755,000 members, in 20,000 centers. It planned and coordinated workers' recreational facilities in sports: track meets, gymnastics, boxing matches, soccer games, bicycle races; in cultural activities: concerts, musical recitals, public singing, amateur writing, film festivals, staging of plays; and numerous hobbies and popular crafts. Local, provincial, and national contests were held regularly. In addition, there were parades, celebration of important dates in the state calendar, rousing speeches by the *Duce* and lesser personalities, calculated to stimulate oneness. Correspondence was drawn between the competitive drive in sports and the desire to excel in cultural pursuits and the fight to increase production, curb inflation, and maintain the value of the lira, and to sharpen the spirit for war.

These organizations worked in a subtle manner for the socialization of the people. They gained much support for the regime. *Dopolavoro* members freely selected their pastime and probably hardly noticed that it was carried on within a fascist context. Although the affiliations drew the Nationalists' high approbation, they eventually provoked displeasure and uneasiness because they were increasingly placed under party domination, especially after Federzoni and Rocco had been removed from center stage. After the Ethiopian conquest, what the Nationalists had suspected became a reality. Many Italians who participated in these cultural-physical-social enterprises concluded that they were primarily regime agencies for mass psychology and mind control.

In early 1935, the ministry of press and propaganda was established under Galeazzo Ciano, married to Edda, Mussolini's daughter. Dino Alfieri, once president of the Milan Nationalist Club and an early opponent of union with fascism, was under-secretary. The ministry developed a list of Italian and foreign authors and books to be proscribed. The most celebrated fifth-grade reader of the period was the nationalist Forges' *Balilla Vittoriosa* (*Victorious Balilla*), which glorified the typical fascist's dedication and nationalistic sentiment. Beginning on December 27, 1933, and continuing until his untimely death in June 1936, Forges had the favorite news broadcast. Called "Chronicles of the Regime," it was a fifteen minute nightly commentary on the day's happenings. Interspersed among the news of scandals, divorce, unemployment, and crime statistics plaguing the Western Democracies, were the accomplishments of the fascist state: urban reconstruction, interclass harmony, stability of the Italian family, reinvigoration of youth, social welfare programs, and the conquest of Ethiopia.

When Ciano left the ministry for Africa in October 1935, Alfieri took charge. All cultural materials were to reflect, in his own words, "a clear and sincere Fascist outlook." Mussolini's position appeared contradictory. He commanded that literature and the arts should remain free of ideological restraints and he also advocated a partnership between culture and fascism. Early in 1932, Alfieri conceived of the idea for the *Decennale*, a nationwide display-festival of the first decade of fascist rule. The *Duce* agreed with the concept and appointed a commission of Alfieri, Luigi Freddi, Cipriano Oppo, and Alessandro Melchiorre, all Nationalists, for implementation. Inaugurated in October, the Exhibit of the Fascist Revolution, housed in a large building in Milan, featured graphic and illustrative memorabilia of fascism's rise, development, and achievements. Italians thronged to see it. It was a tremendous propaganda success for the regime and a personal triumph for the *Duce*.

Alfieri's ministry had an important assignment during the Ethiopian war. Morale had to be reinforced and Italians had to endure privations due to war, aggravated by the economic sanctions imposed on Italy by fifty-two countries through the auspices of the League of Nations. The ministry's services were extended in many cultural directions. All institutions, from the Royal Italian Academy, and the Fascist Institute of Culture, to the Dante Alighieri Society, and others of lesser note, rallied around the official theme of Italy's "civilizing mission." Representatives of the organizations, journalists, and radio news broadcasters were escorted to the field to report on the feats of Italian arms. Following the creation of the Italian Empire, Mussolini thought Fascism was sufficiently secure to shift the emphasis from censorship and sheer propaganda to reaching out to the Italian masses. The objective was to elevate cultural tastes within a fascist totalitarian mold. In May 1937, the ministry of press and propaganda gave way to the ministry of popular culture headed by Alfieri. It is impossible to say if it was the Fascist version of the institute of nationalist culture anticipated in the opening article of the Pact of Fusion. In short order, the number of employees multiplied, from 183 to 800.

For reasons unknown, the ministry appeared to escape the encroaching and all-inclusive party net. Intellectuals, artists, musicians, novelists, poets, play-wrights, movie-script writers, and producers were placed under a strict regimen of conformity and surveillance. In close contact with Joseph Goebbels, his counterpart in Germany, Alfieri strove to unite all Italian cultural societies and subordinate them to his ministry's close supervision. It was done in name only. Alfieri was not Goebbels; Mussolini was not Hitler; and Fascist Italy was not Nazi Germany. Whether required or not, a uniform policy was never realized. The building constructed for the Decade Exhibit ran the gamut in architectural and decorative stylistic accents, from the classical, the baroque, the modern, and the futurist, to sheer individualistic innovation. One need only to review the films of the fascist period to note that along with cheerful adherence to the party line, there was restrained spoofing and prudent criticizing of fascist rule, and those movies which, in true Hollywood fashion, deliberately accorded ideology second place to adventure and entertainment.

On October 29, 1933, Alfieri left the popular culture ministry and became ambassador the Holy See. Before leaving, he had the task of explaining to a stunned and complacent people the rationale for the regime's anti-Semitic legislation of 1938–39. He was assisted by many, including the nationalist Roberto Paribeni. In 1938, he marked the tenth anniversary of the Italian Academy's founding with an anti-Semitic diatribe. He focused on the deleterious influence Judaism presumably exerted on

Italians from Ancient Rome to the present. To think that Ernesto Nathan had been mayor of Rome between 1909–13 at the head of a Radical Masonic coalition.

EMPIRE. The foreign policy unfolded at the start of the fascist period was a mixture of defiance and cooperation. The extreme militarist, the nationalist Coppola, was appointed the Italian delegate to the League of Nations between 1923 and 1925, and Italy's representative to the Geneva Disarmament Conference of 1925. Mussolini, himself, derided and explicitly declared that Fascist Italy did not subscribe to the standard of international good will and world cooperation which was being advanced by the League and the World Court. Italian diplomats and naval experts left the Washington Naval Conference of 1922 quite satisfied, because they had succeeded in obtaining for Italy parity with France in capital ships, that is ships over 10,000 tons and having guns larger than eight inches. The ratio established was 5-5-3 for Britain, the United States, Japan, and 1.67-1.67 for France and Italy. At the same time that fascist Italy served notice that she intended to build up the rank accorded her, she proceeded toward the imposition of Italian cultural uniformity on the 200,000 Austrian minority people of the Alto Adige (South Tyrol), which Italy had inherited in 1919. Cultural freedoms were denied, with Italian imposed as the official language in the schools and administration.

In terms of international collaboration, Italy was a signatory power of the Locarno Pact, December 1, 1925. Germany and France, and Germany and Belgium formulated treaties pledged to the maintenance of their respective borders. Britain and Italy were the guarantors. Germany was to be admitted to the League as a permanent member. Fascist Italy was in the forefront protecting Austria's independence against Nazi German plots. On July 25, 1934, the Nazis attempted a coup, during which Austrian Chancellor Englebert Dollfuss was assassinated. In swift reaction, Mussolini despatched several divisions to the Alpine frontier. Mussolini's resolve compelled Chancellor Adolf Hitler to back down. Because Britain and France were concerned over Germany's rearmament, which had been expressly prohibited by the Versailles Treaty, a conference was called of World War allies to organize a common policy. This produced the Stresa

Front, so-named from the site in northern Italy where the prime ministers of Britain, France, and Italy met on April 11–14, 1935. Stanley Baldwin, Pierre Laval, and Mussolini agreed on the preservation of Austria's territorial integrity, and denounced all treaty violations, which, they warned, could only provoke war. Mussolini's prestige and Fascist Italy's stock were never higher than at the Munich Conference of September 28–30, 1938, when the Italian dictator had a significant part in preserving the peace which had been severely threatened by the German-Czechoslovakian Sudentenland deadlock.

That all this was a prelude to empire is unmistakable. There should be no equivocation on that score. Fusion did not lessen the nationalist drum beat for empire. If anything, it made it more insistent and bombastic. In an article, entitled, "*La lotta della nazione*" ("The Nation's Battle"), appearing in the widely read Fascist review, *Gerarchia* (*Hierarchy*), Corradini submitted that "Nationalism, Fascism, and Imperialism are the same thing" because of Italy's primacy and proletarian status. If Federzoni had been inexplicably dropped from Mussolini's cabinet in December 1928, the inevitable chagrin did not deter him from publicizing, like Corradini and Coppola, Italy's imperialist calling. In 1928, the Kellogg-Briand Pact was signed by all the major powers, including Italy. It pledged the signatory states to renounce war as "an instrument of national policy." Having perceived that Italy had no choice but to sign the document, Coppola then scathingly and sarcastically dubbed "the law to outlaw war" as the most flagrant piece of sophistry concocted by the liberal-democratic mentality. It was a reactionary device of the United States, Britain, and France, to perpetuate the *status quo*, designed to protect their huge empires while disarming late arrivals like fascist Italy and preventing Italians from finding their rightful place in the world.

Autarchia (Autarchy), the means of realizing economic self-sufficiency, was another way by which to ready the country for its coming encounter with destiny. It became fascist Italy's stated policy in March 1936 over the Ethiopian war. Already, however, by 1925, Italy was being set in the direction of a stern economic nationalism. Proletarian Italy had no other choice. The drive to increase grain production, given high priority in the so-called "Battle for Wheat" symbolized the citizens' will and single-mindedness of purpose in all phases of the autarchical program. Self-reliance in agricultural production led to similar rigorous measures in other fields. Dependence on foreign sources of critical materials had to be reversed. Introduction of domestic substitutes, *ersatz* as in Germany, alleviated many shortages. Stockpiling was instituted. A prized by-product was that Italians were being taught to sacrifice, labor, serve, make do, even do without, if need be, for priority number one—the fascist state. Coppola saw enough stamina, vitality, unanimity, and inspired leadership to be convinced that Fascist Italy was girding itself for world power. (*See reading No. 51.*)

If the conquest of Ethiopia, October 3, 1935 to May 9, 1936, was a test case for Fascist Italy, it passed with flying colors. Even if the herd psychology whipped up by authoritarian regimes is taken into consideration, there is no doubt that nearly all the populace related to the myths and values which underlay the fascist state and that they inwardly believed they were adhering to fascism on their own volition. Among the many immigrant centers in North Africa, and North and South America, stories of repression were discounted as fabrications, politically inspired, or merely incidental. What came up in bold relief was order, national pride, military prowess, closing-of-ranks, perseverance—in sum, the qualities which spell victory and which Italians had lacked, whose realization were credited to Mussolini and fascism.

The war for Ethiopia had many functions to serve. Comprising 450,000 square miles, or four times Italy's size, Ethiopia had space to spare for Italy's teeming population, as Turiello, Oriani, and Crispi had averred, and sizeable stores of mineral wealth to supplement the meager fare nature had bequeathed Italy. It would compensate for Ouchy and erase the stinging memories of Custozza, Lissa, Dogali, and Adowa. Primitive, Ethiopia would allow Italy to resume her civilizing mission. Sectors of the Catholic Church reacted favorably, as they had over Libya, and many high and low officials bestowed blessings on the armed forces and the Italian people. In many church and lay centers, Rocco's hopes for a state-church alliance for Italian expansion assumed momentary reality. The overseas dimensions and the complicated diplomatic, military, logistic, terrain, and climatic obstacles, together with the Ethiopians' resistance, were exactly what Nationalists had ordered to vindicate the Italians' national self-consciousness. Clever to the core, Mussolini utilized Corradini's theory of proletarian nationalism to give to his people the supreme meaning of what they were about in Ethiopia and to put the Western Democracies on the moral defensive. (*See Reading No. 52.*) Because Italy triumphed in spite of the economic boycott of fifty-two states, victory was *prima facie* evidence of the nationalist fervor in which soldiers and civilians had personally committed themselves to the challenge. Such was the pull exercised by nationalism that Mussolini who as a Socialist had derogated the flag as "a rag to be planted on a dunghill" was now as a fascist regaled as the leader who had hoisted the national colors, green, orange, white, over Ethiopia. With Ethiopia added to Libya, Eritrea, and Italian Somaliland, Italy was assembling an impressive African empire. Strategy called for linkage of Libya with the three colonies comprising Italian East Africa.

MUTUAL DISENCHANTMENT. The state's and party's respective roles, which had been from the beginning a major bone of contention between Nationalists and Fascists, had remained unresolved. If anything, the problem had become more insidious and exchanges more heated. Fascist radicals accused Federzoni of muzzling the party with legalitarian measures and Rocco of sabotaging fascism's essence with a syndical-corporative state of rightist orientation. Nationalism's prewar recommendation for cartels and industrial combinations was neither circumstantial nor temporary but an integral and permanent facet of its exclusive business mentality. What they had feared and warned against from the first had been borne out. Nationalism had inveigled itself into Fascism and derailed it from its original course, that of being a genuine revolutionary force for economic opportunity and social justice. Nationalists reciprocated with their own recriminations. Assisted by conservative Fascists, they decried the left Fascists' opposition to their idea of the organic state. They lamented the absence of a central theme. The regime was fast stagnating. Enforced indiscriminate ideological conformity was no substitute for moral cohesion. The cadres which were to train and be mentors of the new ruling class were not forthcoming. No generation of competent and devoted public servants was being produced. Nationalists grieved because left Fascists led by Panunzio openly discussed the possible abolition of the monarchy as an integral aspect of the evolving fascist state. Resentment focused on Mussolini's dictatorship, which was rapidly reaching ridiculous and monstrous proportions. As much as they must share blame for the development, it is difficult to see Nationalists as abiding psychophants of the *Duce*. Mussolini's many maneuvers and sudden cabinet changes had Nationalists conjure Fascist Italy as one huge principality, in which the Duce was titular overlord, but at the price of tolerating many local party and bureaucratic enclaves of power at the public welfare's expense.

How logical and ironic that Corradini should have been the first one known to vent his spleen against the sordid state of affairs. Notes discovered on his desk at his death, December 11, 1931, revealed his revulsion over the personal despotism and partiocracy which had emerged. It was a crude and inefficient variant of Giolitti and *Giolittismo*. Corradini's distempers and the baring of his feelings are not surprising, because his love was exclusively for Italy and the Italians, however questionably formulated. Corradini's biting and negative observations were immediately brought to Mussolini's attention. Although Mussolini in his Senate eulogy extolled the Florentine as "a Fascist of the very first hour," the last minute curtailment of announced plans for statewide commemoration indicated that old wounds had been reopened. Nationalist grumbling became more pronounced, even though, like Corradini's, it was muted and restricted to personal reflections and private gatherings. (*See Reading No. 53.*)

Confronted by the challenge, and for other reasons as well, Mussolini chose his dictatorial rule and the party as the main line of defense. He publicly stated that the party was an indispensable organ of the fascist regime. To underscore the point, on December 12, 1931, he relieved the former nationalist Giovanni Giuriati, and brought in the ultimate subaltern, Achille Starace, who remained as general secretary in 1939. Although the move was effected the day after Corradini's death, it had been pending and not necessarily connected with Corradini's hostile remarks. Building on Farinacci's prior efforts, Starace compiled a unique set of gestures and rituals, called *Costume e Mistica Fascista*

(Fascist Customs and Myths). They elevated Mussolini, the *Duce*, into a veritable cult figure. Whenever he appeared in public, he was accompanied by hordes of party functionaries who shouted his praises. This, together with Starace's all-out use of the party to enforce fascism, filled the Nationalists, and most Italians, with disgust.

Mussolini tried to put distance between prominent Nationalists and himself. Rocco, in July 1932, was relieved of his duties as minister of justice, with no explanation offered for the departure of the individual who has been universally declared to be "the legislator" of the fascist regime. Federzoni went to the Senate on November 28, 1928, and was its president from April 10, 1929 until March 15, 1939. On March 7, 1938, he became president of the Italian Academy, and served until July 1943. It is apparent that while Mussolini felt compelled to move such frontline Nationalists from the major seats of power, he still relied on their connections with critical segments of Italian society. Alfieri, named ambassador to the Holy See on October 29, 1939, was lifted on May 13, 1940, at Hitler's personal request, and sent to Berlin, where he remained a faithful executor of the *Duce*'s will until the Grand Council's meeting, July 24–25, 1943. Suvich served as undersecretary for foreign affairs from August 1932, and was a reliable spokesman for a more independent foreign policy. When Ciano assumed the foreign ministry portfolio, July 9, 1936, Suvich was prevailed upon to accept the ambassadorial post in Washington, where, it was believed, his relations with international trade would prove beneficial to Italy.

Dissension between Nationalists and Fascists was attenuated by the Ethiopian conquest. While it gave Fascism a reprieve, victory was very costly. Although human losses were not heavy, 400,000 men were sent to East Africa, supported by hundreds of airplanes, thousands of trucks, tractors, tanks, rifles, machine guns, artillery pieces, and millions of rounds of ammunition. The empire having been created, time, money, and manual resources in large quantities were needed to open Ethiopia up to colonists and extractive industries. By 1939, 130,000 Italians dwelt in Ethiopia and Eritrea, hardly the number Nationalists had originally expected to relocate to the Italian African colonies. What is also clear is that the considerable number of men and huge financial outlays deployed in Africa stood to be denied to the home land. Furthermore, Fascist Italy decided over Ethiopia on a venturesome course in foreign policy, which proved impossible to check. It demonstrated a tragic incapacity to order priorities.

The emergence of the Rome-Berlin Axis described the growing intimacy between Fascist Italy and Nazi Germany, following the latters' political and material assistance for Ethiopia. By the Convention of October 25, 1936, Germany recognized Italian sovereignty over Ethiopia, and the two powers agreed to draw up an economic treaty and to pursue identical objectives toward the League of Nations and Communism. On November 6, 1937, Italy joined the Anti-Comintern Pact, entered in by Germany and Japan, November 25, 1936. It called for consultation and unified action against the Third Communist International and had the effect of extending the Rome-Berlin Axis to Tokyo. In cooperation and competition with Germany, Italy intervened in the Spanish Civil War in favor of General Francisco Franco's Insurgents against the Loyalist forces backed by the Soviet Union. Involvement began in July 1936, within two months of the Ethiopian annexation. This, added to the outlays required by Ethiopia, stretched Italy's commitments to a dangerous point. All told, between 50,000 and 75,000 Italian soldiers saw action in Spain, and Italy sent ninety-one warships and submarines. Military success could not nullify the fact that the price of participation was $410,000,000, that 4,000 Italians had been killed, 4,000 wounded, 800 captured, and that 4,000 Anti-Fascist emigrés had fought in the international brigades. The general undermining of Italy's international position was dramatically revealed by Germany's uncontested absorption of Austria on March 13, 1938. German troops were now encamped on the Alpine frontier.

DEFEAT AND OVERTHROW. Nationalist attitude toward the Second World War, which began on September 1, 1939, appears to be uneven and indecisive. Italy would welcome a nationalist-imperialist-ideological conflict which would prove once and for all fascism's superiority over democracy and communism, and which would reclaim for Italy Nice, Savoy, Corsica, and gain Malta, Tunisia, Egypt, British and French Somaliland, and allow the reorganization of Europe on a corporative basis. Italy's mission was sufficiently expansive to include the destruction of atheistic communism, a possibility most inviting to Catholics and the church. Still, in spite of the nationalist myths of war, empire, and their exaltation of Fascist Italy as the Second, Third, or Fourth Rome, it is conceivable that Nationalists would not have found it contradictory to their maxim of Italy First had they preferred neutrality or entrance in the war on the side of the Western Democracies against Nazi Germany. They had faced a similar situation in 1914–15. The Pact of Steel between Nazi Germany and Fascist Italy, signed May 22, 1939, could be made to suffer the same fate as the Triple Alliance. The conservative Fascist Grandi, ambassador to Great Britain from 1932 to 1939, minced no words in the Grand Council in refuting the status of "non-belligerence" decided by Mussolini for the opening phase of the war. He drew an analogy between Germany's behavior in 1939 and Austria's in 1914. Germany, he charged, had violated the Pact of Steel by going immediately to war, a step which the alliance forbad for three years as a concession to Italy's need for additional time for preparation. If he urged renunciation of the pact, there is no evidence Nationalists bestirred themselves in behalf of Grandi's counsel. In Liberal Italy, 1914–15, Nationalists had the vigor, independence of thought, and concern for the fatherland to campaign for the abrogation of the Triplice and war against Germany and Austria. By 1939, thanks to nationalist-fascist Italy, the vigor and independence of spirit had vanished, and concern for the fatherland had withered.

As *Duce* and dictator, Mussolini alone undertook the decision for war. Based on unlimited confidence in Germany's ability to strike hard and fast and a dismally low evaluation of Britain's and France's capacity for endurance, Mussolini concluded that the conflict would be over within a year. He needed, he said, a couple of hundred fatalities to get him a seat at the peace table. Other motives may have been his personal resentment for having been overshadowed by the upstart, Hitler, and deep apprehension, as in 1914, that neutrality would summon a victorious Germany's revenge. Nationalists must shoulder a major part of the responsibility for Mussolini's personal determination, for, from the fascist's regime inception, they had done their utmost to strengthen the premier's powers and position at the expense of such important institutions as the Crown, Court, Council of Ministers, Fascist Grand Council, and parliament. Although Victor Emmanuel was consulted, the king, it is reported, raised serious objections, but in the end went along with the *Duce*'s desires. Surmising or hoping that the nationalist theory of proletarian nationalism had enough compelling influence, Mussolini deferred to it in the rationale he offered his people for their involvement in the Second World War, on June 10, 1940. (*See Reading No. 54.*)

The war was anything but swift and productive. Italian armed forces suffered one crushing defeat following another. If Italians could relate to proletarian nationalism during the wars for Libya and Ethiopia, they could not in this war. The war was senseless, foolhardy, divisive, and most demoralizing, as Federzoni lamented. (*See Reading No. 55.*) As Fascist Italy's misfortunes multiplied and the war was brought home to Italy proper through the Allied invasion of Sicily on July 10, 1943, the Councillors prevailed on an unsuspecting *Duce*, and had him convoke the Grand Council in special session, held through the night and morning of July 24–25. After heated discussions, Federzoni and Alfieri voted with the majority nineteen, against seven opposed, and two abstentions, for the Grandi-Bottai-Ciano Resolution, which urged return to constitutional government, and Victor Emmanuel taking command of the armed forces and active direction of the state. This move set in motion a chain reaction which led to the overthrow of Mussolini and Fascism. The Anti-Fascist Resistance burst forth. In his memoirs, Grandi relates that Federzoni was a constant source of encouragement in the appeals for drastic change he personally transmitted to the king and other highly placed individuals. On September 3, 1943, the Marshal Pietro Badoglio government accepted the Allies' unconditional surrender terms for liberated and occupied Italy. A month later, Italy declared war on Germany, and achieved co-belligerent status. A peace treaty was signed on February 10, 1947.

It is recalled that Mussolini and fascism were toppled because of wartime difficulties and not due to peacetime revolt. We are reminded of the probability that a sizable number of Nationalists, of lower and intermediate rank, were among the thousands who perished with the Salò Republic, Mussolini's pro-Nazi,

Neo-fascist regime in the north. Like their fascist colleagues, they chose death out of loyalty to the *Duce*, to fascism, with their dreams of a nationalist-fascist Italy still vibrant in their hearts. Because of their vote in favor of unseating Mussolini, Alfieri and Federzoni were tried in absentia by the Salò Republic Verona Trials, in January 1944, and condemned to death for high treason. Within Free Italy, or in Italian immigrant colonies abroad, there was nothing even remotely comparable to the Mazzinian Society of New York, 1938, or the Garibadlian International Alliance, formed in Mexico City, November 1941. There was no apparent interest to perpetuate the memory of nationalist and fascist leaders and their ideals. Among the many political parties, the Italian Social Movement is the one entry which harks back to Italy's fascist past. It was founded by Giorgio Almiranti in Rome, December 1946, Almiranti having served as head of cabinet in Fernando Mezzasoma's ministry of popular culture of the Salò Republic. With 40 Deputies out of a total of 630, it speaks for the preservation of fascist and nationalist values. It was unsuccessfully monarchist, for the retention of colonies, in favor of a strong military apparatus, and against proportional representation. Of late it has been for ethnic pride, defense of Italian culture, independence in foreign policy, prochurch, and against divorce, abortion, and women's demands for equal rights.

What remained of Nationalism? Fascism? Gone was the repressive, one-party, rightist corporativist state. Gone was the *Duce*, the magnetic leader. The monarchy was also banished by the referendum of June 2, 1946. Mazzini's republic was thereby assuming political reality. Lost were all of Italy's overseas possessions. Strict limitations were placed on the country's military establishment and Italy had to pay $350,000,000 in reparations to her former enemies. In April 1949, Italy became a charter member of the North Atlantic Treaty Organization and allowed Naples to become the naval command of NATO's Mediterranean fleet. She has permitted the United States to establish air and nuclear bases on her soil and received $1,515,000,000 in economic assistance from the same between 1948 and 1952. Italy hosted the talks which led to the Pact of Rome, February 23, 1953. It created the European Economic Community, a way station on the road to the Common Market, and, along with

NATO, a major step toward eventual European union. The Mazzinian vision as articulated in his Young Europe was being gradually realized. Republican Italy is loosing the close and confessional ties between the Catholic Church and the state, and is negotiating treaties with her Protestant and Jewish religious minorities for the full exercise of their constitutional liberties. With 900,000 Africans, Middle Easterners, and Asians, Italy, for centuries a nation of emigrants, is currently attracting immigrants of her own. In spite of the south's lagging economic growth, International Monetary Fund studies predict that by the year 2000 Italy will most likely be the world's third economic power, behind the United States and Japan.

Nationalists, as well as Fascists, would have adjudged foreign aid as a handout, the offspring of a supplicant's mentality. They would have condemned participation in multilateral security arrangements and international economic cooperation as rank servility, the abnegation of Italy's singular greatness and uniqueness, the transforming of the Italian republic into an American client state. This was abject subjugation to alien forces all over again. Most likely, they would never have admitted that true and permanent progress could be registered under the aegis of the liberal-democratic state and would certainly have branded Italy's sharply rising standard of living as illusory and outlandishly materialistic. Because peaceful and individual efforts were antithetical to natural and historical laws, all such alleged accomplishments were bound to be evanescent. The grant to Sicily of a form of regional autonomy, Red Brigade terrorism, and right-wing violence would have been underscored by the Nationalists as indisputable proof that Italy was not yet one and united, but even more dangerously divided than ever before. Foreign athletes playing on Italian sports teams frequently comment that Italians as participants and spectators do not approach the games from a purely professional point of view, or for love of the sport, but for *campanilismo*, the visceral satisfaction experienced in observing the home squad defeat Rome, or Turin, Milan, Genoa, Venice, Pisa, Bologna, Naples, Catania, or Palermo. One severe and protracted economic depression or a major political crisis and Italy would be crushed and would disintegrate.

What contribution did proletarian and imperialist nationalism make to Mussolini and fascism? Nationalism gave Mussolini and fascism what they requested, the men and ideas, which were elaborated into institutional structures and governmental policies. Without the timely and extensive assistance of the Nationalists, Mussolini would not have been able to organize his administration effectively, normalize the fascist takeover, and remain at the helm for two decades. Without nationalism, Mussolini and fascism would have rapidly deteriorated into another one of the many ministerial crises which had troubled postwar Italy. For nationalism, fascism offered it the opportunity to advance from a modest exercise of influence to a vigorous attempt to give practical life to its more salient political, social, economic, and imperialist theories.

Examining the phenomenon of proletarian and imperialist nationalism in broad perspective, there were legitimate historical reasons why it arose. Nationalism was disposed to fill a void—to give Italians a sense of ethnic pride and national purpose, tackle the problems of emigration and alleged cultural decline, improve living conditions, adopt a more realistic foreign policy, achieve moral and spiritual solidarity, essentials of the well-ordered state which liberation and unification, understandably, could not adequately address. For the possibilities and the lurking nemesis, there is the judgment of an Italian academician rendered in 1905, in connection with Corradini's *Regno*. (*See Reading No. 56.*)

PART III

READINGS

READING NO. 1

ITALY'S STRATEGIC POSITION DIVINELY ORDAINED*

Italy's geographic centrality and its consequent unique role as determined by the divine scheme was articulated by the former priest, ex-Piedmontese statesman, and proponent of the confederationist solution of the problem of Italian unification, Vincenzo Gioberti (1801–1852).

γ   γ   γ

Because of its location, the peninsula is the moral center of the civilized world. . . . Providence selected two civilizations which emerged from the messages announced by Noah and Christ. They developed between two bodies of water in order to facilitate their diffusion throughout the world. Just as the first was born between the two rivers, the renewed and more advanced civilization arose between two seas: the former in fertile Mesopotamia, between the Tigris and the Euphrates, from which it spread rapidly to Asia, Africa, and our West; the latter in Italy, between the Tyrrhenian and Adriatic, which, due to Italy's considerable extension from Central Europe, puts Italy in the privileged position of dominating the rest of the hemisphere. . . . Only she can give mankind all the benefits of civil society. Having been the creator, preserver, and redeemer of European Civilization, Italy is destined to become universal. Therefore, she deserves the title of mother nation of mankind.

---

*Dal primato morale e civile degli italiani (3 vols., Brussels, 1843), I, 42, 46–47.

READING NO. 2

ATTACK AGAINST PROVINCIALISM*

Regional suspicions and the resulting social-cultural animosity infuriated many Italians, including Gino Rinaldo d'Carli.

γ γ γ

The day before yesterday a Stranger entered [Demetrio's] store and . . . requested to be served coffee. . . . Unfortunately, a young man named Alcibiade was sitting nearby. . . . He looked at the Stranger with an air of superiority; then he asked him if he was a foreigner. The foreigner quickly sized up the inquirer and in a tone of subdued scorn replied, "No Sir." "Are you then Milanese?" Alcibiade further inquired. "No Sir, I am not Milanese," the visitor added. The inquirer was surprised by such a reply, and well should he have been because all of us present were struck by this introduction and the dialogue which followed. After the surprise and the most sincere apologies for meddling, our Alcibiade asked the Stranger for an explanation. "I am Italian," responded the Stranger, "and an Italian in Italy, unlike a Frenchman in France, an Englishman in England, a Dutchman in Holland, etc., is never treated but as a foreigner." The Milanese [Alcibiade] unsuccessfully attempted to defend his line of inquiry by alluding to the custom everywhere in Italy of labelling a foreigner anyone who is not born or does not live within the immediate confines. But the Stranger interrupted him and continued, "Among the popular prejudices in Italy, there is a most singular one. . . . This bias may be described as the inscrutable genius of the Italian people of being inhospitable and of transforming themselves into their own worst enemies. . . . It certainly does not," he went on, "bring honor to an Italian thinker to meet everywhere scandalous reminders of being by nature or by nationality different from his neighbors, and to note that everyone greets one another with the salutation, *foreigner*.

*"*Della patria degli italiani* (The Italians' Fatherland)," *Il Caffè*, II (1765), 298–300, 302.

This is so flagrantly the case that there are in Italy as many foreigners as there are Italians. . . .

"How happy [the Stranger concluded] Italy would be if all our common inclination toward independence . . . were combined and directed toward one goal, that is the total good of the nation. . . . That being admitted, what difference really would there be found between Italian and Italian, if our origin, our talents, and the conditions be the same for all? And if there isn't any difference, for what reason is there in Italy such readiness among us to disparage each other, and for what reason is there in Italy such reluctance, not to say outright refusal, to believe that the good of the entire nation is not something odd?"

READING NO. 3

NEITHER IMPERIAL ROMAN, HOLY ROMAN, NOR ROMAN CATHOLIC, BUT ITALIAN*

As he opened the first parliamentary session of the Kingdom of Italy in Turin, April 2, 1861, King Victor Emmanuel II uttered the following declaration.

γ   γ   γ

MESSRS. SENATORS! MESSRS. DEPUTIES!

As we prepare to give [Italy] new ordinances, we dare not refer to old factions but to remember the service rendered by all to the common cause. All sincere parties are invited to emulate them so that we can achieve the fatherland's greatness and the highest standard of living for our people. Henceforth, [Italy] is no more the Italy of the Romans, neither is she the Italy of the Medieval Age; nor can she be any longer a field open to foreign ambitions. Rather, she is the Italy of the Italians.

*"The Inaugural Royal Session of 1861," *Atti parlamentari Discussioni della camera dei deputati*, VII Legislature (Session 1861–1863), (Turin, 1863), I, 1.

READING NO. 4

APPEAL FOR A LIBERATOR*

Machiavelli had thought of Pope Alexander VI or his son, Cesare Borgia, the Duke of Valentino, as a potential rescuer, only to have been disappointed.

γ   γ   γ

Having carefully considered the subject of the above discourse, and wondering within myself whether the present times were propitious to a new Prince, and whether there were elements that would give an opportunity to a wise and virtuous one to introduce a new order of things which would do honor to him and good to the people of this country, it appears to me that so many things concur to favor a new prince that I never knew a time more fit than the present.

And, if, as I said, it was necessary that the people of Israel should be captive so as to make manifest the ability of Moses; that the Persians should be oppressed by the Medes so as to discover the greatness of the soul of Cyrus; and that the Athenians should be dispersed to illustrate the capabilities of Theseus; then at the present time, in order to discover the virtue of an Italian spirit, it was necessary that Italy should be reduced to the extremity she is now in, that she should be more enslaved than the Hebrews, more oppressed than the Persians, more scattered than the Athenians; without head, without order, beaten, despoiled, torn, overrun; and to have endured every kind of desolation.

Although lately some spark may have been shown by one, which made us think he was ordained by God for our redemption, nevertheless it was afterwards seen, in the height of his career, that fortune rejected him; so that Italy, left as without life, waits for him who shall yet heal her wounds and put an end to the

---

The Prince, trans. and with an Introduction by W. K. Mariott (New York, 1908), pp. 205–206. Written in 1513.

ravaging and plundering of Lombardy, to the swindling and taxing of the kingdom and of Tuscany, and cleanse those sores that for long have festered. It is seen how she entreats God to send someone who shall deliver her from these wrongs and barbarous insults. It is seen also that she is ready and willing to follow a banner if only someone will raise it.

READING NO. 5

MAZZINI AND ITALY AS THE THIRD ROME*

Mazzini believed in the Italians' messianic calling. In the passage below, he urged them to combine unification with the freeing of all subject people and their inclusion within an international political system founded on liberty and justice.

γ　　　　γ　　　　γ

If she intends to become great, prosperous, and truly powerful, Italy must plant resolutely on her frontiers a banner that proclaims to the peoples: LIBERTY, NATIONALITY, and direct to that *end* every act of her international life. It is our third mission in the world. Rome and the Caesars unfolded with the Republic the idea of *political* unity, and when and where it was possible she realized it with her Legions' arms; the Rome of the Popes promoted the idea of *moral* unity and partly succeeded through the priests' and the believers' preaching; but neither one nor the other acknowledged—and they could not have then—the providential collective movement of the nations. . . . Rome of the People, of the Italian Nation, having faith in Progress, in Humanity's unified life, and in the special purpose of each nation, must hasten its fulfillment as its advocate and guide.

*Giuseppe Mazzini, "Missione italiana," *Scritti (Writings) di Giuseppe Mazzini, 1832–71* (Milan, 1921), pp. 58–59.

READING NO. 6

GIOBERTI INTRODUCES AND JUSTIFIES ITALY'S PRIMACY AND AN ITALIAN CONFEDERATION UNDER THE POPE*

Gioberti was an articulate spokesman of an Italian primacy. In the following passage, he involved pope and princes in the unification process and he expressed his expectations for united Italy, church, and mankind.

γ   γ   γ

. . .When it is affirmed that Italy is universal, supernatural, spiritual, priestly, creative, and so on, these varied gifts do not express properties as much as different facets of one attribute, that is of that primacy which is hers. . . . To express the same in one word, one can say that Italy is the supernation and the head people because there is eminently contained in her all those many elements of which the national genius of the various races consist, and make of the human species, not the least less than any individual, *an image and likeness of God*. . . . And what more beautiful spectacle can the mind of an Italian grasp than that of his fatherland, one, strong, powerful, devoted to God, compact and serene in herself, respected and admired by peoples? What more blessed future can be imagined? What happiness more desirable?. . . . I imagine her [Italy] mighty and of one soul, thanks to a stable and permanent alliance among her several princes which, by increasing each's strength in proportion to the other's addition, will elevate their armies into an Italian militia which will protect the peninsula's gates against foreign aggression. . . . I await the festive wonder when an Italian fleet will once again plough through the waves of the Mediterranean and the legitimate domination of the seas, usurped for many centuries, will return to the command of that powerful and generous race which cleared its [Mediterranean]

*Vincenzo Gioberti, *Del primato morale e civile degli italiani*, III, 156–157, 259, 262.

174

lanes and gave it its name. I see the eyes of Europe and the world fixed on this future, resurgent Italy. . . .

I see, finally, religion placed at the top of every human interest and the princes and the people vying in reverence and in love toward the Roman Pontiff, acknowledging and venerating him not only as Peter's successor, the Vicar of Christ and head of the Universal Church, but as the doge and standardbearer of the Italian Confederation, Europe's arbiter and peacemaker, spiritual father of the human race, the world's civilizer and stabilizer, the heir and natural and powerful builder of Latin greatness.

READING NO. 7

A SPUR TO RALLY ITALIANS BEHIND SAVOY'S CHARLES EMMANUEL I AGAINST SPAIN*

In 1614, the Duchy of Savoy went to war to oust Spain from Lombardy. In the excerpt below, the writer Alessandro Tassoni supported Duke Charles Emmanuel I's appeal to pope and princes to join in Italy's liberation from the foreign intruder, Spain.

γ　　　　　γ　　　　　γ

How long will we, Italian princes and gentlemen, . . . endure being downtrodden by the arrogance and conceit of foreign peoples who . . . confuse courtesy with cowardice? I speak to the princes and nobles. . . . All other people . . . have nothing more dear than their fatherland. They forget their hostility and hatred and unite to defend her against foreign depredations; indeed, dogs, wolves, lions inhabiting the same region, the same locality, the same forest, join together for the common defense; we Italians alone, so different from all other people and from all other animals, abandon our neighbor, abandon our friend, abandon our fatherland, to join with alien foes! What a sorrowful destiny for Italy this is!. . . .

What fear or hope can induce us to forsake the Duke of Savoy at such a momentous occasion, who is embattled for the reputation of the princes of Italy and for our common liberty, to submit to people, who instead of thanking us for our help hold us in no regard?. . . . Of whom do we have fear? That kingdom [Spanish] which once had a robust body is now exhausted by luxury . . ., and is now an elephant with the heart of a helpless wretch. . . . And if [Spain] succeeds to occupy Piedmont, to gain control of the door into Italy, and roam throughout [the peninsula], I am asking you Italian princes and nobles what hope

*Alessandro Tassoni, "*Filippiche contro gli spagnuoli,*" *Prose politiche e morali,* ed. Giorgio Rossi (Bari, 1930), pp. 341–342, 345, 351, 361. First published in 1614.

league against the Turk in favor of the Austrians and the Hungarians, more friendly to the Turks than to us; we are concerned with our very safety.

Chief Pontiff, Republic of Venice, Grand Duke of Tuscany, . . . Italian princes and nobles, do not be treacherous to yourselves. . . . Spain in herself is through. . . . Italy alone gives her assurance because she is at war with herself at the expense of the Duke of Savoy. . . . Take head of this brave prince [Charles Emmanuel], shame yourselves for your past fears, and combine your forces to his.

READING NO. 8

ECONOMICS AS A POSSIBLE LEVER FOR UNIFICATION*

In the following brief, almost parenthetical insertion, there is a guarded hint of an assumed centripetal spin-off resulting from expanded economic activity.

γ   γ   γ

. . . .If the liberty of commerce were to be extended from the narrow confines of each state to all Italy, what would be the consequences?

*Antonio Genovesi, *Lezioni di commercio ossia di economic politica* (3 vols.; Naples, 1766–67), II, 45.

READING NO. 9

ITALY'S LACK OF A CULTURAL CAPITAL DEPLORED*

The excerpt below is from "The Second Letter" of an anonymous English admirer of Italy, written to a Venetian acquaintance named Miladi.

γ   γ   γ

. . . .I cannot hide the fact that your literature annoys me more than that of any other people. . . . In Italy every province has a Parnassus, one style, its own taste, and one school in keeping with its local outlook, one league, one system of evaluation distinct from others. . . . Naples, Rome, Florence, Venice, Bologna, Milan, Turin, and Genoa are all capitals of a multitude of literatures. An author approved in one is criticized in another; and the greatest writer, the oracle of this province, is hardly mentioned in that one. . . .

It was bothersome to me not to be able to know Italy and where its essence was. Rome claims it civilized everyone. Its reputation is sufficient. Florence has the *Crusca* and has had the De Medici; Bologna is the mother of scholarship and has the university to prove it, which is the greatest of all institutions of higher learning; Turin, Padua, and Pisa have universities of their own; Venice boasts of more publishing houses and booksellers than any other city; but Naples and Genoa brag of their wealth, Milan of sumptuous dishes. . . . Each exalts its own tribunal, features its own literary parliament and exercises sovereign power in its district in matters of opinion as London does in England, Paris for France. To tell you the truth, I think that if Italy had one center, one point of reference, it would be far richer in the arts, in letters, and possibly also in the sciences, than any other people. . . .

---

*Saverio Bettinelli, "*Lettera seconda*," *Dodici lettere inglesi* (*Twelve English Letters*) (Venice, 1766), pp. 84–85.

READING NO. 10

REPUBLICAN UNITARY STATE PROPOSED*

In the following extract, the victorious Gioja of the Cisalpine Republic's essay contest offered a classic summary for the unification and incorporation of the peninsula into a comprehensive republic. To Mazzini, it was the only plan "since the French invasion which contemplated the political unity of the common fatherland."

γ   γ   γ

. . . .The disorders characteristic of independent republics and the inherent rivalry and reluctance to act in a confederation of republics invite Italy to be united in one indivisible republic. In fact, the nature of the Italian territory, whose internal parts are not separated by any natural obstacles; the climate which varies little from one end to the other; the prosperity of the cities situated in continent[al Europe]; the many rivers which facilitate rapid transportation of native and foreign products; our surpluses of every kind which provoked the cupidity of others and keep alive the temptation to invade; the many convenient ports; . . . the inability of any city to resist hostile forces alone, their schemes and ambitions; the solidarity that union can give the Italian masses, thereby making them the eternal shoals of would-be conquerors; the past experience which admonishes Italy that when divided it was prey for conquest and tyrannized by foreign nations; the state of depression in which our navy finds itself, which would become the guardian of our liberty were it to be revived by union; commerce which is everywhere arrested due to the thousands of impediments chargeable to the petty jealousies of small independent and rival states; that lack of confidence [and] indecision, that lingering unrest which follows

---

*Melchiorre Gioja, *Quale dei governi liberi meglio convenga alla felicità dell' Italia (Which Form of Free Government Suits Italy Best)?* (Milan, 1797), 269–271.

revolutions and tends to produce anarchy . . .; the intellect that extends itself in corresponds with the extension of its activity; the influence of political objectives which by eliminating passions destroys special interests and envy, parent of discord and seditions; similar customs which give public opinion direction and constitute its strength; identical language which assists in the communication of sentiments and reminds us of our origins; the same love for the arts, for crafts, for the sciences; the same defects, the same hopes, the same fears, in a word, the physical, moral, the political, everything, invite us to unite with the most intimate bonds in the bosom of one indivisible republic.

READING NO. 11

FOSCOLO CHALLENGES NAPOLEON
TO HIS HISTORIC DUTY*

In the winter of 1799, the poet despatched from Genoa his "Bonaparte Liberatore, Oda [Ode]." Excerpts from the preamble, "A [To] Bonaparte," are reproduced below.

γ   γ   γ

I am dedicating this ode to you . . . not to flatter you with your accomplishments but to show you by contrast Italy's misery, which rightfully awaits the restoration of the liberty by the individual who first announced it. . . . Because of your benevolence and because of your genius, which surpasses that of all others of our age, we have no choice but to appeal to you. You are obliged to help us not only because you are of Italian blood, and the revolution that occurred in Italy is your work, but to have the centuries forget that Treaty [Campo Formio] which bartered away my fatherland [Venice], stunned nations, and heaped reproach on your illustrious name. . . .

You are a great man and yet mortal, and you were born in an age in which universal wickedness places enormous obstacles in the way of magnanimous undertakings, while offering powerful inducements to do evil. Conscious of your superiority and aware of the desperateness of our situation, you might be tempted to take a path you inwardly dislike. Not even Caesar before he crossed the Rubicone aspired to be a dictator. In the most discouraging of time great revolutions have summoned forth tremendous courage and great ability. If you, aspiring to supreme rule, freely disregard the first [magnanimous undertakings], and, reaching for immortality, . . . you succomb to the second [powerful inducements to do evil], our century will find a Tacitus, who will commit your judgment to posterity's severest reprobation. Best wishes.

*Opere (Collected Works) (12 vols., Florence, 1888), I, 37–38.

READING NO. 12

MUTUALITY BETWEEN HIGH CULTURE AND A FREE AND UNIFIED STATE*

Requested by a Signor Ranieri de' Casalbigi to express his views on the theater and political society, Alfieri replied thusly.

γ　　　　γ　　　　γ

It is my strong belief that men must be educated by the theater to be free, courageous, gracious, to embrace virtue, and to be intolerant of every form of violence, to love their country, to be aware of their rights, and to be zealous, honorable and magnanimous in all their desires. . . . To have a theater in modern nations as in the past presupposes the existence of a true nation, not ten divided peoples who, though superficially united, have really nothing in common; . . . it assumes education, private and public culture, armies, commerce, navies, war, patriotism, the fine arts. . . . The best protection for the theater, as of every noble art and virtue, is a free people.

*Alfieri to Casalbigi (no date), *Opere* (11 vols., Turin, 1903), VII, 197–198.

READING NO. 13

ALFIERI'S BATTLE CRY FOR LIBERATION AND UNIFICATION*

The dramatist opened and concluded the Misogallo *with a dedication and a resolve. The components of hope, determination, personal sacrifice, intense dislike of anything un-Italian, and the strategic involvement of literature add up to make the* Misogallo *a signal document of the nationalist psychology.*

γ   γ   γ

To the Past, Present, and Future Italy . . .[,] the August Matron, for so long the principal seat of all human wisdom and values, and now disarmed, divided, despised, enslaved . . .; to Italy, which some day will undoubtedly rise again, virtuous, gracious, free and one. . . .

The day will arrive, the day will return, in which
Italians, alive again at last, will be bravely engaged
On the battlefield, and not with another's arms
In cowardly defense, but attacking the Gauls.
At their side two sharp spurs,
They will have, their pristine courage and my songs:
So that recalling what they were, and what I was,
They will burn with irresistible fire.
And armed then with that heavenly fury
Breathed into me by the words of their Fathers,
They will make my rhymes deadly to the Gauls.
Already I hear them say to me: Oh our dear Seer in wretched
Times born, yet you have created these
Sublime years, which you prophesied.

Il Misogallo (1797), *Opere*, IV, 103, 209.

READING NO. 14

LEOPARDI MOURNS FOR ITALY*

The poem, "All'Italia (To Italy)," consists of 140 lines in free verse. Thirty-eight are offered here.

γ   γ   γ

Oh my dear fatherland, I see the walls and the arches
And the columns and the monuments and the deserted
Towers of our forefathers
But the glory I do not see.
I do not see the laurel and the steel with which
Our ancient fathers were crowned. What an indictment.
Our face has fallen and our chest is bare.
Alas! how many wounds,
Bruises, blood stains! I see you as an obese
Woman! I implore heaven
And the world: tell me, tell me:
Who reduced her to such a pitiful condition? And this is worse,
Her arms are chained;
Her hair is disheveled and she is without veil
She sits in the gutter sad and abandoned,
Hiding her face
Between her knees, and weeps. . . .
Why? But why? Where is your ancient power?
Your arms, valor, constancy?
Who stole your sword?
Who betrayed you? By what trick and what deceit?
Or what force was able to remove your mantle and your wreath of
    gold?
How did you fall
From such heights to such a dismal abyss?

*Opere (5 vols., Milan, 1937), I, 137–138. Originally published in 1818, in Rome.

No one battles for you? None defends you
Of all your people? Arms, here the arms: I only
Will battle, will die for you.
Grant, Oh Heavens, that my blood
Will be fire in Italian breasts.
Where are your children?. . . .
Italy's youth? Oh gods, Oh gods:
Italian swords are drawn for other countries.
How sad is the lot befalling one who dies in war,
Not for his patriotic shores and for his chaste wife and his dear
    children,
But for the common enemy
For other people, and cannot say while dieing:
Blessed land of my birth,
The life you gave me I hereby return to you. . . .

READING NO. 15

A HOME SPUN REVOLUTION URGED*

Having exhaustively studied the Neapolitan revolution of 1799, Cuoco pointed to a number of lessons which, he hoped, would elicit the attention of Italian patriots.

γ   γ   γ

From the start the Neapolitan nation developed a frivolous mania for copying foreign ways. . . . A tailor in Naples would not know how to sew a suit unless the design had come from London or Paris. From the imitation of clothing habits, we went to social customs and manners and to the adoption of foreign languages. . . . Adoption of foreign languages brought with it the acceptance of foreign opinions. The rage to imitate foreign countries first weakens, then impoverishes, and finally ruins a nation, destroying in her every desire for her own things. . . . How many of us were democratic simply because the French were democratic?. . . .

The principles of the Neapolitan revolution would have been more known had they surged from the nation's depths. Taken from a foreign [French] constitution, they were very strange to us, based on concepts too abstract. They were alien to our instincts. . . . Since our revolution was a passive one, the only means for success was by winning the people's approval. . . . Among us patriots, . . . many paid lip service to the republic, many had it only in their heads, very few in their hearts. . . . What meaning did the phrase have that was incorporated in all the proclamations addressed to the people—"At Last You Are Free?". . . . People had no inkling of what liberty was. It is a

Saggio storico sulla rivoluzione napoletana del 1799, ed. Fausto Nicolini (Bari, 1913), pp. 28–29, 83, 90, 94, 104, 258, 323, 328. First published in 1804.

sentiment and not an idea; it must be demonstrated by facts, not explained in words. . . . Constitutions that endure are those which people formulate for themselves. . . . They must be made for people as they are and ever will be, imperfect, error prone. When a constitution fails, I blame its drafters in the same manner when a shoe does not fit I fault the shoemaker. . . .

READING NO. 16

YOUNG ITALY*

The unsuccessful conspiracies of the late 1820s and early 1830s convinced Mazzini that the Carboneria *was elitist and distant from the people. In July 1831, while in exile in Marseilles, he founded Young Italy as a more popular instrument of Italian unification.*

γ　　　　γ　　　　γ

Young Italy consists of the brotherhood of those Italians who believe in a law of *Progress* and of *Duty*; who are convinced that Italy is called to be a Nation—which can through her own strength make herself the same—that the short-comings of past efforts are not to be charged to intrinsic weakness, but to the ineffective direction of the revolutionary elements—that the surest of one's power is in perseverance and in the unity of effort—they consecrate, united in association, their thoughts and their action to the great objective of restoring Italy as a Nation of free and equal (citizens), *One, Independent, Sovereign*. . . .

Young Italy is republican and unitary. *Republican*—because, theoretically, a Nation's people are called, by divine law and humanity, to be free, equal, and brothers; and the republican institution is the only one which can guarantee those goals since sovereignty resides essentially in the nation, the only progressive and faithful interpreter of the supreme moral law. . . .

Young Italy is Unitary—because without Unity there is no true Nation—because without Unity there is no strength and Italy, surrounded by powerful and envious unitary nations, needs above all to be strong. . . .

Education and Insurrection are the means by which Young Italy intends to achieve its ends. . . .

*Mazzini, *Scritti edite e inedite [Published and Unpublished Writings]*, ed. G. Mazzini (2 vols., 1861), I, 107, 111–112, 114–115, 117.

Insurrection must present the initial program of the future united Italian Nationality. Wherever it occurs, it will feature the Italian flag, have Italian aims, use the Italian language—all destined to form one People. It will act in the name of the people and will depend on the people, hitherto ignored. It is destined to conquer all Italy. . . . Destined to rehabilitate Italy in the affection and its influence among peoples, it will act to validate its cause. . . .

Insurrections and revolts by bands are the [subject] People's wars, through which they emancipate themselves from foreign overlords. . . .

Young Italy's colors are *White, Red, Green.* Inscribed on the flag's colors are: *Liberty, Equality, Humanity*; on the reverse side: *Independence, Unity.* . . .

READING NO. 17

WHAT REMAINS TO BE DONE*

From his abode in France, the Neo-Guelph Gioberti surveyed the post 1848–1849 scene and offered his opinion on the nationalists' task.

γ   γ   γ

. . .In her Renewal, Italy must trust to the maximum in herself because the national conscience has arisen and only requires nourishment. . . . It would be folly to invite the anti-liberals, that is, the municipalists, and the puritans to the undertaking. The former are not comfortable with the new; in fact, they would want to return to the stultifying repression of earlier days. . . . The latter, who do not understand the *Risorgimento*, and wanting to curb it they lay waste to it, are even less in a position to understand the Renewal. Their arrogance, inexperience and absolute lack of foresight, their deficiency in practical judgment, the excessive reliance on their own counsels, their intolerance toward others, and above all their factious egoism, personal ambitions, and the corrupt doctrines they profess in their selection of means and ends, are such that wherever they are and whatever the circumstances, they can only ruin political undertakings. . . .

Therefore, there remains only the preparatory labor. Nursing of public opinion depends on the dialectical relationship between liberals and democrats. Neither one nor the other can succeed unless each assists the other in the enterprise. Only through their union could Italy develop a national political school which is bold and equal to the times; which discovers energy in moderation and knows how to be patient and ready according to the moment; which flees from the opposite exaggerations of the anxious and the cowardly; which is pregnant in

Del rinnovamento civile dell'Italia [Italy's Civil Renewal], ed. Fausto Nicolini (3 vols., 1911), III, 205–208. First published in 1851.

anticipation; knows how to initiate, pursue, achieve, to seize the opportunities and adopts them with confident prudence, irksome to the extremists' camp; which wins to itself those disillusioned and still teachable from the querelous factions, and above all the youth, more forthright by nature and more disposed to abandon unwise instructions and to accept sound ones; and for the last item can reconcile religion with culture and Catholic liberty with respect due higher authority. . . .

READING NO. 18

ITALIAN NATIONAL SOCIETY:
LIBERATION AND UNIFICATION
OF ALL THE PENINSULA*

The society was primarily the work of Daniele Manin and Giorgio T. Pallavicino. After Manin's decease on September 22, 1857, Pallavicino became president and the Sicilian revolutionary Giuseppe La Farina secretary, with Garibaldi vice president.

γ   γ   γ

I. Program

The Italian National Society declares: 'That it prefers the great principle of Italian Independence and Unification above the question of political organization and municipal and provincial interests; That it will be for the House of Savoy as long as the House of Savoy will be for Italy by every reasonable and possible means; . . . That it believes that Italian popular action is necessary to achieve Italy's independence and unification and that the Piedmontese government's cooperation is vital'. . . .
Political Creed

February 24, 1858

We place Italy's independence ahead of any question of form of government and of every municipal interest because our fatherland will never be able to enjoy the benefits of a civil order, and much less that of a republic, while one of her most cherished provinces [Lombardy-Venetia] and others lie directly or indirectly under Austria's hard and abusive rule. . . . Italian independence must be the hope, not only of public-minded men, but of all intelligent individuals. . . . Whoever therefore loves his

*Giuseppe La Farina, *Scritti politici*, collected by Ausonio Franchi (2 vols., Milan, 1870), II, 81–86.

fatherland, be he Constitutional [Monarchist] or Republican, an intellectual of laborer, educated in the sciences, or a tradesman, born in one or another province, in this or that Italian city, must want with us, above all, that the nation recover her lost independence. . . .

We place *Unification* along side *Independence*. It is impossible for any one who desires Italy's restoration of her independence to succeed without unifying all her energies. [It is also] impossible that her independence can be defended and survive without unifying her civil laws. It is also evident to all that the strength of the armed forces consists in large part in their unity; and all understand that an army of 100,000 soldiers, for example, is more powerful and costs less to maintain than ten armies of 10,000 soldiers each. . . .

For Italy to be strong, powerful, rich, prosperous, happy, it is necessary that she be independent and unified. The union of forces will give us independence; from independence will arise the liberty of which our nation is capable. . . . Everyone feels in his heart that Italy, sooner or later, will be one and independent, and even our enemies sense it. . . . When Napoleon was in exile on the island of St. Helena and could no longer be embarrassed by the trappings of personal power, he meditated on what he had seen and learned, and observed: 'Italy is one nation: Similarity of customs, language, literature will in the future more or less distant bring about the gathering of all her inhabitants into one State. . . . Rome is without doubt the capital which Italians will someday select.'

READING NO. 19

MAZZINIAN MISSION RE-EVOKED*

Victor Emmanuel II (1820–78) was the last king of Piedmont and the first of Italy. In the following section of his inaugural address of May 25, 1863 to the eighth legislature, he reflected on the past and thrust toward the future in a way that legislators and commentators thought gave new life to the democratic-republican dream of a continental crusade headed by Italy for national self-determination and an international order of free peoples.

γ   γ   γ

Senators! Deputies! I as King of Italy open this session. I thank you for your achievements during this hectic period of over two years. You affirmed the Nation's rights by the completion of her unity; I will know how to maintain those rights inviolate. . . . The new kingdom has been recognized by most of the Powers. Our voice in conjunction with theirs will be heard in devotion to the triumph of justice and the championing of the principles of liberty and of nationality.

*Discorsi della corona (Crown) al parlamento nazionale dalla I alla XX legislatura (Naples, 1897), p. 53.

READING NO. 20

A HISTORIAN DEFENDS CAVOUR AND THE RISORGIMENTO AGAINST DETRACTORS*

United Italy's failure to realize the grand promise of the Risorgimento *produced a major current of thought which blamed Cavour and the* Risorgimento *for the lack of fulfillment. In the following excerpt, a Cavourian scholar debunks their presumed shortcomings.*

γ   γ   γ

It is the statesman's responsibility to resolve the problems of his age, not those of the future, to which he contributes above all by creating newer reality which presents newer problems. Cavour contributed to the overcoming of his age by resolving the Italian question which had constituted one of the great themes of European life during the first half of the century on the same level with the revolutionary movements and international relations. . . . It was the creation of the Kingdom of Italy which made the Mazzinians' attempts to resurrect a new edition of 1848 in the years after 1860 impossible and outdated. . . .

In truth, that which [Cavour] possessed, and instead was missing in his successors, was that confidence in the country which permitted him in the span of two years to accommodate all the exponents of the national movement, and which was lost after Aspromonte and Mentana and the 1866 experiences. This was a loss to which the Left Liberals above everyone else did not resign themselves, predisposed to charge the responsibilities for the calamities or the misfortunes of the new kingdom to the mediocrity and weak idealistic bent of the Right Liberal leadership and to those Left Liberal sectors with which [the Right Liberals] had arranged a [political] understanding. This was the

---

*Rosario Romeo, *"Conclusione," Cavour e il suo tempo (Cavour and His Times), 1810–1861* (3 vols., Bari: Gius. Laterza & Sons, 1969-1984), III, 943, 945–946, 949–950. Courtesy of publisher.

Italy which thought to narrow the gap between what Italians had fought for and what they had obtained by appealing to the glamour of the ideal. It believed it could prevail until events of the first half of the nineteen hundreds, with the world wars and the totalitarian [Fascist] experiment, resulted in the complete dissolution of the *Risorgimento* heritage, now replaced, in the conduct of Italian life, by principles and criteria, fundamentally different.

READING NO. 21

FATE OF ITALY'S MISSION AND PRIMACY LAMENTED*

In the lines reproduced below, the restless genius Giovanni Papini, critic, journalist, novelist, poet, and social philosopher, expressed dismay over the Risorgimento's *unfinished business.*

γ　　　　γ　　　　γ

[Italy] was unified by sheer compromise. . . . There was *little nationality*, . . . and '*Italy will make herself*,' however famous, remained just a pharse. . . . But the *Risorgimento*'s most painful and doleful legacy is that it has not been completed, that it is a work left half done and for some time abandoned by all. The *Risorgimento* was not, at least not in the propositions of the greatest minds that conceived them, only a political movement. In Mazzini's and Gioberti's minds, Italy's unification had its justification in a civilizing and cultural mission which our country was to unfold in the world. But, having realized unity and independence, this spiritual promise, this ultimate objective of Italian resurrection, was little by little forgotten by all, even by those who have the audacity to label themselves Mazzinians. The national program's most noble part was ignored.

---

*"*Il mestiere dell'Italia e il sogno d'una grande missione* (Italy's Profession and the Dream of a Great Mission)," *Giornale d'Italia* (Rome), August 31, 1906.

READING NO. 22

BRIGANDAGE IN THE NEAPOLITAN PROVINCES*

Refusal to submit to the unitary regime, dramatized by outbreaks of banditry, moved the Chamber to authorize an investigation. Excerpts are from the Commission of Inquiry's Report, 1863.

γ γ γ

The primary causes of brigandage are the background factors, and first among these is the social question. The peasant's economic status, especially in those provinces where brigandage has reached the densest level, is most unsatisfactory. . . . The tiller of the soil has no bond that ties him to the land. His lot is the same of that of the propertyless, and even were his wages to be raised, his economic situation would not necessarily improve.

Extreme poverty alone would not probably cause such pernicious effects were it not related to the other evils produced by the Bourbons' disastrous rule. . . . These evils are ignorance, zealously preserved and extended, superstitution, accepted and diffused, and, most importantly, the absolute absence of confidence in the system of justice and the law. . . .

The war against brigandage from May 1, 1861 to March 31, 1863 has resulted in the following losses to our army: . . . 21 officers and 286 enlisted men killed, that is 307 fatalities. . . . The toll of wounded is 5 officers and 81 enlisted personnel, in all 86. During this period, 6 soldiers were taken prisoners by the desperados; 19 soldiers have not been heard from. The losses suffered by the brigands are as follows: . . . 1,038 executed, 2,413 killed in battle, a total 3,451 deaths, and 2,768 ar-

*Giuseppe Massari and Stefano Castagnola, *Il brigandaggio nelle provincie napoletane* (Naples, 1863), pp. 14–5, 32, 118, 121–122.

rested. . . . The approximate number of brigands who died,
were apprehended, or voluntarily surrendered was 7,151. . . .

Brigandage is real war, indeed it is the worst type of warfare
imaginable; it is a battle between barbarism and civilization; it is
rapine and murder lifting the standard of rebellion against civil
society.

READING NO. 23

ITALY'S MESSIANIC ORIGINS RECERTIFIED*

In January 1863, the Poles revolted against Russia. Left Liberals desired to question Foreign Minister Giuseppe Pasolini on Italy's official attitude. He declined the invitation. On February 9, Crispi spoke out.

γ   γ   γ

I understand that the conditions of our country, or rather the conditions in which the King's Government has placed itself, are such that it is almost impossible for it to announce to the Chamber that it is determined to inaugurate the policy of freedom toward worthy people which should form the basis of Italian foreign policy. Our Government has denied its origins which is one of revolution. It has forgotten that we are arisen in the interest of the principle of nationality, that we are a people who had vindicated itself in liberty after many centuries of slavery, and that all the nations, which are in the same situation in which Italy found herself, must have our help, lest our own cause run the danger of perishing. . . . There are two policies: the official policy, cautious, also fearful, the Government unable to break the ties which it must maintain with a number of northern powers, and the people's policy. [The people] are ignorant of diplomacy and as a consequence they gloriously and instinctively can, indeed they must, neither accept nor respect the treaties which tore Poland to shreds. . . .

---

*Excerpted from Francesco Crispi, "*Polonia*," *Discorsi parlamentari* (3 vols., Rome, 1915), I, 292–294.

Let us recall, gentlemen, that the Poles after 1830 sought refuge throughout Europe, shedding their blood for the cause of all the peoples who would strike a blow for freedom. Let us recall that they fought in the south for Italian unity and that we, gentlemen, ought to repay them for the sacrifice and blood shed for us. If the Government cannot and will not, it ought at least leave the people free to do their duty.

READING NO. 24

MAZZINI REPUDIATES THE KINGDOM OF ITALY*

In August 1871, the Mazzinian republican democratic national-ist Carlo Bini died. Invited by the Young Italy Livornese Brother-hood to participate in the official mourning, Mazzini declined and gave the following explanation.

γ   γ   γ

Citizen. Because of ill health and other reasons it is impossi-ble for me to assist at the commemorations planned in honor of Carlo Bini. But even in the absence of those reasons, I do not keep from you that I would hesitate to become involved. What would await me? Silent and broken among the brothers inter-ested in paying a tribute of love to a noble soul taken from our more deserving life, I would be nothing but a discordant note. . . . And you must, rather than complain about me, con-sole me. Perhaps the years and disillusionment have produced within me a sense of severe melancholy which inures me against the more normal feelings of my brothers. But I glance at the Italy that is, I remember the Italy for which Carlo Bini and those who gave and wore themselves out, I think at the little which he accomplished, at the nothing which we today do to realize that ideal, and I hold myself unworthy to relate to the period honored by our dead. . . .

The idea [for which we fought] was that of an Italy risen from the grave through her people's virtue and sacrifice, purified of every defect by an expiation which endured for more than three centuries, resplendent in faith and zeal, strong in the awareness of the battles won and of exploits wrought with her own blood,

*Guiseppi Mazzini, *Scritti edizione nazionale (Writings, National Edition)*, Third Series, Vol. XCII, *Scritti politici*, Vol. XCI, *Epistolario (Correspondence)*) (Imola, 1941), 159–162.

just like an angel crowned with a double baptism of past and future glory, a messenger to the nations of the good news of a coming age of justice and love. . . .

Whether satisfied or sorrowful, today we represent a lie of Italy. . . . The people who had arisen, excited and expectant of marvelous deeds as they contemplated the resurgence of the ancient masters of the world, in disillusionment search elsewhere, and declare among themselves: "this is but a phantasm of Italy."

Goodbye. Yours, Gius. Mazzini.

READING NO. 25

ORIANI INDICTS PARLIAMENTARY DEMOCRACY AND SUMMONS ITALY TO MISSIONARY DESTINY*

Against the backdrop of defeat at Dogali and the Crispi government's decision to reopen the Abyssinian conflict, the novelist and political writer Alfredo Oraini (1852–1909) penned a commentary, extracted below.

γ   γ   γ

. . . .All Italy's millenial strivings to constitute herself a nation, the blood of her heroic activity, and the many tragedies experienced in her great history were now tending to this day when [Italy as an] immortal protagonist was re-entering history, to sail once again on the high seas as the carrier of a new civilization, after having isolated herself within her own territory. Without a doubt, the people sensed the hour's greatness. Trembling with inexpressible emotions, they thronged to the port, greeting warmly the soldiers who were returning to Africa. Yes, they were returning to Africa because the war between Italy and Africa has lasted 3,000 years, and Italy already had deposed Hannibal. . . .

But parliament and government, the one more debased than the other, did not comprehend at all the momentous significance of the expedition. . . . Italy's triumphal entry into contemporary world history was changed into an entrance of stealth, with Italy unconscious of herself, and with excessive worries for her powerful neighbors who were envious of her. What should have been a moment of glory became a moment of shame. Garibaldi, Mazzini, and all the revolution's heroic personalities were dead; a vulgar democracy perverted their character and genius into the

---

*Fino a Dogali (Until Dogali) (1889), Opera omnia (Collected Works) (Bologna, 1923), VII, 334–339, passim.

most vile interpretations. There was no desire for a war with Africa. . . .

Since Italy has been twice the world's center and has been resurrected today as a nation, it cannot withdraw from this universal civilizing labor. . . . The reason for the third Italian reappearance has not been sufficiently investigated. Evidently, history did not permit it for the sole interests of the Italians, having denied the same to many other people which disappeared in other ages. If Italy has again become a nation, the secret of this historical phenomenon lies in the need world history has of her toil and in the capacity of our people to meet it. Having forsaken the great revolutionary spirit, democracy did not understand the meaning of the African campaign. . . . The African undertaking was for Italy the first consequence of her *Risorgimento*.

READING NO. 26

PLEA FOR AN ITALIAN COLONIAL EMPIRE*

Pasquale Turiello (1836–1902) fought in the wars of unification. Lawyer by training, he also became a teacher, journalist, and political polemicist. Here is a sample of the thinking that made him the most consistent exponent of imperialism of his day.

γ   γ   γ

We therefore believe and confess that it is only our new generation's indolence and laxity which is responsible for the fact that soon after the conquest of Rome Italy finds herself with no ideals and political tasks worth pursuing. By contrast, history universally teaches that it is the glory and destiny of all virile nations to expand beyond their boundaries once they have acquired independence. . . . The day we restrict ourselves between the Alps and the sea, we would within these limits soon find ourselves increasingly pressed by foreign pressures, based on power, population, commerce. . . . From North Africa to the Plata [Brazil], many parts of Italy are already located outside Italian geographic confines. This represents our nationality's greatest vulnerability. The risk of servitude is not only as in Trent and Trieste today or within Italy as she was occupied in the past. Our blood in involved. Indeed the risk is greater, for it threatens, if forgotten, the total loss of our sensibilities as Italians. Even more than a legal right, we must develop a civil and political responsibility toward our own no matter where they live and have relocated themselves. We must find, rescue, and immediately unite them to us with every means possible. . . .

The most natural and available remedy for the dangers described lies indeed in the possibility of a broad extension of the Italian race onto Africa's most salubrious plateaus. Our race is

*Pasquale Turiello, *Governo e governanti in Italia* (*Government and the Governed in Italy*) (2 vols., 2nd ed.; Bologna, 1889), I, 35–37, 41–43.

probably the most adaptable of all the European races to a variety of climates. Occupation of half of the Abyssinian high lands and its division among several million of our families would be sufficient. . . .

In conclusion, the future for the Italian race appears ominous, since it is the nation which requires more than any other its own lands. Meanwhile it is the slowest to acquire them, while more than 1,000,000 Italians live outside the fatherland, under constant alien domination which wants to deprive them of their ethnicity. Depending on our country's decision to meet the challenge in time, our race will be able to compete or not with those few peoples that have similar birthrates and like potential. . . .

READING NO. 27

"WHITHER ARE WE HEADED?"*

The question of national goals was raised in 1900 by Sidney Sonnino, leader of the conservative Liberals, treasury minister under Crispi, future prime minister, and foreign minister during the First World War. The following extracts offer answers to the question posed.

γ   γ   γ

The country is sick, morally and politically. This is proven by the riots of 1893, 1898, and by the results of the 1897 elections and those of this year, by which the subversive parties [Socialist, Republican] have tripled their representation, the continuance of the brutal plague of political assassination which has stained the good Italian name for more than a half century. Since our public conscience is not thoroughly outraged, it must indicate a serious flaw in our national education. Political discontent is on the increase and spreading; the administration of justice has lost prestige among the population. At the same time, ministerial instability, with one ministry dizzily succeeding another, makes it almost impossible to realize a mature and stedfast reform policy, and contributes to the undermining of institutional confidence. During the twenty-two years of Humbert I's reign, twenty-one governmental crises occurred. . . .

The dangers and extraordinary difficulties in which the monarchical-representative government finds itself in Italy, the march of extreme parties, with little scrupulosity in the selection of their means and of [political] alliances, nourished by the revolutionary traditions they shared before the Kingdom's unification; the Vatican's implacable hostility which gives antidynastic and antiunitary tone to a party (Clerical), which would

*"Quid Agendum?" *Nuova Antologia* (Rome), September 16, 1900, pp. 342–343, 363–364.

amount to being nothing more than a ultraconservative endeavor—all these things and others combine to make it impossible, in my opinion, for the great Liberal and Constitutional Party to enjoy the luxury of remaining divided into two distinct organizations and blocs which alternately govern the country. Each stands to become victim of the extreme party which is closest, the Left (Liberal) by the subversives, the Right (Liberal) by the Clericals. . . .

By closing ranks around the Crown, which personifies the Italian State, one, independent and free, of that Italian State which our fathers dreamt about for centuries, whose formation is due to the House of Savoy's elevated and patriotic perspicacity, we will resolve the numerous and thorny internal problems which press upon us from every side, inspiring us to a higher sentiment of justice, love, and harmony; externally, we will succeed in safeguarding the vital moral and material interests of the fatherland for today and tomorrow. . . .

READING NO. 28

CORRADINI'S CONVERSION TO NATIONALISM*

Entitled "Abba Garima," the exact locality where the Adowa battle took place, the statement appeared in an unsigned editorial in the Marzocco, *a Florentine review of art, literature, and sculpture, cofounded and edited by Corradini.*

γ   γ   γ

In a moment in which it seemed to us that our spirits were locked within ourselves, we youths, who thought to have forgotten so many things, who were being suppressed by so much tedium, or by so much ardor of individual ambitions, suddenly communicated to our country's soul. From the news of the first massacres until the last, we experienced continuous rebirths within us. . . .

*"Abba Carima," *Il Marzocco*, I, 6 (March 8, 1896), 1.

READING NO. 29

ANNOUNCEMENT OF THE *REGNO**

Corradini's Florentine political review began publication on November 2, 1903. It ceased on December 25, 1906. The following is excerpted from the opening number.

γ　　　　　γ　　　　　γ

In founding this review, my friends and I have but one purpose: to be a voice among the many raised in protest and contempt at the degradation of the nation. . . . And first and foremost against vile and disgraceful Socialism. . . . Noble thoughts were everywhere replaced by the fury of the lowest instincts of greed and destruction. All the classes were outlawed for just one, and the manual laborer's wages became the be-all and end-all of human society. Every value was subjected to furious attack by the masses. . . . All this state of affairs is disgusting, . . . but few are daring enough to speak out. We who must be true to ourselves wish to be one among those few voices, as outspoken as indignation itself which knows no fear.

It is also a voice to vituperate . . . the Italian bourgeoisie which reigns but does not rule. . . . I am not referring to the cowardice that lends strength to its aggressors' audacity, nor to the even more headlong retreat from its pursuit. I am referring to something that twists our lips into a bitter laugh full of anger and revulsion: the fact that it is a willing accomplice to its own destruction. Must the class struggle enjoy a free ride within the country and, externally, to batter down those great harmonious ethnic and historical entities which are called nations? The Italian bourgeoisie is bent on weakening itself daily by its love for the doctrines of freedom and internationalism. It is the sewer into which sentimental socialism drains. . . . Every sign of

*Enrico Corradini, *"Per coloro che risorgono* (For those Who are Resurgent)," *Il Regno*, I, 1 (November 29, 1903), 1–2.

decrepitude, tenderheartedness, dogmatism, outdated respect for transient human life, outmoded pity for the weak and lowly, utility and mediocrity accepted as the canons for wisdom, disregard for the higher human potentialities, mockery of the heroic—all these most fetid signs of the putrified state of degraded people can be found in the contemplative life of the bourgeoisie. . . .

And its practical life corresponds to its contemplative life. Base democracy has set up its congregations, schools, agencies, cliques, clans, intrigues, its schemes whereby the greater is driven out by the less, in every organism and body that rules, governs, controls, inspires and represents the Italian people, which creates and conducts their civic acts. . . . Just as the infantile barbarians in Rome overturned the statues of emperors, of heroes, of the gods, our townreared citizens, even worse barbarians, have trampled upon the lofty values of man and the nation. . . .

And thus the Italian middle classes who rule and govern the Italian people are not the same as the people who have shaken themselves loose from their torpor. Over this land which was called the land of the dead and is now the land of those who have risen from the grave to a life of industry, the only truth that remains is that the suffocating atmosphere of deadly deeds is being dispelled.

In founding this review, we oppose both [Socialism, bourgeoisie], for, although enemies, they are associates in their liking for that which is basically materialistic. Our voice will be lifted to re-erect the statues of the higher human and national values before the very eyes of those who are awakening to a new life.

READING NO. 30

NEW JOURNALISTIC VENTURES

Shock and revival of a nationalist nature are illustrated in the passages below lifted from public opinion organs which owed their inception to the Bosnian episode.

γ γ γ

1. We wish to sing the love of danger, the qualities of energy and of fearlessness;

2. The essential elements of our poetry are courage, boldness, and revolt . . .;

9. We desire to glorify war—the world's only hygiene—militarism, patriotism, the destructive acts of the anarchists, the beautiful ideas that kill and that despise women;

10. We want to demolish museums, libraries, fight all moralisms, feminism, utilitarian and opportunistic cowardice. . . .*

Program: In the darkness of the present hour we shout our nationalist and imperialist faith against every advance of pacifism and democracy, against every humanitarian sentimentalism. . . . We are against the policy of renunciations, . . . of humiliations, and of fear. . . . We urge those who are seeking to organize the bourgeoisie to rally around the fatherland's standard. . . . On the day of our victory, we will no longer have an antibourgeosie soul. . . . We affirm that nationalism is the doctrine and practice of national solidarity. . . . Private life must be nationalized on the basis of individual liberty, consonant with the power of the state. . . .

---

*Filippo T. Marinetti, *"Manifeste du futurisme,"* Le Figaro* (Paris), February 20, 1909. Reprinted in his Milan review, *La Poesia* (*Poetry*), March 1909.
†Gastone Calosci, *"Programma,"* La Prora* (Florence), June 15, 1910, p. 1. Subtitle: Fortnightly Review of Italian Nationalism.

And we are imperialists. In theory, always. In actuality, when and to the extent it can be useful. . . . Imperialism is the consequence and extension of nationalism. . . . It wants to dominate in order to create. It does not want to impose its civilization because it is its own but because it is the best. . . . We are also Africanists. . . . We have the primacy of emigration. Therefore, let us profit from our people's diffusive energy, . . . [this form] of unconscious imperialism. We hold the army to be the bedrock of our national strength . . . The navy is the instrument most suitable for the confirmation and realization of imperialist ideals. . . . We also know that alliances and international friendships have little worth if not backed with powerful forces. . . .

As we are advocating an energetic policy, we are also advising the return to a culture that is classical, noble, manly, to the lofty thought of which Italy was repeatedly the most marvelous and admired teacher in the world. . . . Let us prepare our immortal race for our supreme role.[†]

READING NO. 31

CONSTITUTION OF THE FIRST NATIONALIST CLUB OF TURIN, JULY 1909*

The driving force behind the club was the Tricolore, *a Turin political weekly founded on the morrow of Austria's seizure of Bosnia in October 1908.*

γ   γ   γ

Article A). The Nation is the greatest and ultimate unit of collective life. Italian Nationalism is Irredentist.

B). It is understood that Nationalism is not a class party but a solidarity for the union of all classes; it is understood that Nationalism has faith in the elevation of the working classes, and desires it; it is affirmed that the class struggle is to be contained within the limits of national solidarity, and that Nationalism's seeks to ally the two nation's two productive classes, the industrial and the worker. . . .

C). It is affirmed that the Monarchy is the living personification of the nation's active conscience. . . .

D). It is affirmed that the army and the navy are the instruments of an active, expansionist policy, of commercial and also of military expansionism, when necessary. Imperialism is the action of Nationalism.

E). It is affirmed that Nationalism's duty is the promotion of all forms of Italian culture, the nation's supreme goal being the enrichment of world history with a more heightened civilization.

F). Nationalism is also: cult of the traditions, the magnificent heroes, of Imperial Rome, mistress of the world.

G). [Nationalism affirms] unflagging hostility to any tendency which leads to state democracy. . . . Affirmation on economic grounds of integral nationalism and opposition to any social legislation that enchains individual liberty. . . .

*Statuto del primo gruppo nazionalista (Constitution of the First Nationalist Club)," *Il Tricolore*, July 16, 1909, p. 1.

READING NO. 32

NATIONALISM AND SYNDICALISM FOR EMPIRE*

In 1910, Corradini published La patria lontana (The Distant Fatherland). *The setting was an Italian immigrant settlement in Brazil. Having heard that Italy was at war, the syndicalist organizer Giacomo Rummo and scores of workers accompanied the nationalist campaigner Piero Buondelmonti back to the homeland. The event described below occurred as the ship was nearing Italy.*

γ γ γ

At dawn Piero Buondelmonti, feeling on his forehead the breeze from the Roman lake [Mediterranean], addressed his companions to praise what they had done and would do. "You," he began to say, "have given the fatherland a good example. You are just a few but your return has a most notable meaning because you, my friends, you left as emigrants and you return as soldiers. . . . Italy's future generations will be grateful. If Italy wins this war, it will take heart and will return to her ancestors' ways. And then those who will come later will have no more need to do what you had to do, emigrate to strange lands, armed only with hands and grit, and will be able to emigrate to the lands the fatherland will have conquered for herself. Then Italy will not only be where she is today but will be wherever there are Italians, just like England is today wherever there are Englishmen. And then the Italians will no longer speak their overseers' language but will speak their own tongue. Then, even those who will come, will do what you have done, will return to fight in the fatherland's great wars, but many of them and not a few hundred like you. . . . And then, as you do, others will return, but not to fight, indeed to admire the beautiful works with which the

*Corradini, *La patria lontana* (Milan, 1910), pp. 254–256.

fatherland will be glorified, in the new empire as already in the old. Cities which are today ancient, will be resplendent in the eyes of those who return one day, older and more venerable, true sanctuaries of the race, and others will arise, equally beautiful and immense. Then wherever the Italians will be, they will hear their fatherland spoken of with reverence because it will once again be at the top of the world, it will be at the head of a world which will have surpassed in size, pace, and power our modern world as it surpassed in the ancient world. . . ." Thus spoke Buondelmonti.

READING NO. 33

CASE FOR PROLETARIAN NATIONALISM*

On December 3, 1910, Corradini addressed the Florence inaugural convention of Italian nationalism with a major speech.

γ　　　　γ　　　　γ

. . . . We must start by acknowledging this principle: there are proletarian nations just as there are proletarian classes; nations, that is, whose conditions of life are as disadvantageously subordinated to those of other nations, as are classes. With this premise, Nationalism must above all consistently hammer at this truth: Italy is a nation morally and materially proletarian and it is proletarian in the period before her recovery. That is to say, before she is organized, at a time when her vital parts are full of folly and weaknesses. Subjected to other nations, she is feeble not in her people's vigor but in her nation's strength. Exactly like the proletariat before Socialism came to its rescue.

The workers' sinews were as strong as they are today but what will did they have to better their lot? They were blind to their state. So what happened when Socialism met the proletariat? It awakened, it caught a glimpse of its situation, understood the possibility of changing it, and for the first time conceived of the ideas of how change comes about. And Socialism drew the proletariat unto itself, it urged it to fight, fashioned its unity by means of the class struggle, its conscience, strength, its own weapons, its new rights, its will for victory, its pride to overcome decisively. It freed it and enabled it to dictate its class law to the other classes, to the nation, and to other nations.

Well then, my colleagues, Nationalism must do something similar for the Italian nation. It must become our National Socialism. That is, just as socialism taught the proletariat the value of the class struggle, we must teach Italy the value of the

---

*"Classi proletarie: socialismo; nazioni proletarie: nazionalismo," *Atti* (*Proceedings*) *del congresso di Firenze* (Florence, 1911), pp. 27–29.

international struggle. You ask, but the international struggle implies war? Well, let it be war! And let Nationalism arouse in Italy the will for the victorious war. . . .

To summarize, our foreign policy and home policy are both failures. What are the causes? There is need for a thorough re-evaluation. Nationalism intends to undertake this reappraisal. There is need for a change in the system in order to have a better one, both human and material. Nationalism desires to discover such as system. Herein lies its justification.

READING NO. 34

ITALIAN NATIONALISM'S UNIQUENESS*

Following Milan, Rocco penned a pamphlet for the Association in which he explained nationalism and detailed its objectives. In Part Three, he discounted the four main objections critics had raised. First, Italian nationalism was war-oriented; second, it was intensely pro-clerical; third, it was superfluous since every Italian was patriotic; fourth, it was nothing more than a carbon copy of French nationalism. Rocco's rebuttal to the last charge detains us.

γ   γ   γ

There does not exist a single nationalism just as there does not exist one single Socialism. There are various kinds of nationalisms. Just as races and nations are different, so their attitudes are different. For that reason alone, Italian Nationalism differs from the French variety. In France, a country rich but in political decline as a result of the shocking rate of depopulation, nationalism means regret for a vanished past that will never return, when the country was economically poor but rich in men and for that reason was expansionist, progressive, and energetic. And because at that time France was ruled by an absolute monarchy in alliance with the Church, French Nationalism is absolutist, clerical, and Anti-Semitic. In Italy, however, a poor but prolific country, Nationalism does not mean regret for the past but confidence in the future. And because Italy was wretched and oppressed when governed by absolute monarchies in alliance with the Church, Italian Nationalism is neither absolutist nor clerical nor Anti-Semitic. What is more, since the main problem for the French is the reinvigoration of their race, French Nationalism is directed inwards. Since our main problem is that of wealth and the expansion of our race, our Nationalism is outward

---

*Che cosa è il nazionalismo e che cosa vogliono i nazionalisti [*What is Nationalism and What Do the Nationalists Want*] (Padua, 1914), p. 88.

looking and imperialistic. In sum, since France has achieved power but lacks manpower, although more than adequately supplied with territories, French Nationalism is conservative and defensive. In Italy, a country short of territories but wealthy in manpower, Nationalism is aggressive and expansionist. Therefore, any similarity between these two forms of nationalism is purely one of name!

READING NO. 35

WAR FOR NATIONAL INTEGRATION AND INTERNATIONAL ESTEEM*

An original member of the Association's central committee, cofounder of the Idea Nazionale, *Francesco Coppola was frantically antidemocratic, fanatically imperialist, and hysterically prowar. In these excerpts he delineated war's opportunities and Italy's responsibilities.*

γ   γ   γ

It is said in Italy that the war being fought today is the war between a democratic and authoritarian outlook, between the principle of nationality and imperialism, between civil society of a humanitarian pacifist type and that of a military character, that it represents the last of wars, the supreme war because after it there will be no more need for war, at least not among the so-called civilized states. It is, in a word, a democratic war, the democratic war *par excellence*. . . . Now, all this is infinitely puerile.

What will be Italy's war and for what purpose will Italy fight? Italy will undertake war to finish the work of her *Risorgimento* and to solidify her political unity. But not just for that. She will also fight for other, and perhaps even, greater reasons, of a moral and political character. She will war because in her recent history as a nation Italy has not had a great war, a real war which would have made Italy a reality truly sacred in the heart of her sons and genuinely respected in foreigners' minds. War alone is the melting pot in which the national soul is repeatedly tempered in the

*"Per la democracia o per l'Italia [For Democracy or for Italy]?", *L'Idea Nazionale*, October 3, 1914.

likeness of its basic virtues, becomes increasingly sublime as it purifies itself in pain and through sacrifice and becomes a marvel to itself and in the sight of the world. If Italy, alone among the great European powers, were not to experience this selfless consecration, the war would end with Italy irretrievably demoralized within and diminished without.

READING NO. 36

"SACRED EGOISM" AND WORLD POWER*

Premier Salandra introduced "sacred egoism" on October 19. On the same day, Coppola submitted a "Nationalist" interpretation of Salandra's concept and guide.

γ　　　　γ　　　　γ

We must agree on what we mean by "sacred egoism". . . . Italy's "sacred egoism" cannot and should not be restricted to Irredentism. . . . Beyond the issue of Irredentism there is that of the Adriatic, beyond that of the Adriatic that of the Mediterranean, beyond that of the Mediterranean there is the issue of world power, which the present war will resolve for at least half a century. Italy cannot and should not allow the latter to be settled without her input, which unavoidably would be the case were she not to decide in time to participate in the war. Italy is, and must become all the more, a World Power. The war undoubtedly will open vast opportunities in the Adriatic, the Mediterranean, and especially in the Eastern Mediterranean, in Asia Minor, which, even if it does not include the Ottoman Empire, will consist of sizeable gains in the belligerent powers' political and economic influence. If Italy does not want to be suffocated and wither politically and economically in the Mediterranean, she cannot be indifferent to the availability of this inheritance. The war raging today will open immense opportunities in the rest of the world for hegemony and for influence. It will certainly generate new ranks of Powers and also updated moral and cultural classifications in which the highest positions will be reserved for those nations which have conquered them with arms, boldness, and will, and with actual sacrifice of blood and

*"Il 'sacro egoismo,'" L'Idea Nazionale, October 20, 1914.

sorrow, and, most of all, with a fearless and resolute soul. In the new order, Italy must, under penalty of falling helplessly into the lowest ranks, conquer her place for herself. And there will be no place for the fainthearted. Italy is, and must become even more than she is, one of the prime movers of world politics. Italy's "sacred egoism" is neither more nor less Italian imperialism.

READING NO. 37

CORRADINI'S STERN WARNING
TO THE KING*

Believing that the government was unbearably slow in responding to the opportunity represented by the First World War, the Nationalist Corradini published the following threat to King Victor Emmanuel III.

γ   γ   γ

It was first said by me and then by others. This is not a European war. This is a revolution. We want the Crown to remain. . . . But we cannot forget that we are citizens first and subjects second, and that we therefore accept the monarchy as long as it is an organ of the nation and fulfills a national function. . . . Up to this moment [the Salandra ministry] has been a government without purpose, which has failed to take . . . notice of the challenge of the historic hour. . . .

*Corradini, "Il governo e la corona (The Government and the Crown)," L'Idea Nazionale, November 22, 1914.

READING NO. 38

MUSSOLINI'S BLUNT ADMONITION
TO THE MONARCHY*

Suspicious and fearful that Premier Salandra and Foreign Minister Sonnino would succomb to mounting neutralist pressure and keep Italy out of the war, the Fascist Mussolini formulated the following ultimatum to the monarchy.

γ   γ   γ

The situation is this. If the monarchy is willing to face war, the great war, against the Central Powers, the entire country . . . will have to rally around the government because victory can only be achieved at that price. . . . If the monarchy remains neutral and satisfies itself with meagre territorial gains offered by its diplomats with their insidious strike-a-bargain mentality, or if the monarchy goes to war only against Austria and not also against Germany, it is simple and obvious to anticipate that the resulting "moral disaffection" . . . will provoke disparate factions to unite in one decisive revolution. The nation will arise against the betrayal and the monarchy will have knitted its own shroud in the bosom of neutrality.

*"Moniti sempre più precisi [Warnings Ever More Precise]," *Il Popolo d'Italia* (Milan), April 8, 1915.

READING NO. 39

GIOLITTI EXPLAINS HIS NEUTRALIST STANCE*

Giolitti requested of Camillo Peano that his letter be published on the prominiterial, La Tribuna. *Peano, and Olindo Malagodi, the Rome daily's editor, changed* molto *(much) to* parecchio *(quite a bit). The message, which appeared on February 2, 1915, was contemptuously referred to as "the* parecchio *letter."*

γ   γ   γ

Cavour [Piedmont], January 24, 1915

Dear Friend,

. . .It is certainly true that I, unlike the Nationalists, do not regard war as desirable but as a misfortune, which should be incurred only when the country's honor and vital interests are at stake. I do not think it justifiable to push the country into war due to sentimentalism toward other peoples. For sentimentalism a man can risk his own life but not his country's. But if it became necessary, I would not hesitate to confront war, as I have already demonstrated.

Given Europe's actual conditions, it is my belief that quite a bit can be obtained without becoming involved in war, although a person out of government is not fully qualified to claim a complete understanding of the possibility.

As for the rumor of conspiracy and crisis, I refuse to put any stock in them. I have supported and support the government and pay no attention to the insolence of those who profess to be its friends but are, in fact, its worst enemies.

"Parole chiare dell'On. Giolitti (Clear Words from the Hon. Giolitti)," *La Tribuna*, February 2, 1915.

READING NO. 40

VENGEANCE URGED AGAINST GIOLITTI*

Rabid interventionists, including governmental officials, enlisted D'Annunzio's vocal support. General belief was that Giolitti was secretly meeting with Prince Bernard von Bülow, former German chancellor and past ambassador to Italy, who was on a special mission to facilitate an Austro-Italian agreement. Had it not been for security forces guarding Giolitti at his residence on Via Cavour, his personal safety would have been in serious jeopardy. Following are extracts from D'Annunzio's harangue of May 13 in Rome.

γ   γ   γ

Comrades, there is no more time to talk but to move; there is no more time to meet but to act, and to act as Romans. . . . Any extreme force is legitimate, if we want to prevent the Fatherland's betrayal. You must stop a handful of pimps and tricksters from selling and giving Italy away. All necessary actions are sanctioned by the law of Rome. Listen to me. Understand me. The betrayal is by now obvious. . . . The betrayal is taking place in Rome, in the city of the future, in the city of life! In your Rome there is a plot to strangle the Fatherland with a Prussian rope, tied by that old thick-lipped hangman, whose fugitive heels are familar with the road to Berlin. The assassination is taking place in Rome. . . . Listen. We are on the verge of being sold like an infected herd. There is the threat that the stamp of servility will be branded on each of our foreheads, on mine, on yours, on that of your sons, on those of the still unborn. The term Italian will be

*"*La legge di Roma* (The Law of Rome)," *Per la più grande Italia* (*For the Greatest Italy*) (Rome, 1915), pp. 73–78, *passim*.

a name of humiliation, a name to be concealed, a name which will scorch the lips to pronounce.

Do you understand? Have you heard? That is what the intriguer, the repulsive pirate, from Dronero desires to inflict on you, against which those of ancient Roman blood must decisively react. . . . Let us now vow that they [Giolitti, von Bülow] will not succeed.

READING NO. 41

AN ANTI-GIOLITTIAN AND ANTI-PARLIAMENTARY WAR*

In the following editorial, the Idea Nazionale, *the Association's semi-official organ, discerned the potential internal implications of the struggle for war.*

γ　　　　γ　　　　γ

. . . .Parliament is Giolitti; Giolitti is Parliament: the byword of our shame. That is the old Italy, the old Italy that ignores the new, the true, the sacred Italy resurgent in history and for the future. It ignores her because she does not have eyes to see, no mind to understand her, has no heart to will her, no ideology worthy of her. It ignores her precisely because she is Parliament, Parliament, which is the falsification of the Nation.

But today that which was inevitable has come to pass. In the decisive hour of the new Italy's destiny, the Nation had chosen her path, the path of strenuous effort, sacrifice, the life of greatness: war. Her heart and arms had been prepared for the supreme test. Her will shone as a sword, her thirst for life and for her future enlivened her blood for the dawn of a new day; the soul, extended toward duty and hope, requested sacrifice for victory. Italy's sacred name was breaking forth from the confused memories of historic light, for so long extinguished.

And behold, Parliament, because of its gesture, has unexpectedly thrown itself across the path. The collision, which is inevitable, has occurred. The collision is fatal. Either Parliament

*"*Il parliamento contro l'Italia* (Parliament against Italy)," *L'Idea Nazionale*, May 15, 1915.

will batter down the Nation, and, resume, on her holy and quivering body, its occupation as a procurer to prostitute her also to the foreigner; or the Nation will overthrow Parliament, dismantle the swindlers' benches, purify the pimps' alcoves with fire and steel, and proclaim to the entire world her life's resolve, her life's ideals, her immortal life's majestic beauty. . .

READING NO. 42

MUSSOLINI POSES AGAIN THE ISSUE OF WAR OR REVOLUTION*

On the afternoon of May 13, 1915, at the Piazza del Duomo *in Milan, Mussolini addressed an interventionist rally. Excerpts are reproduced below.*

γ   γ   γ

. . .Fainthearted Deputies, mercenaries, charlatans, who are subservient to the Kaiser's will, dine with Prince von Bülow. . . . They should be arraigned before a war tribunal.

As for me, I am all the more convinced that it is necessary for Italy's health to shoot, I say *shoot* in the back, about a dozen Deputies and consign former ministers to penal colonies. Not only that, but I maintain, with a conviction becoming daily more profound, that Parliament in Italy is the pestiferous disease which poisons the Nation's lifeblood. It must be extirpated.

---

*"*O la guerra o la rivoluzione* (Either War or Revolution)," *Il Popolo d'Italia,* May 14, 1915.

READING NO. 43

NATIONALIST IDEOLOGY AND POLICY*

After the Nationalist Association's March 1919 Rome convention, Rocco was authorized to summarize the resolutions approved. The result was "The Nationalist Program." Below are extracts from the more crucial sections.

γ   γ   γ

Nationalism's Essence and Task. . . . . Since the objectives of Anglo-Saxon superimperialism have drained the League of Nations of every ideal and practical content, the nature of the great conflict just ended is by now evident. It was simply the struggle of peoples and empires for power and world domonation. No doctrine, no political movement leaves history's severest test as triumphant as nationalism. Formulas were and continue to be internationalist, humanitarian, pacifist; sentiment and will are nationalist. (Georges) Clemenceau labors for French nationalism, Lloyd George for English nationalism, (Woodrow) Wilson for American nationalism. The proof offered by a fact too obvious and evident provokes no denial. This evidence also indicates that besides other nationalisms there must exist an Italian Nationalism.

. . .Nationalism, therefore, even today places nations on the guard against the facile illusions of those who believe that ideologies can be diverted from history's inevitable fate. The struggle among peoples is an eternal law and most necessary in the world; let the bloody battles cease, the bloodless struggles of political and economic competition immediately ensues. If they do not want to perish, Italians must prepare themselves for the latter struggles. Consequently, all of nationalism's assumptions remain valid. The subordination of the internal struggle to the external remains valid; the need for national solidarity and

---

*"*Il programma nazionalista,*" Rocco, *Scritti, discorsi politici* (3 vols., Milan, 1938), II, 493–494, 498–499, 504.

internal discipline remains valid. . . . [Nationalism] alone in-
sures our survival. . . . Nationalism resumes its place in the
battle for Italy, for victory, against Bolshevist anarchy, destroyer
of the Fatherland. . . .

*The Corporative and Syndical Principle and Its Application in
the Constitutional Field.* National solidarity is the fundamental
and organic law of the nation's life, through which alone the
Italian nation can realize the social and economic rebuilding
necessitated by the war. But the national solidarity principle
implies that of national organization. In the nation, the most
advanced and differentiated social organisms, the essential organs of social life, are not isolated individuals nor heterogeneous
masses but organized collectivities. Internal discipline, the indispensable condition for the existence and development of
national society, is not only the individual's subordination to the
nation but at the same time the individual's subordination to the
secondary collectivities to which he belongs, and from them to
the nation. Removed from the political exploitation of professional demagogues, extended beyond the working classes to
include the categories of producers, the syndicate must become
the hinge of national economic organization and the instrument
through which the unsuppressible class antagonisms are automatically disciplined and resolved by the State's energetic intervention. . . .

We are in fact convinced that a solid and integral syndical
system will not weaken the State but will reinforce it. It will
determine the creation of a labor magistracy which would close
an epoch in the State's evolution and open another. It is hardly
necessary to mention that State involvement must include and be
preceded by all those provisions that work toward assuring
workers the best working conditions, protection against injuries,
and also retirement pensions.

READING NO. 44

FASCISM-NATIONALISM HISTORICAL-IDEOLOGICAL CONVERGENCE*

On January 5, 1922, Rocco, in a major address at Viterbo, compared Nationalist and Fascist development. Impressed, Mussolini urged colleagues to study it carefully. The following is excerpted from the speech. Subtitles are omitted.

γ　　　　γ　　　　γ

. . .We [Nationalists] who wanted and fought the war for the conquest of Trent and Trieste, and Fiume and Dalmatia, for Italy, and to obtain her rightful place as a world power, but above all to give the Italian people a national conscience and a national will, can finally say that we have won the battle. Alongside the Nationalist movement the Fascist movement is forming and affirming itself. It has increased its strength tenfold and is spreading rapidly and confidently, gaining Italy's cultivated youth. It is formidable in the number of adherents and for its influence among the petite bourgeoisie, workers, and peasants. As it evolves and becomes more concrete, it appears increasingly to be a movement essentially Nationalist. . . .

Fascism has travelled the same difficult road. Like Nationalism, it was born as a spontaneous expression of national instinct and sentiment. The tests during the years of national mortification had a determining impact on Nationalism; the epic ordeal of the great war, and those sorrowful ones of the postwar period, have had decisive effect on Fascism. In 1919, Fascism was still a romantic movement, nominally national, the same as Nationalism in 1910. It was composed of a few left interventionists, by veteran Socialists and Syndicalists, disgusted over the cowardice and antinational attitude predominant among Socialism's

*"*Il fascismo verso il nazionalismo* (Fascism Towards Nationalism)," *L'Idea Nazionale*, January 6, 1922.

237

various factions. . . . As a voluntary militia in defense of national and the social order against Communism, Fascism has quickly lost the pseudorevolutionary character which had marked its beginnings. As a school of courage and sacrifice, it immediately understood the democratic myth's error and the deception which had mesmerized the ignorant, ugly, and egoistic mob. . . .

At this point begins the Fascist movement's reflective phase. From instinct and sentiment, as was Nationalism from 1910 to 1911, Fascism tends to become doctrine. . . . Assuredly assisted by more than ten years of Nationalist elucidations, the national conception of the State and society, and of relations among the State, classes, and individuals, has penetrated Fascism deeply. And that is natural. Fascism is national instinct and sentiment and will. To connect them to principles and ideology, is to do nothing else than to explain national activity in terms of a national doctrine, that is to become Nationalist. . . .

We who have seized upon this truth by means of bitter struggle and an extended internal travail, witness, not merely without envy, but with infinite pleasure, how it is illuminating our younger companions of the battle of faith. And we ascertain with satisfaction that our labor has not been in vain, that Fascism's understanding of national truth is proceeding even more rapidly than it did among us, as is natural and right. The road which we trod in four years Fascism has trod in just a few months. . . . It can be certified that, as Fascism is accepting and disseminating the national conception of State and society, it is meeting the same hostility and ignorance which victimized Nationalism. . . . Together we deny the philosophy of the French Revolution, from which Liberalism, Democracy, also Socialism, as political theories, descend. . . .

Our greatest pride, our deepest contentment, is that we, finally, have separated ourselves from that spiritual anarchy which surrenders to all compromises and errors, and to have as the guide of all our political activity the beacon light not only of a grand sentiment but also of a matchless idea and of a complete and superb system of doctrine and principles [Nationalism].

READING NO. 45

PACT OF FUSION BETWEEN NATIONALISM AND FASCISM*

γ   γ   γ

Article 1. The Italian Nationalist Association renounces political and social activity as a party and unites with the National Fascist Party. There will arise in Rome an Institute of Nationalist Culture, presided over by Benito Mussolini and as a direct emanation of the NFP and under its control, which will have the assignment of strengthening and diffusing the party's political doctrines.

2. The INA's members will be enrolled *en masse* in the National Fascist Party. . . .

3. The Nationalist syndical associations will enter the corresponding National Fascist Corporations. Those from Nationalism who qualify will gradually enter Fascism's journalistic, propaganda, and recreational organizations.

4. The President of the Council of Ministers [Premier Mussolini] will assign an adequate representation of Nationalists to the Grand Council of the National Fascist Party and to the other directing organs.

5. The President will impart instructions to the General Command of the Voluntary Militia for National Security for the admission of those who belonged to the Minutemen. The President of the Council will consider the military rank, war pension, and service experience of the members of the loosed militia of the Minutemen to determine their rank in the National Militia. . . .

7. The Little Italians and the Nationalist Vanguards will combine with the Balilla and the Vanguards of the National Fascist Party. The Balilla and the Vanguards will wear blue ties under the collars of the black shirts.

*"*Il patto di unione,*" *L'Idea Nazionale*, February 28, 1923.

8. The Nationalist and Fascist Parliamentary Groups will unite as will the representatives of the two parties in local administration.

9. The Italian Nationalist Association's flags and pennants will be preserved at the National Fascist Party's headquarters in Rome.

10. The Commission is responsible for implementing these norms and for working out local situations. Commissioners Paolucci and [Nicola] Sansonelli are specifically delegated to direct and supervise the effectuation of fusion.

READING NO. 46

SOLEMNIZING FUSION*

On March 6, 1923, the Association's central committee met with Mussolini in Rome's famous Chigi Palace. Federzoni introduced the last committeemen and read a prepared statement. Mussolini returned the gesture.

γ   γ   γ

Federzoni: As the Italian Nationalists are preparing to enter Fascism's ranks with unfrangible discipline and unshakable faith, the Central Committee extends to you . . . its respectful and devoted greetings, and remembers with legitimate pride the old battles which united . . . Fascism and Nationalism, the indestructible patrimony of the common faith, and secure harbinger of the splendid fortunes of the imperial Italy of tomorrow.

Mussolini: I do not believe it is necessary for me to use so many words to tell you that your salutation . . . deeply touches me. . . . I tell you sincerely that you must give us cadres, men, values. But with all that it is not to be thought that Fascism has not had its own theories, in which case it would be a serious error. . . . There are obstacles to overcome, but I ask myself whether there be anything in this world that does not present some difficulty. . .

In conclusion, the word of order for the new times that await Italy is this: it is imperative to unify. Too much has been destroyed; there has been an enormous waste of energies. The time for the great reconstruction has arrived. I exchange greetings with you and I am happy to count you, I will not say among my soldiers, but among the nation's loyal soldiers.

*"*Il comitato centrale dall'on. Mussolini," *L'Idea Nazionale*, March 9, 1923.

241

READING NO. 47

THE *IDEA NAZIONALE* APPRAISES
THE MERGER*

The Rome nationalist political daily was strong for fusion and assumed that it was inevitable. In the following editorial, it analyzed and drew the significance before the terms of union had been acted upon by the Nationalist Association and the Fascist party.

γ   γ   γ

. . .What is the importance of the act? First of all it has the highest moral value in that it signifies the national spirit's triumph over separatist feelings. Divided, Fascism and Nationalism would have made . . . two parties and nothing more than two parties; united they become something more and something better. They become an organ of the national will and of the national conscience: an organ which must prepare and support the government's efforts directed toward Italy's self-realization and advancement in the world. . . .

Nationalism, which has accepted the greater sacrifice, has obeyed its own precept. It has always been disdainful about becoming a true and proper party, and has even refused the name. Had it organized and acted as a party, it would have had to . . . acclimate itself to the environment created by the democratic mentality and by parliamentary practices. . . . Nationalism has never forgotten that the party has only instrumental purposes and that parties are not ends in themselves: the true and only end is the Nation. In a country such as ours, with its local and municipal traditions, parties have always been a plague on the Nation. They have never considered themselves as means towards a goal superior to themselves but have always attempted

---

*"*Il valore dell'atto* (The Worth of the Act)," *L'Idea Nazionale*, February 28, 1923.

to impose their own thinking and organizations on the nation's objectives and interests. Nationalism has represented a reaction to this particularist mind set and has always affirmed itself as a principle for national unification. . . .

The act of union also has the highest political value. Through it, the Nationalists assume Fascism's name and uniform in the same moment in which Fascism declares itself Nationalist. In fact, the premises underling the act of union unequivocally affixed the spirit of the new unified party. . . .

But there is in addition a recognition even more explicit. In Article 1 of the Convention there is provision for the establishment of an "Institute of Nationalist Culture . . . which will have the assignment of strengthening and diffusing the party's political doctrines." This will be the Institute for Italian expansion in the world, worthy indeed to be adorned with the emblem of the Roman eagle, adopted by the Nationalists as a symbol.

READING NO. 48

INTEGRATION OF ITALIAN HISTORY ADVISED*

In 1929, Croce published Storia dell'Italia dal 1871 al 1915. *His start in 1871 aroused Corradini's disquisition. Excerpts follow.*

γ   γ   γ

Reform of Italy's history. What does it mean? Simply and precisely what the words signify. Reform, that is, revision and correction; Italy's history, that is, narration of our Fatherland's past. In sum, Italy's history from its origins to our day has not been written. It must be rewritten.

We must acknowledge that our Fatherland's history is the most difficult of all national histories because of its vastness in time and space, its variety, indeed, unique diversity. To prove the point, we need only to consider that it includes, leaving aside its very beginnings, the history of a powerful people, the Etruscan, whose origins and language are not known; Rome's history; the church's history; the histories of numerous cities, which were in themselves magnificent, powerful, conquering states; there is, in sum, the history of the most extreme fortunes and the most diverse ordinances: commerce, despots, foreign dominations, decadence in several regions, progress and stability in others, *Risorgimento*, liberation, unification, and all that followed up to the victorious war and all that resulted from it until our present hour.

We come to the central theme. What do we note above all else? We note a mode of conceptualization which is erroneous and yet entrenched: there is the fixed tradition of conceiving of Italy's history as fractured into many bits and pieces: on one side there is the history of Rome and her empire and on the other the

*"Reforma della storia d'Italia," Nuova Antologia, September 16, 1931, pp. 145–153.

history of so-called Italy. . . . All of us, due to culture and education, are formed and taught in that manner. We have in our mind, in brief, a history of Italy that is fragmented and disorganized. . . .

Well, now, all that must cease. The revision and correction, as I was saying above, is necessary and cogent. It is imperative that we begin to conceive and to construct the unity of Italy's history, the essential, organic unity, which it was and is in reality, between the history of Italy and the immense span of time which separates it from Rome and her empire. Italy and Rome must begin to appear as one thing only, to be treated as one thing only, which they were and are by race, in their doing and suffering, in vicissitudes, in everything. . . .

The Nation has its own history as its own territory. [It serves as] the bond of unity, well-spring of patriotism, a school of dedication for its children from generation to generation. Italy's history is a precious thing for Italians. It can make, finally, their beloved Fatherland a greater Fatherland in the glory and reality of the ideal, and in that way instruct them from age-to-age to perform more sublime exploits and endure more severe sacrifices on her behalf. . . .

READING NO. 49

PROSPECTS FOR RAPPROCHEMENT
BETWEEN CHURCH AND STATE*

No one was more vocal, persistent, and pursuasive than Alfredo Rocco in arguing the case for church-state reconciliation. In the extract below of 1914, he outlined the basis and objectives.

γ   γ   γ

Nationalists and Clericals. . . . Today, therefore, there can be points of contact between Nationalists and Catholics. Above all else because Nationalists want national discipline and internal harmony so that the Italian Nation can undertake her national struggle in the world one and united. Now that the Church has accepted unification with Rome as capital as an accomplished fact, and that a serious dispute is about to end, . . . they do not desire to rekindle and perpetuate a strife, which is evident has no reason to exist.

Another point of contact between Nationalists and Catholics is this. Contrary to Democrats, who in their mania to defend the individual against any social organizational tie, are by nature antireligious, Nationalists acknowledge all of religion's high moral and national values. Nationalists, therefore, believe that the State cannot disinterest itself from the most important and fundamental social phenomenon represented by religion. And since the Catholic religion is the religion of the overwhelming majority of the Italian people, the Italian State cannot ignore the Catholic Church nor the Catholic Faith. It must, by all means, take under consideration the interests of Italian Catholics, in so far as they compatible with the nation's interests.

These two points of contact permit the Nationalists, in certain circumstances, to be in agreement with Catholics. But they do not mean that between the two conceptions, the Nationalist and

*Rocco, *Che cosa è il nazionalismo e che cosa vogliono i nazionalisti,* pp. 81–82.

the Catholic, there is a theoretical or practical connection. Nationalists are not Clericals for this basic reason: they consider the nation's concerns as pre-eminent and absolute and the religious as subordinate and ancillary. Therefore, Nationalists do not believe that the State is to be an instrument of the Church; they believe, rather, that the State must affirm its sovereignty even in the face of the Church.

Because, however, they admit religion and the Catholic Church are very important factors in national life, they [Nationalists] want, without endangering State sovereignty, to safeguard Catholic interests as far as possible. And in this moment of Italian life to safeguard means to respect the Italian Catholics' liberty of conscience against antireligious persecutions of democratic anticlericals. Perhaps in the future it will be possible to go beyond and work out with the Catholic Church, even tacitly, an understanding by which the Catholic establishment might serve the expansion of the Italian nation in the world.

READING NO. 50

THE SYNDICAL-CORPORATIVE STATE IN HISTORICAL-IDEOLOGICAL PERSPECTIVE*

Francesco Ercole, professor of Italian literature at the University of Palermo, was an early nationalist. In the excerpts below, he offered a most perceptive summary analysis of corporativism from a nationalist-fascist perspective.

γ   γ   γ

What else is true but that Fascism has achieved the efficient conjunction of two theoretical tendencies already in existence and active in *antebellum* Europe: voluntaristic syndicalism, which was being unfolded, particularly in France, through George Sorel's merits; and political nationalism, which was being unfolded, particularly in Italy, through the merits of Enrico Corradini, Luigi Federzoni, Alfredo Rocco, Francesco Coppola? From that moment, Syndicalism and Nationalism were tending to converge under the influence of historical affinities, despite the almost antithetical differences in their points of departure. Sorelian Syndicalism's disposition to acknowledge the bourgeoisie's and middle class capitalism's historic value and the justification of national solidarity as above that of the class struggle was evident before and during the war. The exertion was no less evident in Nationalism as it sought to account for the underlying causes of the economic struggle among classes and of the need to redirect the struggle to the supreme demands of national destiny through insertion of the amenable syndical phenomenon into the state organism. The one and the other of these two theoretical initiatives would have continued, similarities between them on the contrary, to fight or ignore each

*"Le origini del corporativismo fascista," Politica, XXIX, 81 (1928), 35–36.

other . . . had it not been for that fusion which suddenly, almost as if by magic, had been realized in a solid unity of faith in the conscience and will of one of the most powerful integrating Men and Achievers history knows. From the unifying synthesis of Syndicalism and Nationalism within Benito Mussolini, there was indeed originally formed the Fascist Faith; and from Benito Mussolini, this Faith immediately spilled over into the political movement of the *Fasci*. . . .

READING NO. 51

ITALY FINALLY RESTORED TO HER PRIMACY AND MISSION*

In the following lines, the nationalist Coppola offered as far-reaching a statement and justification of Italy's messianic role as was to be forthcoming from either nationalism or fascism.

γ   γ   γ

Italy, prolific and growing, youthful and sober, one of blood, of culture, and of soul, all Catholic and thoroughly monarchical, fervent in patriotism and confident in her destiny, is today the most compact, the most unified, and the most dynamic among the great nations of the world. . . .

Having rediscovered her new unitary youth, tested and tempered in the war and victory, the ways and signs, the sentiment and the Roman pride in her destiny, Italy has also rediscovered the millennial sense, the tradition and the vocation, secret and worth, of her universal mission.

. . .If there exists in the world a universal genius, as a capacity both to think and act universally, it is Roman and Italian. All that which has been and is spiritually universal in Western humanity has had its origins and its baptism in Rome and in Italy; it has been and is Italian. All Western Civilization rests today on Roman foundations. . . . No other people, in all the course of history, had an international vocation and function comparable to the Roman and the Italian; no other people as this lived, thought, created under universal mandates. All that which is ages past was or strove to be universal was or strove to be Roman. It was born in Rome and sought in the Roman name its mission's entitlement and legitimacy. . . . The same Christianity not only found in Rome the name but also the spirit, the

*"*L'Idea imperiale della nazione italiana," Politica, XXIV, 71 (1927), 25–44, passim.

voice, and the power of radiation, to become truly Catholic, that is, universal. . . .

With the Fascist Revolution, Italy has once again lifted herself, to revindicate and to affirm, for herself and for the world, the classical principles of order, clarity, and of authority, the idea of the State as the fountain of law, and of power as the end of the State, the idea of life as civil and religious warfare, and of national and international society as a hierarchy of men and of peoples—the monarchical and Catholic concept. The Italians feel their universal calling much more strongly because of the triple threat represented by the advancing Germanic, Anglo-Saxon, Slavic domination to the European Latin world. . . . Italy readily accepts the high honor of primogeniture, authentic, direct legate of Europe's Roman and Catholic Civilizations. Perhaps, after fifteen centuries, it is her singular destiny to serve them another time. May the deeds speak.

Therefore, in its triple aspect, from the demographic-territorial necessity, and that is in the need of colonial and Mediterranean expansion; from the reassertion of her own place as a world power; and, finally, from the understanding and will of her universal calling, Italy integrates in her political, ethical, and historic values the imperial idea. It upsurges today in Italy following the twin victories of her arms over the enemies in the Great War and of her spirit over the Democratic ideologies of a decadent Europe. . . .

READING NO. 52

A PROLETARIAN-NATIONALIST WAR*

With the Ethiopian conflict just days away (October 3, 1935), Mussolini granted many interviews. Below is interview with Léo Gerville-Réache of the Parisian Matin, September 15, in Rome. The journalist's internal comments are omitted.

γ   γ   γ

Mussolini: Italy also loves, desires peace, but only if it is established on justice. Italy will therefore pursue what it considers to be just and of vital necessity. It was thought, at the beginning, that I might be engaging in a game of *poker* [bluff]. No one today can have any doubt of our people's and its leaders' unshakable resolve. You've been in Italy for some time. You've certainly been able to note that the country's material forces and morale are equal to our destiny.

We have had a sincere friendship for the English people, a faithful friendship over the years, but we find it today simply monstrous that the nation which dominates the world would refuse us a meagre strip of land in the African sun. . . .

We, certainly, have stated, with utmost candor, what our objectives are in this colonial undertaking: our security above all and the possibility of expansion for a prolific people which having farmed what was arable in its own unyielding territory will not resign itself to death by starvation. . . . You have observed the serenity of our country's people. It is calm because it is conscious of its strength and has decided to have its place in the sun.

You have been able to evaluate the new Italy's indomitable forces. We have one million men mobilized. The country is confident [and] prepared to give more. When I give the signal, you would be witness to the most demonstrative display of a determined people: ten million men mobilized in one day. It is to

---

*"Il *conflitto italo-abissino*," *Tribuna-Idea Nazionale*, September 18, 1935.

be known that I have exempted the syndicates and workers from this practice alarm, to whom just a few minutes are valuable since they labor for national defense. . . . Ten million men; that is more than sufficient. If it is necessary, we'll do even better. Something more impressive will eventuate if it is dared, for example, to inflict military sanctions against us.

Would France, whose friendly and basically European stirrings I acknowledge, want military sanctions? Admitting as I do her delicate position, that is all we would want to ask her. But for the others, let them understand this well, sanctions means the risk of redrawing Europe's map. This is the most brilliant result which will be obtained by those who, due to pure egoism, pretend to deny Italy her right to live.

—And still, it would have been interesting, it would have been highly judicious, had our country been placed among those who wish to preserve. We will see instead what will be the cost of having pushed her among those who are clamoring for a different distribution and, who knows, perhaps a more sound justice. . . .

READING NO. 53

CORRADINI DECLARES THE MUSSOLINI-FASCIST DICTATORSHIP REPUGNANT AND SELF-DEFEATING*

Disenchantment was expressed in notes found on Corradini's desk after his death, December 11, 1931. Federzoni included a fragment of the notes in his memoirs.

γ   γ   γ

Too much is being said of Fascism and too little of Italy
Individuals can be the best of Italians without being enrolled in the Fascist party.

Do we wish to consider forty million Italians pariahs? Do we desire to banish them to spiritual confinement?

Less Fascism and more Italy, less Party and more the Nation, less Revolution and more Constitution. . . .

To project what occurs in Italy as the miracle of a miraculous man is to reduce Italy to a nonidentity in all the other nations' sight.

Fascism's role was not so much that of destroying the old liberal and democratic regime as it was that of giving it a sound successor. . . .

A personal regime does not produce a ruling class. . . .

In a complex, modern state, a dictatorship overburdens itself with a bundle of duties beyond any human capability. It follows that many and wide areas of national life remain beyond the scope of vigilance and at the mercy of corruption. The consequences of a personal, absolute government are many and serious. First: the development of a shocking servile and obsequious spirit. Second: an absolute government distances the

---

*Luigi Federzoni, *L'Italia di ieri per la storia di domani* (*Yesterday's Italy's for Tomorrow's History*) (Verona: Arnaldo Mondadori, 1967), pp. 17–19. Courtesy of Argentieri-Federzoni family.

Nation, that is its constituent elements, which are the citizens and classes, from the exercise of their true and proper political activities, which cannot be that unless they are connected with the right of discussion and of initiative. Therein consists the task of real government, that of promoting coordination and collaboration among national activities. . . .

READING NO. 54

MUSSOLINI RALLIES PROLETARIAN AND FASCIST ITALY TO THE SECOND WORLD WAR*

At 6:00 P.M., on the tenth of June 1940, speaking from the Palazzo Venezia, in Rome, before a subdued multitude, the Duce *made the following announcement.*

γ   γ   γ

The hour assigned us by destiny has struck in the horizons of our fatherland. The hour of irrevocable decisions. The declaration of war has already been handed to the ambassadors of Great Britain and France. We are going to war against the plutocratic and reactionary democracies of the West, who have always hindered our march and often threatened the very existence of the Italian people. . . . Today we have decided to face the risks and sacrifices of war because our honor, our interests and our future urge it. A people is truly great only if it holds its obligations sacred and does not evade the supreme challenges which determine the course of history.

Today we are taking up arms in order that, having solved the problem of our land frontiers, we can fix our maritime borders. We want to break the territorial and military chains that choke us in our own sea, for a nation of forty-five million souls is not really free unless it has access to the oceans. This gigantic struggle is but one phase of the logical development of our revolution; it is the struggle of people who are poor but rich with energy against the exploiters who cling fiercely to their monopoly of all the earth's gold and resources; it is the struggle of fertile, youthful peoples against sterile ones on the threshold of decline; it is the struggle between two centuries and two

---

*POPOLO ITALIANO! CORRE ALLE [RUN TO] ARMI . . .!, Popolo d'Italia, June 8, 1940.

ideas. . . . Italians! At a memorable meeting in Berlin, I said that, according to the law of Fascism morality, when one has a friend, one stands by him to the end. We have done that, and we shall do likewise with Germany, her people, and her marvelous armed forces.

On the eve of an event of historic proportions, our thoughts turn to his Majesty the King and Emperor who, as always, has faithfully interpreted the soul of the fatherland. And we salute the Führer, the leader of Germany, our great ally.

Proletarian and Fascist Italy is for the third time on her feet, strong, proud, and united as never before. We have but one categorical and binding watchword for all. It already has taken flight and sparks hearts from the Alps to the Indian Ocean: Victory! And we shall win, to give finally to Italy, to Europe, and to the world a long period of peace with justice.

Italians! Rush to arms, and show your tenacity, your courage, your valor!

READING NO. 55

A DISTINGUISHED NATIONALIST AND FASCIST REFLECTS*

Federzoni was one of the founders of the Association and served fascism in many prominent posts. At the Grand Council meeting of July 24–25, 1943, he voted with the majority to divest Mussolini of his dictatorial powers. Condemned to death in absentia by the fascist Salò Republic's Verona trials, January 8–10, 1944, Federzoni was tried by the Italian Supreme Court, sentenced for life, and pardoned in 1947. The following passage is from his postwar recollections.

γ γ γ

In truth, Italy's intervention in this war was through Mussolini's personal initiative. In the regime's official circles, only one or two of the usual professional frenetics, lacking any moral authority, had dared with brutal insensitivity to welcome that venture even riskier than the others before it. Among the Grand Council veteran members there was not a few who had candidly opposed it; and precisely because he was aware of their thinking Mussolini had decided against convoking the Grand Council before arriving at the fatal decision. . . .

After all the optimistic prophecies had been gradually proven false, there surfaced a moral declension entirely unprecedented in Italy: let the war go as it might, everyone felt compelled to reduce one's sacrifices and his discomforts. The Nation's spiritual disgregation had begun, a frightening thing seen also among the youth. It was the negative result of many years of absurd rhetoric with which the sacred words Enrico Corradini had taught us to use with caution, measure, and respect had been emptied of idealistic content and satisfying substance. . . .

*Luigi Federzoni, *Italia di ieri per la storia di domani*, pp. 207–210. Courtesy of Argentieri-Federzoni family.

Nothing had served to make one rally behind the war, not in the slightest. Not the proclaimed territorial aspirations, which lacked the emotion of poetry and the light of memory which had consecrated others in the past; and least of all the hate propaganda against the enemy, sterile propaganda because hate cannot be urged as a duty, and most of all because the ally [Germany] was much more loathed than the enemy, and that without the need of propaganda. The Italians, therefore, had even ceased to love Italy. Alas, they had learned to discriminate between that Italy and the genuine Italy, mother of us all, eternal in her faith, in her glories and in her traditions, superior to parties and men. This real Italy, already ours and of our ancestors, . . . did not exist anymore. Fascism had tried to kill her by taking her place in the Italians' hearts. It had denied the past with the nonsensical pretension of having invented everything, the ideals, institutions, mental inclinations, and habits. It had attempted to have people forget the *Risorgimento* and had endeavored to eliminate from history the first eighty years of our national unity by summarily condemning them as mediocre in ideas and in achievements. It had deigned to arrogate unto itself the heritage of Imperial Rome, with a panaroma of vain phantasms in place of concrete action set in our time. For the present and the future, it had spoken of revolution rather than of the fatherland. In that fashion history's educational value had been lost, which is first of all the appreciation of continuity. There was always in the best, admittedly, the sentiment of high duty, for which one had also to die; and many went to their death in combat with supreme detachment, as if in obedience to a law of honor. But the spiritual fervor for the Italian Nation's ends seemed spent.

READING NO. 56

AN EARLY AND PROPHETIC EVALUATION OF NATIONALISM-IMPERIALISM*

Submitted in 1905 by the Neo-Kantian Alessandro Chiappelli, professor of philosophy, University of Naples. Extract below.

γ   γ   γ

By now there is no cultivated person in our country who is not acquainted with the political program of the youthful Florentine writers which have as their organ the review, *Il Regno*, founded and directed with much effectiveness until recently by Enrico Corradini, authoritative head of the group and one of the most lucid geniuses of the rising generation. . . . No one, meanwhile, would want to limit the praises due to the labors so animated and original as is that of these youthful champions of expansion, whose propulsive ideas are continually expressed with vigor of form, even if occasionally hyperbolically and foolhardily, but always inspired by a lively and high love of the fatherland. . . .

. . . It is not my intention to indulge myself and show how this program [of expansion] resolves itself into a blatant inversion of current moral values, and is the denial of the most legitimate human idealities. . . .

Life, for the spokesmen of force, is equated with the will to dominate; and is, according to the concept by which Nietzsche meets with Darwinism, the destruction of the many for the victory of the strongest. It follows that the life envisioned by them is the heroic life: and hero signifies lord and ruler. They do not suspect that life can be, as indeed it is, association, coopera-

*Alessandro Chiappelli, "*Energia politica e imperialismo* (Political Energy and Imperialism)," *Nuova Antologia*, October 16, 1905, pp. 552, 554–555, 557. (*Note*: Due to the confusing discrepancy in bibliographical detail between individual issues and their compilation in volume form, scholars simply use the initial date and page number.)

tion, equilibrium; that destruction does not represent but a subordinate, ephemeral moment, which redounds to a superior harmony of multiple elements. . . Is not the historical process the way by which liberty gradually entwines itself in the very necessity of things? And how can one deny that modern life continually opens ways to the lower people so that they can progress in life?. . . . Our age, therefore, comes to be less heroic as it becomes more humane. . . .

Rights of spirituality and of moral values can be ignored as the writers of the *Regno* and the apostles of force too frequently do; but it cannot be denied that these truths are forces also, and sovereign and guiding forces of life; forces which do not conduct to violence but to the equilibrium of peace. Let us remember that power does not mean arrogance and that true force is not aggressive and tyrannical; it is rather normally calm and serene because it is sure of itself like that of the lion and the athlete.

There is, in sum, something even stronger in peoples' lives than the power of arms and it is justice: that justice through which Dante saw the vision of the imperial eagle, and by which we were restored in the sight of all the consenting and applauding nations.

FOR FURTHER READING

Alfieri, Dino, *Dictators Face to Face*, trans. by David Moore (New York, 1955).

Burckhardt, Jacob, *The Civilization of the Renaissance in Italy* (London, 1955).

Burke, Peter, *The Historical Anthropology of Early Modern Italy* (New York, 1987).

Casale, Ottavio (ed. and trans.), *A Leopardi Reader* (Urbana, 1981).

Ciano, Galeazzo, *The Ciano Diaries, 1939–1943*, ed. Hugh Gibson (New York, 1973).

Clough, Shepard B., *The Economic History of Modern Italy* (New York, 1964).

Colli, Leandro (ed.), *La cultura italians tra'800 e'900 e le origini del nazionalismo* (Florence, 1981).

Coppa, Frank J., *Pope Pius IX* (Boston, 1979).

Corradini, Enrico, *La patria lontana* (Milan, 1910).

——————*Discorsi politici* (Florence, 1923).

Croce, Benedetto, *A History of Italy, 1871–1915*, trans. by C. M. Ady (Oxford, 1929).

Denoto, Giacomo, *The Languages of Italy*, trans. by V. Louise Katainen (Chicago, 1978).

Delzell, Charles, *Mussolini's Enemies. The Anti-Fascist Resistance* (Princeton, N. J., 1961).

Drake, Richard, *Byzantium for Rome. The Politics of Nostalgia in Umbertian Italy 1978–1900* (Chapel Hill, 1980).

English Songs of Italian Freedom, chosen and arranged with an introduction by George Macaulay Trevelyan (London, 1911).

Felice, Renzo de, *Interpretations of Fascism*, trans. Brenda Huff (Cambridge, Mass., 1977).

——————*Mussolini*, 5 vols. (Turin, 1965–81).

Gaeta, Franco, *Il nazionalismo italiano* (Naples, 1965).

Gentile, Emilio, *Le origini dell'ideologia fascista (1918–1925)* (Bari, 1975).

Glauco, Cambon, *Ugo Foscolo, Poet of Exile* (Princeton, N. J., 1980).

Gottman, Jean, *The Significance of Territory* (New York, 1973).

Grand, Alexander De, *The Italian Nationalist Association and the Rise of Fascism in Italy* (Lincoln, Nebraska, 1978).

Grazia, Victoria De, *The Culture of Consent* (Cambridge, London, 1981).

Gregor, James A., *Young Mussolini and the Intellectual Origins of Fascism* (Berkeley, Calif., 1979).

Grew, Raymond, *A Sterner Plan for Italian Unity* (Princeton, N. J., 1963).

Halperin, S. William, *Mussolini and Italian Fascism* (Princeton, N. J., 1964).

Kent, Peter L., *The Pope and the Duce* (New York, 1981).

Landy, Marcia, *Fascism in Film* (Princeton, N. J., 1986).

Ledeen, Michael A., *The First Duce. D'Annunzio at Fiume* (Baltimore, 1977).

Lyttleton, Adrian, *The Seizure of Power. Fascism in Italy 1919–1929* (New York, 1973).

Marraro, Howard R., *Nationalism in Italian Education* (New York, 1927).

Mazzini, Giuseppe, *The Duties of Man and Other Essays* (London, 1860).

Megaro, Gaudens, *Vittorio Alfieri: Forerunner of Italian Nationalism* (New York, 1930).

Moore, Michael, *Vico in the Tradition of Rhetoric* (Princeton, N. J., 1985).

Mussolini, Benito, *Fascism: Doctrine and Institutions* (New York, 1968).

Noether, Emiliana, *Seeds of Italian Nationalism, 1700–1815* (New York, 1969).

Nolte, Ernst, *Three Faces of Fascism*, trans. from the German by Leila Vennewitz (New York, 1965).

Pollard, John F., *The Vatican and Italian Fascism, 1929–32* (London, 1985).

Renzi, William A., *In the Shadow of the Sword. Italy's Neutrality and Entrance into the Great War, 1914–1915* (New York, 1987).

Roberts, David D., *The Syndicalist Tradition and Italian Fascism* (Chapel Hill, 1979).

Rogger, Hans and Weber, Eugene, *The European Right. A Historical Profile* (Berkeley, Calif., 1966).

Romano, Sergio, *Crispi* (Milan, 1986).

Romeo, Rosario, *Cavour e il suo tempo 1810–1861,* 3 vols. (Bari, 1969–1984).

Rota, Ettore, *Le origini del Risorgimento, 1700–1800*, 2 vols. (3rd ed.; Milan, 1938).

Salvadori, Massimo, *Cavour and the Unification of Italy* (Princeton, N. J., 1961).

Salomone, A. William, *Italy in the Giolittian Era* (Philadelphia, 1945).

Salvatorelli, Luigi, *Nazionalfascismo* (Turin, 1923).

——————*The Risorgimento: Thought and Action*, trans. Mario Domandi, introduction by Charles Delzell (New York, 1970).

Salvemini, Gaetano, *Under the Axe of Fascism* (New York, 1939).

Sforza, Carlo, *The Real Italians* (New York, 1942).

Smith, Denis Mack, *Cavour and Garibaldi 1860* (London, 1985).

Taeye-Henen, Monique de, *Le nationalisme d'Enrico Corradini et les origines du fascisme dans le revue florentine "Il Regno"—1903–1906* (Paris, 1973).

Tannenbaum, Edward R., *The Fascist Experience. Italian Society and Culture, 1922–1945* (New York, 1972).

Thayer, John A., *Italy and the Great War. Politics and Culture, 1870–1915* (Madison, Wis., 1964).

Trevelyan, George M., *Garibaldi and the Thousand (May 1860)* (New York, 1928).

Valsecchi, Franco, *L'Italia nel seicento e settecento* (Turin, 1967).

Vaussard, Maurice, *De Pétrarque a Mussolini. Évolution du sentimente nationaliste italien* (Paris, 1961).

Whyte, A. J. B., *The Early Life and Letters of Cavour, 1810–1848* (London, 1925).

——————*The Political Life and Letters of Cavour, 1848–1861* (London, 1936).

Whol, Robert, *The Generation of 1914* (Cambridge, Mass., 1979).

Zeppi, Stelio, *Il pensiero politico dell'idealismo italiano e il nazionalfascismo* (Florence, 1973).

Zunino, Pier Giorgio, *L'ideologia del fascismo* (Bologna, 1985).

INDEX

265